Formulaic Genres

Also by Koenraad Kuiper

BOUNTY

INTRODUCTION TO ENGLISH LANGUAGE: Word, Sound and Sentence (*with W. Scott Allan*)

NEW ZEALAND ENGLISH (*co-editor with Allan Bell*)

SEMANTICS: A Course Book (*co-editor with Li FuYin*)

TIMEPIECES

SMOOTH TALKERS

MIKROKOSMOS

SIGNS OF LIFE

Formulaic Genres

Koenraad Kuiper
University of Canterbury, New Zealand

palgrave
macmillan

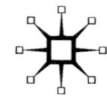

© Koenraad Kuiper 2009

All rights reserved. No reproduction, copy or transmission of this publication may be made without written permission.

No portion of this publication may be reproduced, copied or transmitted save with written permission or in accordance with the provisions of the Copyright, Designs and Patents Act 1988, or under the terms of any licence permitting limited copying issued by the Copyright Licensing Agency, Saffron House, 6-10 Kirby Street, London EC1N 8TS.

Any person who does any unauthorized act in relation to this publication may be liable to criminal prosecution and civil claims for damages.

The author has asserted his right to be identified as the author of this work in accordance with the Copyright, Designs and Patents Act 1988.

First published 2009 by
PALGRAVE MACMILLAN

Palgrave Macmillan in the UK is an imprint of Macmillan Publishers Limited, registered in England, company number 785998, of Houndmills, Basingstoke, Hampshire RG21 6XS.

Palgrave Macmillan in the US is a division of St Martin's Press LLC, 175 Fifth Avenue, New York, NY 10010.

Palgrave Macmillan is the global academic imprint of the above companies and has companies and representatives throughout the world.

Palgrave® and Macmillan® are registered trademarks in the United States, the United Kingdom, Europe and other countries.

ISBN-13: 978–0–230–55352–1 hardback
ISBN-10: 0–230–55352–4 hardback

This book is printed on paper suitable for recycling and made from fully managed and sustained forest sources. Logging, pulping and manufacturing processes are expected to conform to the environmental regulations of the country of origin.

A catalogue record for this book is available from the British Library.

Library of Congress Cataloging-in-Publication Data
Kuiper, Koenraad.
  Formulaic genres / Koenraad Kuiper.
    p. cm.
  Includes bibliographical references and index.
  ISBN 978–0–230–55352–1
  1. Discourse analysis—Social aspects. 2. Language and languages—Variation. I. Title.
  P302.84.K84 2009
  417′.2—dc22   2008042645

10 9 8 7 6 5 4 3 2 1
18 17 16 15 14 13 12 11 10 09

Printed and bound in Great Britain by
CPI Antony Rowe, Chippenham and Eastbourne

Contents

List of Tables and Figures	vii
Preface	ix
Acknowledgements	xii
List of Abbreviations	xiv

Part I Formulaic Genres

1	What are Formulaic Genres?	3
2	A Day at the Races	26
3	Forecasting the Weather	42
4	Polite Genres in a Multilingual Community: Greeting and Eating in Singapore	58
5	Playing a False Part: Projecting and Perceiving Fraudulent Identities on the Internet	75

Part II Genrelects

6	Idiolectal Variation: Ritual Talk at the Supermarket Checkout	95
7	Genrelects, Gender and Politeness: Form and Function in Controlling the Body	116
8	Regional Genrelects in Engagement Notices	138
9	Revolutionary Change: Formula Change during the Cultural Revolution, People's Republic of China	157

| 10 | Historical Variation: The Historical Reconstruction of Proto-English Auction Speech | 177 |
| 11 | Volitional Variation: Humour and Formulae | 191 |

Notes	207
References	214
Index	222

List of Tables and Figures

Tables

5.1	Writers of fraud letters	78
5.2	Examples of formality level of formulae	82
5.3	Examples of domain-related formulae	83
5.4	Stylistic homogeneity levels in fraud letters	84
5.5	Domain specificity of formulae in fraud letters	84
5.6	Error rates in fraud letters	85
5.7	Error rates in selected fraud letters	86
5.8	Error type by standard ESL criteria	87
6.1	Greeting formulae used by each operator	111
7.1	Examples of square dance calling formulae	132
7.2	Examples of round dance cueing formulae	132
8.1	Frequency choice of formula in the Australian engagement notices	143
8.2	Variant forms of formula 3 in the Australian engagement notices	143
8.3	Adjective phrase selection in the Australian engagement notices	143
8.4	Distribution of formula 4 variants in the Australian engagement notices	143
8.5	Who announces the engagement in the Australian engagement notice?	144
8.6	Forms of address in the Australian engagement notices	144
8.7	Formula selection in New Zealand engagement notices	145
8.8	Adjective choice in New Zealand engagement notices	145
8.9	Parental naming in New Zealand engagement notices	146
8.10	*'To family and friends'* and other binary variables in New Zealand engagement notices	146
8.11	Subject of active formulae in New Zealand engagement notices	146
11.1	Number of PLIs per cartoon	199
11.2	Substitutions within a PLI	200
11.3	Relationship between the lexical items	200

| 11.4 | Exchanges | 201 |
| 11.5 | The PLI deformation signature of Cathy Wilcox | 205 |

Figures

3.1	The opening formula of a National Radio forecast	49
5.1	Perceived origin of the writers of the fraud letter	88
5.2	Impression of the writers' social class	89
5.3	Impressions of the writers' educational level	90
5.4	Impressions of the writers' style	90
5.5	Impressions of writers' personality traits	91
6.1	Greetings (starts plus information elicitation)	101
6.2	Introduction to exchange section formulae	106
6.3	Cash call formula	106
6.4	Receipt of cash formula	106
6.5	Introduction to change counting formula	107
6.6	Change counting formula	107
6.7	Back reference formulae	108
6.8	Positive face stroke formulae	108
6.9	Termination formula	108
6.10	Greeting formulae of individual checkout operators	110
7.1	Form of instructors' utterances	127
7.2	Function of instructors' utterances	128
7.3	Forms in square vs round dance calling	133
7.4	Functions in square and round dance calling	134
7.5	Forms of dance callers' utterances	135
7.6	Functions of dance callers' utterances	135
8.1	Passive and active formulae in engagement notices	142
8.2	Formula frequency in engagement notices	147
8.3	Frequency of mention of parents' domicile	148
8.4	Order of mention of couple	149
8.5	Affect of adjective in engagement notices	149
8.6	Frequency of parental naming	150
8.7	'To family and friends'	151
10.1	Sample formula	186
10.2	A new track through the formula	186
10.3	Lexical addition to the formula	186
10.4	The chants of three tobacco auctioneers	188
11.1	Cartoon by Cathy Wilcox	202
11.2	Cartoon by Cathy Wilcox	206

Preface

Some years ago, colleagues suggested that this might be a worthwhile book. A number of the studies contained in it have appeared in various places, many of them where one might not necessarily look for such studies. Others are new. Putting them together is an attempt to make a narrative out of them. It is my hope that each makes its own contribution so that the whole becomes more than the sum of the parts.

All of them were conducted in the conviction that native speakers acquire many genres as a result of acquiring many social roles, a conviction supported by the views of Bakhtin which figure in chapter 1. Consequently, when we look at human linguistic capacities, we should not only marvel at the abstractness of the empty category principle and the universal taxonomy of phonologically null syntactic constituents such as pro, PRO, trace and e (Chomsky, 1981); we should also marvel at the array of genres which humans have created for all the purposes they have for speaking.

The more one looks at genres, the more one finds them associated with formulae. So this book sets out to examine what makes a formulaic genre, and to show that we are often formulaic in our linguistic repertoires.

But genres are not linguistic or social straightjackets. They allow for variation. That variation can be idiolectal, geographic, social, ethnic and diachronic. Genres can also be used for pastiche, parody, satire and various other forms of linguistic play, as, for example, Monty Python's Flying Circus amply showed (Python, 2000). The second half of this book therefore looks at genrelects, a term I have coined to deal with distinct varieties of a genre. It is not my purpose to survey the field of research relating to formulaic genres but to present case studies which illustrate the propositions above. In doing so, I am not suggesting that there is no other work of note on formulaic genres. As the bibliography of work contained in the following web sites (http://kollokationen.bbaw.de/bib/index_de.html, http://www.europhras.org) shows, there is, on the contrary, so much work that a survey within the confines of a book such as this could not do it justice.

As well as the content and outcomes of the research reported in this book, I draw attention in an informal way to some of the methodological considerations which have arisen in doing these studies. This is for the purpose of showing how I approached these studies, as well as suggesting ways other students and scholars might pursue research on formulaic genres. Social scientists live in an increasingly method-and-control milieu. While that has its positive effects, it can also have a dampening effect on the creative imagination which is required to undertake research. So I have been catholic in my methodological tastes.

I now turn to three aspects of presentation. Since these studies have been made over a long period, their relevance for the here and now might be questioned. My view on that is that all case studies are snapshots. All of the social traditions illustrated in these case studies could have changed since the time the studies were conducted, just as the conventions, no doubt, were different in the years before I happened upon them. Does this invalidate the case studies? The answer must be no. A photo of a person is not invalid because they were once a baby and years later they will be elderly. The crucial element is that it be a good photo, one which presents the person at that particular time. For that reason, I have tended to use the historic present tense in many of the following accounts.

For many of the studies, the research was cooperative since others were more enculturated than I in the genre being studied and therefore in many cases we worked on the study together. This has resulted in an amount of uncertainty about the use of first-person pronouns. If they were all singular, that would give the impression that I was the sole author of this work (taking author in the widest sense). That isn't the case. On the other hand, if the choice were uniformly for the plural first person, then that would suggest either the authorial and rather old-fashioned *we* or the plural *we*. So I have been inconsistent. When I use *I*, I am referring to myself and when I use *we*, I mean *we*, plural; I and the person (and in some cases people) with whom I conducted the study; or I and you, the reader. I hope I may be forgiven the inconsistency. It arises, as with the case of the selection of tense, from an attempt to provide the reader with the feel of how the work went at the time. The other parties involved in the second-person plural are named in the Acknowledgements section and in the references to the earlier publications which arose from these studies.

The level of formality with which you present work is a third area of concern. I have tried to present work in an accessible way without, I hope, short-changing the complex nature of many of these genres. Much of the data is presented in illustrative, rather than complete, form.

I have only presented quantitative data on some occasions. While there are doubtless other ways to present this material, my aim has been to reach the widest audience and still do justice to the genres and their users. My intent has also been to look at formulaic genres from a variety of perspectives.

Finally, this book has no concluding chapter or even an epilogue. It has, in other words, only an opening bookend. I have become suspicious of generalizations in the human sciences. I am happy to let these case studies stand as emblematic rather than representative. There are so many studies of formulaic genres done by others and so many left to do. So I hope that this book, rather than leading to a conclusion, will stimulate further work on formulaic genres and if, when you, the reader, have reached the end of chapter 11, you wish for the closing bookend, you might return to chapter 1, since I outline my views of formulaic genres there.

Koenraad Kuiper

Acknowledgements

I have a large number of people to thank who have made it possible to do the work undertaken over the last three decades which is reported in this book. Not least among these is my employer for the last few decades, the University of Canterbury. Periods of study leave and other research support have been invaluable. Host institutions where I have undertaken research have also been vital. They include the Linguistics Department at the University of Massachusetts at Amherst, Bard College, the Linguistics Department at Utrecht University, the Max Planck Institute for Psycholinguistics, the Netherlands Institute for Advanced Studies and the Berlin-Brandenburgische Akademie der Wissenschaften.

My students have also been a great help. They have researched formulaic genres from wall-climbing instructions to second-hand motorcycle advertisements, frequently with panache. Colleagues from many places who have contributed commentary include Tony Cowie, Rosemarie Gläser, Andy Pawley, Diana van Lancker-Sidtis and Alison Wray.

I have been grateful for funding from the following: the New Zealand University Grants Committee, The University of Canterbury, De Nederlandse Organisatie voor Wetenschappelijk Onderzoek in the Netherlands, the Fulbright-Hays Fund, the Netherlands Institute for Advanced Studies.

Particular mention can be made of help for research conducted as reported in the following chapters. Chapter 2 was inspired by research done with Paddy Austin and by discussions with Reon Murtha. Chapter 3 was the result of research collaboration with Francesca Hickey on weather forecasting. We were grateful, in conducting this work, for cooperation from the New Zealand Metereological Service. For help with Chapter 4, my thanks are due to Daphne Tan, without whom the research reported in this chapter would have been impossible, to R. K. S. Tan and S. K. L. Tan for their much appreciated taping of speech in Singapore English and to Singaporeans who found time to discuss their use of Singaporean English, and to C-P. Tan who provided commentary. The research reported in Chapter 5 was conducted with Georgie Columbus. Chapter 6 began life as a research project conducted with Marie Flindall who was a native speaker of checkout operator talk. Her and my supermarkets were helpful in allowing us to record operators and clients. Justine Coupland provided many helpful comments. In Chapter 7, the speech of pump aerobics instructors was recorded by Michelle Lodge. I recorded the dance callers and am grateful to the callers for allowing themselves to be recorded for the research reported in Chapter 7. In Chapter 8 I have to thank Corinna Geisser who first drew my attention to engagement notices as a genre and as a source of variation. Jen Hay and I discussed the project and the data. Marie-Elaine van Egmond did some of the data processing. Chapter 9 owes a great deal to the memories of Ji Fengyuan and Shu Xiaogu who provided all the data and much of the analysis of the formulaic genres of the Cultural Revolution. Chapter 10 was helped by recordings and analysis performed by Douglas Haggo. Various auction rooms around the planet allowed Doug and me to record auctions. I am grateful to Frederik Tillis for help with the analysis of nineteenth-century black musical traditions of the southern USA. For help with Chapter 11, I am grateful to Cathy Wilcox for permission to reproduce her work and for the pleasure that her work has provided. I am also grateful to Andrew Biddington with whom I have discussed the Wilcox cartoons, and to John Paolillo for his paper on Gary Larson's cartoons (Paolillo, 1998) which takes a different tack but with similar material.

Chapter 3 is based on Hickey & Kuiper (2000). Parts of this publication are reprinted with kind permission from John Benjamins Publishing Company, Amsterdam/Philadelphia. [www.benjamins.com].

Chapter 4 is based, in part, on Kuiper & Tan (1989). Parts of this publication are reprinted with kind permission from Mouton de Gruyter.

Chapter 5: versions of sections 5.1–5.3 were published in an earlier conference proceedings (Kuiper & Newsome, 2006). I am grateful to the editors of the volume for permission to re-use this material.

Chapter 6 is based on Kuiper & Flindall (2000). Permission to use this chapter has kindly been given by Pearson Educational.

Chapter 7 is based, in part, on Kuiper & Lodge (2004).

Chapter 10 is based in part on Kuiper (1992) and Kuiper & Tillis (1985).

Chapter 11 is based on Kuiper, K. (2007), parts of which are reprinted with kind permission from John Benjamins Publishing Company, Amsterdam/Philadelphia. [www.benjamins.com].

All co-authors of previously published versions of parts of these chapters have given their permission to have those sections in which they had a stake reworked and republished. My thanks again to them.

I here record my thanks too to Alison Kuiper who, in reading through this manuscript made numerous felicitous suggestions. Our discussions of human talk over the years have always been enriching.

List of Abbreviations

ADJP	adjective phrase
EFL	English as a foreign language
IS	idiomatic sense
NP	noun phrase, used to represent a slot in a formula
LT	literal translation
MOG	Met. Office Guidelines for the writing of scripts for weather forecasts
NZ	New Zealand
PEAS	proto English auction speech
PLI	phrasal lexical item
SE	Singaporean English
UK	United Kingdom
VP	verb phrase

Notational conventions for discourse structure rules

- → The discourse constituent on the left hand side of the arrow has the discourse constituents on the right hand side of the arrow in the given order.
- \+ indicates sequential order of constituents
- { } braces surround alternative choice
- ( ) parentheses surround optional choices
- [ ] square brackets surround free orders
  superscript indicates any number of iterations of the constituent

Notational conventions for finite state diagrams

- → The arrows in finite state diagrams show the directions that speakers may proceed through the diagram from START to STOP. Each such track through the diagram is a realization of a PLI.

Part I
Formulaic Genres

1
What are Formulaic Genres?

> All ritual has a notable tendency to reduce itself to a rehearsal of formulae.
>
> Veblen (1994:75)

1.1 Introduction

This book is about becoming a proficient native speaker of a language, that is, becoming someone who is both a native speaker of a language and who is communicatively competent in the language(s) they have acquired. There are many elements to such proficiency. One significant element in being a proficient native speaker is acquiring and being able to utilize the formulaic genres of the speech communities in which you live and work. Formulaic genres are at the interface between knowing a language and being able to use a language appropriately since such genres integrate these two capacities. The first section of this book will examine the stable features of a set of formulaic genres and thereby illustrate something of their nature. The second section will look at how formulaic genres vary and change.

Becoming a proficient user of a language has two aspects: acquiring it and learning how to use it. To use a hammer you must first have a hammer at hand, while using a hammer for the uses for which it is appropriate is another matter. In many respects this analogy is useful, but not in all respects. Certainly you must be able to produce the sounds of the language you speak and to recognize them in the speech of others. You must know the rules of the syntax of the language and its morphology. The analogy breaks down in the case of the acquisition of vocabulary. Items of vocabulary can have associated conditions for their use, which means that such an item of vocabulary cannot be learned without also learning how it is to be used. Such conditions of use are of two kinds: linguistic and non-linguistic. For example, the word *elephant* is a noun. As such it must be used in certain positions in a sentence and not in others. Syntactic categories essentially specify where a word may be used in the language system. A word like *Balderdash!*, uttered on its own as a sentence, has no syntactic category indicating where in a sentence it may be used. The same is true for the word *yes*. But there are non-linguistic conditions of use for a word like *Balderdash*. These conditions indicate how it may be used socially, in this case as an exclamation of disbelief at something someone else has asserted. A word like *Excellency,* which is used as a polite form of address for (amongst others) ambassadors, has both a linguistic category, that of being a noun, and it also has non-linguistic usage conditions in that it is a polite form of address. Its use cannot be inferred from anything else we know about the item and must therefore be an independent piece of knowledge about the word.

The foregoing discussion suggests that vocabulary items can be distinguished along two parameters, as to whether or not they have linguistic, and non-linguistic, conditions of use:

	yes	no
linguistic conditions of use (lcu)		
non-linguistic conditions of use (nlcu)		

These parameters allow us to provide the following feature specifications for the words below:

elephant [+lcu, −nlcu]
Balderdash! [−lcu, +nlcu]
yes [−lcu, −nlcu]
Excellency [+lcu, +nlcu]

The analogy between languages and tools also breaks down when you look at how the existence of a tool and learning how to use it are sequenced. Unlike physical tools such as hammers and their use, language and its acquisition frequently intertwine. Certainly a child does not have to wait until the whole of their grammar is acquired before being able to speak with and understand other people. People continue to acquire new vocabulary items throughout life; no-one would suggest that a person is a proficient speaker of a language only when all vocabulary items in the language have been learned.

The notion of a proficient native speaker is thus problematic. Linguists have traditionally been interested in the linguistic knowledge acquired by speakers, but the exact nature of that knowledge is not obvious, since it is tacit. The knowledge of a language acquired by a native speaker must therefore be modelled and the model tested against what can be found out from speakers and how they perform. Part of that knowledge is knowledge of vocabulary. The vocabulary which will be in focus in the following chapters requires a distinction to be made between those lexical items which are structurally simple and those which are structurally complex. Structurally simple items of vocabulary are mono-morphemic in that that they have only one meaning-bearing element. *Elephant* is mono-morphemic. Unlike *elephantitis* and *Excellency*, it cannot be broken down into meaningful sub-units. Structurally complex lexical items can have two kinds of structure: word structure or syntactic structure. Those with syntactic structure are phrasal lexical items such as, for example, *Your Excellency* and *take something apart*.

A second set of features can, therefore, be used to distinguish among lexical items on the basis of their structure (Fiedler, 2007:17). In the table all lexical items with the feature [±wlc] are [−ss] and all lexical items with the feature [±dw] are [+wlc]:

	yes	no
structurally simple (ss)		
word level complexity (wlc)		
derived word (dw)		

This set of classifications yields the following feature specifications:

Mono-morphemic words [+ss], e.g. *elephant*
Derived words [+dw], e.g. *elephantitis*
Compound words [−dw], e.g. *elephant reservation*
Phrasal lexical items [−wlc], e.g. *a white elephant*

This classification intersects in obvious ways with the earlier classification according to conditions of use. Since the following chapters will be concerned primarily with phrasal lexical items (PLIs), it should be noted that PLIs always have linguistic conditions of use. This is because phrases by definition have syntactic categories which determine where they may be used in sentences. For example *take advantage of* is a verb phrase and will only fit in those locations in sentences where verb phrases fit. However PLIs may or may not have non-linguistic conditions of use.

For example, the phrase *take advantage of* is part of the vocabulary of English and thus a lexical item but it has no non-linguistic conditions of use. It is not restricted to particular speakers or particular occasions. *Your Excellency*, on the other hand, is restricted to particular situations. It is a form of address used to particular persons on particular occasions. The ambassador's husband would not (except jokingly) address her as *Your Excellency* when they were about to do the dishes, but a guest at a reception at which she was present might well be expected to use this form of address.

Lexical items with the features [−wlc, + nlcu] can be termed *formulae*. The following chapters explore the significance of formulae in the repertoire of native speakers.

Non-linguistic conditions of use which have so far been presented as examples are rather simple. *Your Excellency* is restricted to contexts where formal address is required and it is a form of address restricted to certain persons (Gullen, 2002). Formulae can involve much more complex conditions of use. At this point one illustration will suffice to make this clear: the formula *He's old enough to be your father*.[1] Native speakers of some varieties of English know this formula and, having acquired it, they have acquired a set way of expressing a number of cultural relationships, and mores. In knowing this formula you must know the conditions of its use: who may use it to whom and so forth. The norm is that it should be used only by close female relatives, and perhaps acquaintances, to each other. Others venture to use the formula at some risk. You must also know the general situation in which it is used. The situation is that a young woman is contemplating, or is already involved in, a sexual relationship with an older man. The purpose of uttering the formula is to dissuade the young woman from continuing her relationship with the man. The formula will also normally be used in relative privacy.

There are perhaps deeper cultural messages involved. The first suggestion is that it is not in order for young women to be sexually involved with older men. Second, such relationships are akin to incest between father and daughter and there is an incest taboo prohibiting such relationships. Third, female relatives, particularly older, close female relatives, are responsible for maintaining and controlling the sexual behaviour of young women. That these are a minimal set of conditions of use can be seen from the fact that native speakers share intuitions about this formula. They will, for example, elicit such normative descriptions when asked and will recognize the intent of speakers using this formula in a situation comedy or soap opera. Native speakers also know that there is no formula *She's old enough to be your mother* or an equivalent to it. This indicates that, in the culture which has access to this formula, sexual activity between young women and older men is proscribed more closely than sexual activity between younger men and older women (or perhaps that is beyond proscription). Native speakers also know that there is a threshold of closeness to the addressee. Mother, aunt, grandmother, sister and close female friend all appear appropriate users of the formula.

The two formulae used as illustrations so far have conditions of use which are socially determined. They are also formulae which can be used more or less in isolation. What comes before and after *Your Excellency* is not closely predetermined by the formula itself. That is also true of *He's old enough to be your father*. Other formulae, however, play a subordinate role in larger stretches of discourse. For example, dyadic greetings where one speaker initiates an exchange with a formula and the other replies with a formula dependent on the first (Ferguson, 1976). So if someone says to you *How are things?* and you say *Fine, thanks*, then a discourse pattern has been used as well as individual formulae. Such sequential formulaic dependencies are governed by *discourse structure rules*. Again these two features of linguistic knowledge, the use of formulae and their link to discourse structure rules, are independent of each other. Not all formulae are discourse-indexed and not all discourse structure rules are implemented by formulae. For example, turntaking rules (Schiffrin, 1987) do not necessarily involve formulae, although they may do and we have already seen that some formulae are used independently of more extensive discourse sequencing. Where the two come together, that is, where discourse structure rules are indexed for formulae, a *formulaic genre* exists.

With these preliminary definitions now determined, it is possible to begin the exploration of formulaic genres, based on a range of case studies. Each of the studies has something different to tell about the way in which formulaic genres work in their language communities for the speakers and hearers of a language. Preliminary sketches of engagement notices and ice hockey commentary will illustrate central aspects of formulaic genres. Ice hockey commentaries are an oral genre, while engagement notices, to which we return later, are a written genre.

1.2 Placing an engagement notice in *The Times*

Human beings the planet over tend to pair off in situations akin to Western marriage. This is often accompanied by a ritual which serves as a rite of passage (Gennep, 1960), from the state of being single to the state of being no longer single. Sometimes this ritual is preceded by a preliminary ritual, the announcement of the intent to marry. For centuries in England, this was done by reading, or publishing, the banns in the parish church of the couple concerned. It functioned as a public announcement of a private intention, providing some security that the parties were permitted to marry and thus not undertake an action which would involve them in a breach of the canon law.

In the eighteenth century, with the advent of newspapers it became possible for private individuals to place public notices there. Whether the motivation for publication was the same as that for publishing the banns of marriage, engagement notices have been placed in newspapers for at least a century. One of the newspapers with a history at least this long is *The Times* of London. *The Times* requires the engagement notices placed in it to have a rigid format. This can be called *Times style*. All *Times* engagement notices take the form of a pair of names in bold type at the top of the notice followed by a single formula. *Times* style has the following invariant features.

1. One of two passive-voiced formulae is used. The formulae are:
   The engagement is announced between party 1 and party 2
   where the two parties are the people whose names are given in the header above the formula. The parents of the two parties come after their names in the formula.
   The forthcoming marriage is announced and will take place on NP_1 at NP_2 between party 1 and party 2.
2. Structural variation of formulae 1 and 2 does not occur.
3. The man who is becoming engaged is always mentioned before the woman, i.e. he is always party 1 and she is always party 2.
4. The time and place of the engagement are never mentioned.

Only three areas of variation are possible:

1. Where the parents are mentioned, the domicile of both sets of the parents is mentioned in almost all cases. Where a parent is not mentioned, the domicile of the parties may be. The domicile of a party is mentioned only in such a case.
2. The address form of the parents has four variants:

   a. title plus initials plus surname (where the initials in the case of a married couple are those of the husband), e.g. *Mr and Mrs E. C. Brown;*

    b. title plus given name plus surname (where the first name in the case of a married couple is always the given name of the husband, as in *Colonel and Mrs Alisdair Findlay)*;
    c. as in b. including the mother's given name but without title, e.g. *Rev James and Susan Potter;*
    d. a 'titled' title, e.g. *Count* plus name.

Deceased parents are referred to as *the late*.[2]

3. The birth order of the man and woman being engaged may or may not be given. When it is, over half of the cases are symmetrical in giving the birth order of both the man and woman. Birth order is given only if parents are mentioned.

A typical *Times* engagement notice would thus read:

Mr L. Norriss and Miss A. Sinclair
The engagement is announced between Lester, son of Mr and Mrs Edward Norriss, of Bedford, and Alison, daughter of Mr and Mrs Stephen Sinclair, of Evesham, Cornwall.[3]

By the earlier definition, *Times* engagement notices constitute a formulaic genre. They consist of a heading comprising of two names followed by one of only two formulae. These formulae are used only for engagement notices. The genre therefore has the simplest of discourse structure rules:

    R1   Engagement notice → couple's names + engagement formula
    R2   Names → man's name + woman's name
    R3   Name → title + initial(s) + family name
(The arrow should be read as 'consists of' while the + should be read as 'is followed by'. In later rules, parentheses indicate choices which may or may not be made and braces around constituents indicate alternatives.)

Typographically the names are in bold while the formula is in plain text on the lines below the names.

    These formal characteristics constitute a text type. If one identifies these characteristics in a newspaper notice, then one is reading an engagement notice in *Times* style. However there are non-linguistic features of the context which are linked to the text type and support its existence socially. A couple's intention to marry is being announced. They may have parents living or deceased. They have placed the notice in the newspaper. In the case of *The Times*, they will have contacted the staff member of *The Times* who deals with such notices and who, no doubt, provides oversight to ensure that the notice is in the required form. Her name and contact details are at the bottom of the list of notices. It is the conjunction of these two elements, the formal text type features as a set, together with the non-linguistic contextual features of the situation, which constitute a genre.

1.3 Calling the face-off[4]

Placing an engagement notice is an elementary formulaic genre but this combination of idiosyncratic characteristics of linguistic form and social context recur in many other situations. The next illustration comes from a different environment, the ice hockey rink. Ice hockey is a sport involving furious skating by two teams of six players in pursuit of a flat rubber disk, the puck. The objective is to get the puck into the goal of the opposing team. From time to time, for example when a player is penalized, there is a stoppage in play. Then play is restarted in a manoeuvre termed a 'face-off'. This involves the puck being picked up by one of the officials controlling the game, called a linesman. For the face-off, two players in the position of 'centre' stand facing one another on either side of the linesman. They must have their skates toeing a line drawn under the ice within a circle, the face-off circle. They must be motionless. When they are, the linesman drops the puck between them and they contest possession of the puck. If they are not still, they are waved out of the face-off circle, and two new centres from the bench on the sidelines must come onto the ice and repeat the process. This episode can be described by the following rule.[5]

R1. Episodes of face-offs
Face-off → call + linesman retrieves puck + skates to face-off circle + centres enter circle + (centre(s) waved out + new player(s) enter(s))^n + puck thrown down by linesman + win.

When professional ice hockey is broadcast on television, the commentary is provided by two commentators: a 'play-by-play' commentator and a 'colour' commentator. The former provides an account of the game as it proceeds while the latter provides comments and conversation when play is stopped (Ferguson, 1983). An ice hockey game takes

60 minutes while the intervals, stoppages (and advertising breaks) take about two hours. Both play-by-play and colour commentators can provide commentary of the face-off since there is a stoppage before the face-off. To illustrate the difference between play-by-play and colour commentary, here are two transcripts of commentaries relating face-offs.

Transcripts 1.1
Play-by-play:

> *Minnesota's Broten to take the face-off against McCourt and he got the draw to Lindgren.*

Colour:

> *Broten. McCarthy right behind him hoping that Broten can get it back on this draw against Terrion. Broten won't get the chance from the face-off now. He's waved out. So is Terrion. Cicerelli comes in against Gavin. One fifty-one left in this period. Now they drop it in. Or do they? No. Don Hasseldine, the linesman... Now it goes in and the shot from the line...*

The discourse structure of a commentary is externally driven since it must follow the game and is dependent on the events the commentator sees, i.e. the events in rule 1. However, it is not just a function of external events. If the commentary of face-off events were entirely externally driven then each sub-episode of the visual events would have a verbal analogue. This is not the case. The sequencing of face-off commentaries is different from that of the face-off itself. Here is a set of transcripts of commentators describing face offs. The descriptions used are in play-by-play commentary mode.

Transcripts 1.2

1. *The draw to Minnesota.*
2. *Broten got the draw.*
3. *Acton against Daoust on this draw. One thirty-three left in the period. Acton got the face-off to Hartsberg.*
4. *To the right of Lemelin, they'll drop it in. Derlago going to take the draw for the Toronto Maple Leafs. Harris parked to his right just back a bit. 'gainst Nilssen of Calgary. Nilssen got the draw.*
5. *Lineman Leon Stickle drops it in. Leafs got the draw.*
6. *It's called for a face-off at the Maple Leaf blue line.*
7. *It was gloved ahead so they'll bring that back.*

8. *They'll bring it back to the Maple Leafs' side of centre ice. Now they're set. Dropped in.*
9. *So they'll bring it back for a face-off to the right of Palmateer in that big circle.*
10. *And they force a face-off.*

These commentary portions have omitted the most frequently employed method of describing a face-off, the null method, whereby the face-off receives no verbal commentary at all. On the basis of such commentary portions, we can construct a rule for the commentary of face-offs as follows:

R2. Discourse structure of face-off commentaries in play-by-play mode.

Face-off → $\left\{ \begin{array}{l} \text{(locator)} \\ \text{(call)} \end{array} \right\}$ + ((participants) + (wave out + new player(s))^n + (drop in) + (win)

It can be seen that rule 1 does not map exactly into rule 2. Specifically some portions of rule 1 are routinely omitted. For example, play-by-play commentaries do not describe the process whereby the linesman retrieves the puck and takes it into the face-off circle, gets set, and raises his arm. Other omissions are more sporadic; no commentary ever reports every episode of what actually happens. There are further restrictions. For example, if a play-by-play commentary includes reference to the participants, then it also includes the outcome of the face-off, but not vice versa. This gives the double parenthesis in rule 2 for these two constituents. The fact that a null commentary is possible derives from the fact that all the constituents of rule 2 are optional.

The discourse structure also has frequency properties. The first of these is that the most frequently used way to report a face-off is not to report it at all. The next most frequent occurrences are to report that a face-off will take place in a particular location or that one team or player has won the face-off. Mention of the drop of the puck is unusual and is likely to be in colour mode.

Although visually all face-offs are very similar, their significance varies depending on where on the rink they are taken and on the current state of the game. Thus a face-off during a power play (when one team has a player sitting in the sin bin) is more significant than one in normal play. A face-off in the centre ice area is not as significant as one inside the zone of either team. A face-off in the last minute of play with the score tied is more significant than one in the second period. These factors have an effect on whether the face-off receives any commentary and, if it does, how much. There is a tendency for face-off commentaries to be most detailed during power plays or near the end of a game.

To summarize, ice hockey commentaries have discourse structure rules for face-offs where the visual events and the verbal commentary are not isomorphic. The structure of the discourse is therefore not just externally driven and some elements of more or less arbitrary selection enter into the final structure of the commentary.

What of formulae? In the case of ice hockey commentaries, formulae are not hard to find since most of a play-by-play commentary consists of formulae. All the formulae are indexed for particular constituents in discourse structure; we would therefore expect there to be formulae for each constituent. Below, we illustrate formulae for each constituent as identified earlier in rule 2.

Face-off formulae indexed for discourse constituents.

1. Call formulae:
   a. X [_VP_ *hold on for a face-off*]
   b. X [_VP_ *force a face-off*]
   c. *It's called for a face-off.* (locator)

2. Face-off locator formulae:
   a. *Face-off in N territory.*
   b. *Face-off will be in the N zone.*
   c. *The face-off will come outside the N blue line.*
   d. *They will bring it back to the N side of centre ice.*

3. Participants formulae:
   a. X [_VP_ *take it (for N) against Y (for M)*]
   b. X [_VP_ *take the draw (for N) against Y (for M)*]
   c. X [_VP_ *take the face-off (for N) against Y (for M)*]
   d. *X against Y on this draw* (locator).
   e. *X and Y on this draw* (locator).
   f. *X and Y on this face-off* (locator).
   g. *X against Y on this face-off* (locator).

4. Wave out formulae:
   a. *X is waved out (of the circle).*
   b. *X is thrown out (of the circle).*
   c. *X is waved away.*

5. Drop in formulae:
   a. *The puck is dropped in.*
   b. *It's dropped in.*
   c. *They drop it in.*
   d. *There's the drop of the puck.*

6. Win formulae:
   a. *X [$_{VP}$ get it back (from the draw)]*
   b. *[$_{VP}$ get it back (from the face-off)]*
   c. *[$_{VP}$ get the draw (to Y)]*
   d. *[$_{VP}$ win the draw (to Y)]*
   e. *X with the draw (to Y)*
   f. *X has the draw (to Y)*
   g. *X gets the draw (to Y)*
   h. *X gets it back (to Y)*

Note that, although there are formulae for all of the discourse elements, there are not formulae for some of the reasonably independent episodes in the actual visual structure of the face-off, i.e. in rule 1. What this shows is that only certain episodes have verbal coding. These are the episodes which are seen as significant. In colour commentaries things are different. Colour commentators may discuss the way a linesman takes a face-off but this will not normally be done using formulae. In other cases, although there is coding for various episodes of the face-off, such formulaic coding is used infrequently. For example, the particular linesman taking the face-off is occasionally mentioned but only when there is time to fill. Normally the significant episodes are those relating to the opposing centres and which of them wins the draw. Thus there are a large number of formulae which may be used for relating these aspects of the face-off but only a handful for other episodes. So, like the discourse structure of facing off, the formulae too only selectively represent the game as it is seen.

Thus commentaries represent the game as it is perceived through an abstract representation rather than through its concrete manifestation on the ice. It is for this reason that commentary exists. If a game were just the visual spectacle with associated sound effects such as the swish of the skates and the thump of bodies onto the boards at the edge of the rink, then television would present the game as the fans in the stands see and hear it. But even the camera is selective, showing what seems significant, and the commentator is similarly selective in what he relates.

A team game, therefore, is not just a sequence of set moves on a playing surface. It is also a set of abstract strategies to implement certain short- and long-term goals. The goals range from getting the puck out of one's own zone, to getting it to another player, to getting it into the opposition's zone, to scoring a goal, to winning a game, a division, a play-off, or ultimately the Stanley Cup, which is the trophy handed out at the end of the season to the winner of the National Hockey League competition. Though the short-term goals are evident in the play, the longer-term goals are not, and it is these (among other things) which inform the commentators' selection both of discourse structure and formulae. (Other factors which play a part are, for example, the commercials which appear to be inserted as soon as the whistle blows for a face-off.)

So the reason that face-offs at centre ice are usually not commented on is that these face-offs usually cannot be directly related to longer-term strategies such as goal scoring. The reason why face-offs during a power play are more often included in commentary is that they are considered likely to lead to the scoring of goals. The dropping of the puck is not considered of any significance at all, however well it may be done. The shooting of the puck, by contrast, is considered significant, even if it is done badly.

Looking at the commentary of this brief episode of the game of ice hockey shows that it is a formulaic genre. The discourse rule for face-offs is more complex and the set of formulae which are indexed for it are more numerous than for *Times* engagement notices. But, as in the case of engagement notices, this formal side, which we can call the text-type side, is inextricably linked to the contextual side, namely the event which is receiving commentary. It is not an exact match with the event but rather provides an account and a cultural interpretation of it.

After the description of these two brief examples of formulaic genres, it is possible to ask what theoretical constructs, namely genres and formulae, lie behind such episodes being designated as formulaic genres.

1.4 What is a genre?

The above two formulaic genres are in two different modes; one written, the other spoken. As a written text type with a long history, engagement notices constitute a genre in terms of the external exigencies which give rise to them and in terms of the internal textual regularities which are manifest in them. This determination is further supported as follows. First '[i]n the case of newspaper genres ... we find an unmistakable "generic identity"' (Bhatia, 2001:67). Since engagement notices are clearly identifiable in a newspaper, we may assume that they constitute a well-defined genre. Second, engagement notices constitute part of a folk taxonomy of genres relating to rites of passage, folk taxonomies generally being a reliable way of seeing the external factors of a genre since '[g]enres are text categories readily distinguished by mature speakers of a language' (Biber, 1989:5) and 'for those who share genre knowledge within a culture, there is generally a shared name' (Johns, 1997:22). The folk taxonomy further includes births, marriages and deaths notices.

Ice hockey commentary is also one of a family of commentary genres all spoken ex tempore. Like engagement notices, native speakers who are familiar with these commentaries can tell in a flash whether the commentary is of cricket, rugby union, American football, baseball, basketball or ice hockey. This means each must be an identifiable text type and have a socio-cultural niche in which it is at home and with which the hearer is familiar. So ice hockey commentary is also a genre.

However, the term and concept *genre* is a contested one. Paltridge (1997) provides an overview of many different approaches taken to the construct *genre*. Many approaches stress the communicative function or purpose of a genre as a defining characteristic. For instance Miller (1994:24) suggests that 'a theoretically sound definition of genre must be centred not on the substance or form of the discourse but on the action it is used to accomplish.' Typical of such a view is the proposal that '[c]ommunicative genres are solutions to specifically communicative problems' (Bergmann & Luckmann, 1995:289). Sometimes the relationship is taken to be deterministic, namely that the communicative function is the sole determining factor in deciding the formal properties of the genre. On the other hand it may be that 'communicative purpose can be sufficiently elusive to be largely unavailable for the initial or early identification and categorization of discourses as belonging to certain genres' (Askehave & Swales, 2001:204). But it does seem the case that '[w]herever socially relevant knowledge is to be transmitted we find "convention" instead of "communicative rationality"' (Guenther & Knoblauch, 1995:5). Therefore it is likely that there are arbitrary conventional elements to all genres as well as functionally motivated ones. These elements collectively, the arbitrary and the functional, can be seen as belonging to either external or internal factors involved in how a genre is to be understood. '[T]he inner structure of communicative genres ... consists of rather diverse elements: words and phrases selected from different registers, formulae and entire formulaic blocks; rhetorical forms and tropes, stylistic devices, metric and melodic forms rhymes, adjectival and nominal lists, oppositions etc.' (Bergmann & Luckmann, 1995:292), that is, formal linguistic properties. 'The external structure of communicative genres...exhibits a certain degree of obligation, that is, constraints with respect to milieus, the communicative situation, the type of social relationship as well as social categories of actors (men, women, ethnic groups), relevant in such environments' (Guenther & Knoblauch, 1995:8), that is, contextual factors. The context, however, is to be seen in terms of the way natives in a culture view the context within the purview of a genre. To some extent the internal form of a genre can create its external context. An auction without the verbal performance of an auctioneer does not count as an auction and the external context, is, therefore, dependent on the recognition of the internal properties of the genre's text type.

Like all social phenomena which are seen to be similar in some way and which are conceptualized as recurring, this 'is an intersubjective phenomenon, a social occurrence, and cannot be understood on materialist terms' (Miller, 1994:29). The context must therefore not be invested with any more of a materialist interpretation than a linguist would invest in the concept of the phoneme. Methodologically this leads to the proposal that '[t]o avoid reifying "the context" it is necessary to study the textual details that illuminate the manner in which participants are collectively constructing the world around them' (Bauman & Briggs, 1990:69). Since genres play a role in the socio-cultural life of a community, genres have the capacity to reveal wider features of the culture which sustains them. The following chapters explore a number of formulaic genres for, amongst other things, what they have to tell us about the communities in which they exist.

What then do others have to say about formulaic genres? Recall that the term *formulaic genre* will be used in this book to designate a variety of a language (either spoken or written) which contains discourse structure rules which in turn index formulae for particular roles in the discourse and where a significant amount of the discourse is made up of formulae (Edwards & Sienkewicz, 1990). Recall also that a formula is a phrasal lexical item having associated conditions of use which determine its non-linguistic usage. For more extensive treatments see K. Aijmer (1996), Howarth (1996), Moon (1998), Pawley & Syder (1983), Wray (2002).

We have seen that, even in the tiny genre of *Times* engagement notices, there is variability. There is general agreement that genres are subject to variation and change in both their internal and external features. As Guenther & Knoblauch (1995:6) put it, '[g]enres are ... open to change and cultural variation'. However they also exhibit stabilities since 'genres emerge within a particular socio-historical context and are reinforced over time as a situation recurs ... These genres, in turn, shape future responses to similar situations' (Yates & Orlikowski, 1992:305). If we assume that 'the relationship between formal features and communicative function has generally been treated as one of means to ends, such that form becomes meaningful insofar as it is connected with some kind of content or function' (Bauman & Briggs, 1990:65), then variation in the features of a genre may be significant in some way. So, just as formulaic genres themselves are significant in their communities, the significance of genre variation is also to be sought in the cultural life of the communities of practice whose members place engagement notices in newspapers, perform as auctioneers, or as horse race callers. This is so because 'conventional discourse genres are part of the linguistic habitus that native actors bring to speech, but ... such genres are also produced in speech under various local circumstances' (Hanks, 1987:685).

We would therefore expect to find, in the case of some genres, that variational data would yield to an analysis on the basis, for example, of geographic dialect parameters, idiolectal parameters, housestyle parameters and so forth. In other words, genrelects are likely to exist. Tobacco auction speech, for example, shares linguistic features with other auctioning varieties but has unique features as well. These features are to be heard in the tobacco country of the southern United States (Kuiper & Tillis, 1985). As such they are characteristic of a region as well as an occupation. Engagement notices placed in New Zealand and Australian newspapers also differ significantly, suggesting that there exist regional genrelects of such notices.

1.5 Properties of formulae?[6]

So far only a definition of formulae has been given. Before proceeding further we need to be as explicit about formulae as we have been about genres. The distinctions to be made here will later be important in showing how formulae vary, since all the features which are outlined below are potential sources of variation and thus for differentiating among genrelects. Suppose that formulae are PLIs and that each PLI is a lexical item with its own entry in the mental lexicon of a speaker who knows it. Such knowledge is potentially complex. Furthermore, not all native speakers of a language who know a particular PLI will necessarily know it in exactly the same way, i.e. some will know it as having properties which other speakers will not know (Fraser, 1970:23; Mel'čuk, 1995:171). Since PLIs are phrases, speakers normally know at least two of the words in the phrase. We can think of these words as **lexicalized constituents** and define such a constituent as one where the word-level lexical content of the constituent is given in the lexical entry of the PLI (Verstraten, 1992). For example, in the *let alone* construction discussed by Fillmore, Kay & O'Connor (1988) the words *let alone* are lexicalized constituents of the construction. Testing for this property is often done by substituting for a lexicalized constituent (Gläser, 1986, 1995; Verstraten, 1992:27). If the substitution results in the phrase no longer being recognizable as a PLI then this shows the original phrase was a PLI with a lexicalized constituent. PLIs may also contain a **bound word** (Aronoff, 1976). These are single words which occur only within a PLI. For example *take umbrage at* contains the word *umbrage* which cannot occur freely, and occurs in no other PLI.[7]

Since PLIs are phrases where not every word need be specified, PLIs can contain **slots** (Koopman & Sportiche, 1991; Williams, 1994). A slot in the syntactic representation of a PLI is a position in the structure which requires to be 'filled' with other lexical items but which is not filled in the representation of the item in the lexicon. For example, in the PLI *take NP to task*, the NP is an obligatory complement of the verb which must be filled for the phase to be used grammatically but the lexical content of the NP is not given in the lexical entry of the PLI.

Sometimes slots also have an additional **slot restriction**. While the syntactic category of a slot constrains what it may contain syntactically, there are frequently other constraints of an arbitrary kind. For example, some slots must be filled with animate or human NPs when that is not an inherent requirement of the verb of which the NP is a complement, i.e. not the result of the s-selection properties of the verb (Chomsky, 1996:54). Again examples of slot restrictions are given in Fillmore, Kay & O'Connor (1988) for the *let alone* construction.

Some PLIs have **optional constituents** which may or may not be used. They are part of what the speaker knows when (s)he knows the PLI but their use is optional. For example, in the English PLI *breathe one's last breath* the final noun is optional; speakers can and do just say *breathe one's last*. Note that optional constituents are not just adjuncts which may be added freely. The form of words is particular and is part of what native speakers know of the particular PLI.

In some PLIs there appears to be more than one lexical item functioning in the same position. *To be in a bad mood* is equivalent to *being in a bad temper*. It seems that *mood* and *temper* function as alternatives as last noun in this PLI. But there are no other possible nouns here that are 'known' as part of knowing the PLI. *Mood* and *temper* thus constitute a **selection set**. Selection sets only occur where the PLI is semantically and pragmatically equivalent regardless of which member of the set is used.

Some PLIs will take freely inserted adjunct constituents. Others will not. This can be termed the PLIs' **modifiability** (Nicolas, 1995). For example, one can *get annoyed* or *get very annoyed* but one cannot modify the dismissive PLI *Get lost!* to *Get very lost!*

PLIs have greater or lesser degrees of **flexibility** syntactically under movement, supposing a theory of syntax which allows movement. Classically, the PLI *kick the bucket* will not passivize (Nunberg, Sag & Wasow, 1994).

Restricted collocations occur (Mackin, 1978; Mel'čuk, 1998). For example, if one wishes to use a bus as a means of public transport, one is said to *catch the bus* and then *get on the bus*. One does not *trap the bus* or *get in the bus*. Restricted collocations involve preferential selection of word combinations where such combinations are arbitrary. They may also be idiomatic, i.e. not semantically compositional. Catching the bus is, in some sense idiomatic but getting on the bus could be seen quite literally to be placing one's feet on the floor of the bus or oneself on its seats. Wine is (classically) either white or red; it is not ever purple or light green regardless of the truth conditions of these colours in collocation with *wine*. *To the best of one's abilities* is what English speakers say rather than *at the best of one's abilities*. In terms of their semantic properties neither preposition is preferable. Both create semantically well-formed and appropriate compositional meanings in this construction. Yet one is lexicalized as a restricted collocation and the other is not.

If the meaning of the whole PLI is a compositional function of the meaning of its constituent parts then it is **fully compositional**. Thus PLIs with this property will have all the possible meanings available from the semantic interpretation of the senses of their constituents. For example, the checkout farewell *Have a nice day* is fully compositional but is a PLI.

It is possible for a PLI to be compositional in that the meaning of the whole is a compositional function of the meaning of its constituents, but without all the possible readings of its words being available in the lexicon. For example, a political party could be a social occasion which is political, but in its lexicalized form it is an organization which functions to select and have elected members of a legislature. This is one, but only one, of the possible compositional meanings of *political party*, given that *party* is polysemous. It is thus **selectively compositional**.

A lexical item which is non-compositional in its meaning, i.e. in which the meaning of the whole is not a predictable semantic function of its constituent words is **idiomatic**. In some PLIs only one of the words has an idiomatic sense, i.e. a sense that it does not have when on its own. This sense only exists in combination with the other words in a particular PLI. Such PLIs are **unilaterally idiomatic**. Many restricted collocations are unilaterally idiomatic. In some PLIs more than one word may have a sense that they have only in the PLI. For example a *red herring* is neither red nor a herring, i.e. both words have special senses they have nowhere else but in construction within this PLI (Weinreich, 1969). Such PLIs are **bilaterally idiomatic**.

It seems important in the discussion of the semantic properties of PLIs to differentiate these clearly from the syntactic properties of the same PLI. The work of Mel'čuk, as exemplified in work such as Mel'čuk (1995), makes it clear that PLIs can, in many cases, be seen as mapping semantic predicates idiosyncratically onto verbs for specific arguments. So, for example, the weather is forecast, rather than predicted.

The properties above relate to the formal properties of a PLI in terms of its syntax and semantics but many PLIs also have conventional conditions of use. A **formula** has been defined earlier as a PLI with contextually restricted conditions of use. For example, *I'm sorry.* is a PLI which is used to offer an apology. Speech act theory provides examples of formulae and sub-classifications of types of usage conditions. However this is just a beginning. Every small-scale ritual tends to be accompanied by formulae. On aeroplanes, cabin crew use them: *'What would you like to drink, Sir/Madam?'*; flight crew use them: *'This is your/the captain speaking'*.

1.6 Goffmanian and Bakhtinian native speakers

I now return to the native speaker of a language with whom I started and who is central to everything we shall explore. Who is this person? They are not a Chomskian abstraction 'an ideal native speaker-listener, in a homogeneous speech community, who knows its language perfectly' (Chomsky, 1965:3) but closer to a flesh and blood person.[8] It follows from the descriptions of the two formulaic genres earlier in this chapter that not everyone who speaks English is thereby proficient in placing engagement notices in *The Times*, or in producing fluent commentaries of face-offs in ice hockey games, or even of understanding either genre.

Each of these formulaic genres has text type features of an arbitrary and unpredictable kind and is a cultural artefact belonging to its own speakers and hearers within their own community of practice. Individuals, however, do not all belong to the same communities of practice; they do not all have the same proficiency in the language games that belong to such communities. I might perfectly well understand what an ice hockey commentator was saying without being able to provide such a commentary myself or, in contrast, I might be a fluent cricket commentator but know nothing about ice hockey and its peculiarities.

Such a view of the human condition is akin to that of Irving Goffman. Goffman (1969) sees human beings as being actors on the stage of life. Unlike bees, whose place in the social scheme of bees is genetically predetermined and who can do little about being drones, if they are drones, human beings acquire multiple social roles through acting and interacting in their social environments. It was not predetermined by your genetic endowment that you should be a student, a checkout operator or a member of a jazz band.

Human beings gain social knowledge and the capacity to behave in socially appropriate ways through interacting with other humans. In many ways, you learn to be a child in the way children do, in the culture in which you become a child; you learn how to whine for ice creams, you learn how to thank your grandparents for birthday presents, and cultures differ as to what roles they make available. In New Zealand, for example, I cannot become a shaman (or perhaps an intellectual).

Such socially appropriate ways of being and behaving can be seen in many cases as involving routines. Goffman sees life as having many different routines. Such routines constitute 'a pre-established pattern of action which is unfolded during a performance and which may be presented or played through on other occasions' (Goffman, 1969:27). Each routine is part of a role which we play as we present ourselves to others on the particular stage appropriate to that role. The role may sometimes be played calculatingly and sometimes not. For example, there are times when we may not realize that we are playing the role of supplicant to a superior (although we are). We may listen more attentively and pay close attention to her suit, offering positive backchannels to everything she says. Sometimes we can be calculating in doing the same thing, realizing that by doing so we are more likely to ingratiate ourselves.

There are aspects of the way we perform routines which we can more easily control. For example, we generally control what we say with some care. But there are times when we find it very difficult to control how we perform. For example, we can produce involuntary laughter at quite inopportune times. Generally, Goffman suggests, people present themselves as the social situation dictates and not as they might personally feel. Checkout operators at supermarkets greet us and take their leave of us in ways that they personally might prefer not to do. This is made clear by a letter to the editor in a local newspaper after a previous correspondent had indicated her displeasure at such formulaic greetings. (I shall suggest in chapter 6 that the view below is jaundiced.)

Talking in shops
Sir – Mrs J. Fleming (January 16) complains about staff exchanging pleasantries with her in supermarkets.
After more than 15 years in the supermarket industry I think that I speak for most check-out operators when I say the vast majority do not even care if you live or die, let alone if you have a nice day.
I can assure you that the only reason you are asked how you are or if you have had a nice day is that they are only following an edict from various head offices.[9]

All parties in a situation where routines are being performed will tend to agree about what is mutually required of them when they present themselves. Staff serving in a dress shop and their clients both know that one role of the client is to model the clothes they might be interested in purchasing and it is not for the shop attendant to model the clothes. This situation is different in a haute couture establishment where there may be models present. When serving in a café, waiting staff do not tell clients that they can now go and pick up their coffee from the kitchen; they bring it to them when it has been made. We take such agreements about the nature of our performances for granted, but there is nothing inevitable about them and when disruptions to the social order occur we become aware of the regularities of our routine performances and those of others. This includes the degree of congruence between the performances of all the parties to a routine. The performances of various parties to a performance should be appropriate. Turning up at a high church wedding dressed in shorts and a singlet, drunk, and half an hour after the ceremony has begun, is not in keeping with everyone else who is dressed in formal dress and arrives on time, sober (or at least presenting themselves as such).

Goffman notes that routines are often enacted by teams working in consort. Group members perform with an awareness of how others are performing and what they are performing. For example, an operation in an operating theatre requires all the parties to work together, each with his or her appointed role. Often those roles include scripts. In a business meeting where a team is presenting, one person will hand the floor to the next by saying, *Now I'll hand over to Jo who will explain*.... This view of human beings is seen by Goffman as involving 'the very structure of the self...seen in terms of how we arrange for such performances' where 'the individual (is)...viewed as a performer, a harried fabricator of impressions...;...viewed as a character, a figure, typically a fine one, whose spirit, strength, and other sterling qualities the performance was designed to evoke' (Goffman, 1969:244). We will find that all the factors outlined above are significant in understanding the native speaker as a user of formulaic genres. In Goffman's terms, a native speaker is someone with a range of linguistic and non-linguistic competencies (of various strengths) in playing particular parts. Some of these parts have associated scripts in the form of formulaic genres which go with the role and define the routine. I have already hinted that fluent sport commentators and proficient engagement notice writers have acquired native-speaker competence in these respective genres by being able to command both the text type and the non-linguistic contingencies which are associated with it. I have also suggested that such fluency and proficiency is not universal. No native speaker commands all the roles and knows all the scripts in a culture. For a clearer emphasis on the linguistic side of genres and native speaker competence we now turn to Bakhtin (1986). Bakhtin has this to say about genres: 'We speak only in definite speech genres, that is, all our utterances have definite relatively stable typical *forms of construction of the whole*. Our repertoire of oral (and written) speech genres is rich. We use them confidently and skilfully *in practice*...' (Bakhtin, 1986:78). 'If speech genres did not exist and we had not mastered them,..., speech communication would be almost impossible' (Bakhtin, 1986:79). But as suggested earlier, '[m]any people who have an excellent command of a language often feel quite helpless in certain spheres of communication because they do not have a practical command of the generic forms used in the given spheres' (Bakhtin, 1986:80). In sum, and in line with the argument pursued thus far, 'a native speaker is given not only the mandatory form of the national language (lexical composition and grammatical structure), but also forms of utterance that are mandatory, that is, speech genres' (Bakhtin, 1986:80).

Bakhtin's view of genres thus proposes the genre as a way of shaping utterances into prescribed forms which are socially licensed. A native speaker cannot, according to Bakhtin, be one without such knowledge of genres but such knowledge is always partial since it has to do with the playing of Goffmanian parts. What genres do is link these roles to their prescribed forms of utterance.

1.7 Conclusion

In this chapter the stage has been set for the exploration of a range of formulaic genres which are more complex than the two simple examples provided so far. Each will be examined from both its formal and its social side but with the emphasis on the social. The aim is to place the native speaker as a social being centre stage. I will suppose that such a speaker has already acquired native speaker competence of the Chomskian kind but I will also suppose that this is not enough to be a native speaker in any way that makes being a speaker socially useful, and thus, that being a Chomskian native speaker is not in itself socially sufficient.

In the next chapter I turn to organized horse racing and the way in which it is given voice in the formulaic genre of race calling.

2
A Day at the Races

The wheel has come full circle. I am here.
William Shakespeare *King Lear* (V.iii.ll. 170–4)

2.1 Introduction

In the opening chapter it was suggested that the idealization of model native speakers needs to be deconstructed. In a modern, post-industrial Western society there are no speakers who know even a small portion of the vocabulary of their native language. Most of us, for example, know nothing of the technical vocabulary of aircraft maintenance engineers (Newsome, 2006). We cannot therefore be native speakers of aircraft engineering English. Where communicative competence is concerned, no one is communicatively competent in all the social situations where a particular language may be used. Tao priests are communicatively competent in a large array of ceremonials (Schipper, 1994) whereas the great majority of the billion or more speakers of Han languages are not.

In the place of a generalized notion of native speaker competence, it would therefore be more accurate to think of relativized linguistic competences, both linguistic and communicative. Some speakers have a better grasp of particular features of a language than others, particularly where specialized vocabulary is concerned, and some speakers are more adept, knowledgeable, skilful in manifesting/displaying some communicative performances than others. For instance, I might be a superb writer of used car ads but a terrible teller of jokes, or vice versa.

Such competenc(i)es can be placed within a Goffmanian model of human social competence. This forces us to look, as Goffman does, at the micro level of social action rather than the macro. Here will be found revealed, in small scale arenas of social interaction, some of the essential ways in which humans speak as social beings, as role players in whatever roles have been made available to them and which they have chosen to take up.

Ethnographic work going back at least as far as Malinowski (Malinowski, 1922) suggests that closer-grained work on the rituals of a speech community can be linked with the speech forms used in the performance of these rituals (Herdt, 1980). Again it is customary to think of rituals as being those of exotic cultures such as those of Melanesia (G. Aijmer, 1997) or the Amazon Basin (Chagnon, 1977). But small-scale social rituals occur everywhere in human affairs. This chapter is about a vernacular ritual in a place no more exotic than New Zealand. It shows the way in which formulaic performers (Lord, 1960) code social knowledge of rituals into formulaic speech. This will be illustrated through an ethnography of horse race meetings and the way in which their central ritual event, a horse race, is provided with commentary by race callers. In other words, the ethnography of race meetings locates the formulaic genre of callers socio-culturally.

As with Whorfian hypotheses, a study of this kind runs the risk of circularity. That can be overcome by separating the ethnographic description from the linguistic one and only when these two descriptions have been independently arrived at, showing how they relate. In this case, the relationship is not entirely iconic and certainly not causal. Some aspects of horse racing are foregrounded and others backgrounded in a race call, while still others, though ethnographically significant, play no part in the call.

2.2 A brief ethnography of race meetings.

Horse racing is an old ritual.[1] It is likely that that horses have been raced for as long as humans have ridden horses since there appears to be no society where the latter is done where the former is not also done. Both the ancient Greeks and the Romans raced horses. In central Istanbul one can still see the post around which racing horses and chariots turned when Istanbul was Constantinople. Races may take place on beaches or in deserts but the aim is always competitive, to see who can race their horse the fastest. Organized racing in the Anglo-American tradition can be seen as beginning with the founding of the Jockey Club at Newmarket, England, in 1750. The tradition of horse racing was brought to New Zealand from England during colonial times and much of what happens is based on English traditions (Cassidy, 2002; Fox, 1999). The Canterbury Jockey Club held its first meeting in Christchurch, New

Zealand, in 1855 only a decade or two after Christchurch was founded as a colonial town. However, it is not my purpose to explain the historical evolution of this tradition here but its contemporary significance. To do that it will suffice to narrate the events of a contemporary race meeting and then to interpret them. Most New Zealand towns and cities have at least one racetrack. Many of the larger cities have two: one for harness racing and one for gallops.[2] For much of the year, these tracks are largely deserted with perhaps a horse or two training in the background. The stands are empty and the large parking lots free of cars and horse floats. The track exists to come to life during a race meeting. There are about 20 racing days per year at Riccarton Park, the racecourse chosen for this description. But a race meeting may last a few days, such as at Easter when the meeting held in Christchurch is the Easter Racing Carnival.[3]

2.2.1 Preliminaries

Race day cannot commence without the arrival of the horses, the stars of the show. They are brought in horse floats which have ramps to allow horses to be walked out to their stalls at the back of the grandstands. There they are groomed and looked after until it is their turn to race. Along with the horse comes its human retinue: trainers, grooms, strappers,[4] owners, friends and relatives of owners normally termed the horse's 'connections'. Many spend some time with the horse. The meeting we are imaginatively attending is a gallops meeting. So there are jockeys. They are in the jockeys' room preparing themselves for racing. Jockeys are engaged to ride particular horses at a meeting. The same horse is not always ridden by the same jockey and the same jockey will ride different horses at the same meeting since a horse will only race once in a day. Jockeys wear riding boots, riding breeches, a white shirt and a racing cap with goggles. When racing a horse, the rider must also be wearing a riding jacket and cap displaying the racing colours of the horse's owner. The jockey is therefore identified with the horse only for the period he or she is riding the horse. The jockey is weighed as part of the handicapping process which places various weights on horses to try and even up the odds.

The members of the jockey club and club officials are also busy preparing a host of necessary details for the meeting. The clerk of the course in his red hunting jacket is at hand on his own horse when a race starts in order to escort the horses out to the start, to supervise the running of each race, and then to bring the winner back to the parade ring. The starter must be in the starter's box with his flag for each race to signal that the horses are 'in the starter's hands'. Judges are at the finishing post to determine who is the winner and adjudicate over disputes. A farrier is on hand to shoe any horse which requires new shoes. Since racing is a life-threatening sport, the ambulance and vet must be on hand, one for injured jockeys, the other for injured horses.

The punters (spectators) are also in attendance. They range from beautifully groomed women in the latest fashion accompanied by their male attendants, often also beautifully attired, seated in the members' stand, to picnickers out for a day with their plastic tables and chairs brought along in the car boot. This scene is little different from race day at the Kentucky Derby in the United States (Harrah, 1992) or at race meetings in England (Cassidy, 2002).

2.2.2 Racing

A day at the races involves more than one race. There may be six or seven races 'on the card', the card being the race book in which the names and details of all the races and all the runners in all the races are given. Included is a detailed description of each horse with its relevant details: the owner, breeder, trainer, the weight the horse is carrying on handicap, the jockey, and the owner's racing colours and more. Each race consists of the same events taking place in the same order. First the horses are led around the pre-parade ring at the back of the stands to exercise lightly. They are saddled and bridled, and from the pre-parade ring they are led out onto the parade ring in front of the stands. In the ring the jockeys mount and the horses lightly trot around the ring, often led by the bridle by a walking attendant. From there they go out onto the course through a gate and then, often trotting or galloping to warm up further, they move to the barrier at the start of the race. Here they are placed into the stalls in the position they have drawn on the starting barrier. They move into the back of the stall and the gates are closed behind. This is often a difficult process. The horses are sometimes restless and jockeys run the risk of being hurt by the steelwork of the stall. Sometimes horses move back out of the stall and are then quietened until they are prepared to move into position again. Sometimes jockeys dismount to avoid a fall or stand on the stall's edges. All the while the clerk of the course supervises and various grooms pull, push and drag the horses into position, trying not to get hurt themselves.

When all the horses are in position, the assistant starter raises his flag, the starter opens the gates at the front of the barrier and the horses race from the start to the finish, often a distance of a mile or so. On the way they pass marker pegs which indicate the distance to the finish. In imperial measure these are set a furlong apart; now that New Zealand is metric, they are denominated in 100s of metres. The horses run to the finish by way of the 'straight' which is where the stands are placed, allowing the punters to view the finish at close quarters. As the horses approach the finish, the crowd noise rises to a roar and the pitch increases. The ground vibrates and drums with the sounds of horses' hooves. At the finish post, a camera records the finish. The race over, in the stands excited talk succeeds the roar.

After finishing, the horses slow down, go back to a canter and then a trot and finally a walk. The clerk of the course escorts the winner back into the parade ring where it is again paraded around and receives its prizes: a cheque for the owner, a trophy and sometimes a horse cover for the horse with the name of the race on it. The unsuccessful horses are ridden and walked back to their stalls, warmed down and unsaddled, washed and brushed and, at the end of the meeting, all are taken back to their stables wherever 'home' is.

2.2.3 Gambling

Racing has been associated with gambling for millennia. In New Zealand this is controlled by a public body, the Totalizator Agency Board or TAB. Betting is either 'on course' or 'off course'. For the latter there are a number of options, from visiting a TAB office to betting on-line. On-course betting is done at the TAB offices, of which there are a number in the stands. These offices, where one lines up and places a bet, look rather like ticket offices. There are numerous different ways to bet. One can bet on a horse for a win or a place or 'have a bob each way' meaning to back the horse for either a win or a place. One can bet on 'the double', two designated races at the meeting where one backs a horse in each for a win. One can bet on the trifecta where three races are involved. The odds are given up on a big board and on television monitors. No bookies operate. The odds are determined by the totalizator which adds up all the bets and determines what the pay out will be. Having placed a bet, a punter receives a 'betting slip' and can redeem any winnings directly following the race. At the end of the meeting the ground is covered with the used betting slips of those who did not win.

The Christchurch Casino also has a gambling facility at the course and banks provide credit card facilities including by mobile van. Very large sums of money are involved in a large race meeting. Most money is transacted through off-course betting but significant losses are also incurred on course.

2.2.4 Fashion

Associated with major race meetings there is often a fashion parade and a fashion contest for the best-dressed woman (and man) at the meeting. Just as the horses are paraded around the parade ring, so women parade around the catwalk and the members' enclosure. A recent fashion sensation has been virtual garments painted onto the naked upper body. (Such fashion requires warm temperatures.)

2.2.5 Interpreting race meetings

Racing is a complex ritual. Three significant elements are involved:

- competition among horses (and their 'connections');
- pageantry, as shown in the clerk of the course in his riding habit, the parading of the horses and the jockeys in their colours, and the women in their fashionable clothing; and
- risk-taking, as shown in the risk to life and limb of racing a horse, the financial risks of the owner who expends large amounts of money to purchase and train a horse with the possibility that it will win no money back, and the risk to the punters' bank balances in the wagering on the outcome of a race.

Two cultural patterns appear to govern these elements of racing. The first has to do with the relationship between humans and horses. Racing is a celebration of a long history of interconnectedness between humans and horses. In racing, humans and horses are partners. The breeder who bred the horse has a stake in its future. He or she attempted to get the best stallion and mare together at an affordable price. The owner(s) bought the horse, normally at an annual 'bloodstock auction'. The trainer was engaged to train the horse to race, grooms and strappers looked after it at the training establishment and a jockey was engaged to ride it in a race.

The beauty of the horse is celebrated in the grooming, brushing, clipping, polishing and combing, parading and dressing. The best-dressed horse may be selected from the whole field in the parade ring prior to the race. The parallel with the women who are also groomed, brushed, combed, polished and paraded is manifest. The mastery of rider over horse is on display in the way in which these large beasts are controlled, and, at the finish, whipped to do what they have been trained to do. But mastery is provisional. Riders can be dislodged and fall.

That brings us to the second major pattern, risk-taking. Racing involves risk-taking and the risks are many and real. Horses are able to inflict heavy injuries and death on their riders. Not unusually, jockeys fall and are then trampled by other horses. The ambulance which rides along the outside rail accompanying the race is there for a purpose. Collaterally, racing can inflict heavy injuries and death on a horse. If a rider makes a mistake in riding his or her mount too hard, pushing through an insufficient space, the horse may trip, fall and break a leg or neck. The veterinarian at the track not infrequently has to 'put down' a horse which has been injured. Everyone associated with the horse knows that these risks exist. Owners can lose a large amount of money if a horse is injured, while punters know they can lose their money by placing a bet.

The races provide a rhythm of excitation associated with risk, followed by a counting of the cost, because the ritual of the race meeting organizes the process of risk-taking into a series of events, each of which allowing for the same risks to be taken. At the end of each race the cost can be counted with a few winners and many losers.

Symbolically we can see race meetings as being essentially cyclic. Each day at the races has its cyclical rhythm with people arriving and, at the end, leaving and then returning for the next day's racing. Each race has its cycle with horses leaving their stalls, racing and returning to their stalls. Within each race there are the three circumnavigations: round the pre-parade ring, the parade ring and then the track. The punters place bets, watch the race, and then collect winnings, place bets on the next race and so forth. Informing and congruent with these cycles is fortune's wheel itself.[5] Fortune's wheel is careless of those who follow fortune. It takes them up and it also brings them down. This is its primary topos. Racing being a game of chance, those who follow it should, like epic heroes such as those of the medieval Icelandic sagas, be careless of where fortune's wheel may take them.[6] This is the secondary topos of fortune's wheel.

At the centre of the cycle is the central rhythmic event of the race which the race caller encodes in the form of a commentary. Since race calls are formulaic, the phrasal lexis of the call gives linguistic form to these central cyclical aspects of racing culture.

2.3 Race calling

Horse races have been provided with commentary in New Zealand since radio became a broadcast medium, (Kuiper & Austin, 1990). When radio commentary began, commentators sat in the stands from where their view could be obscured by excited punters. One early commentary contains the sentences, 'Sit down in front please. I can't see a thing'.

Today, however, the commentary box is placed high up overlooking the course.

Race callers provide commentaries of horse racing in the two different modes we have seen at work in ice hockey commentary. Before and after a race the commentary is in colour mode. It is fluent in normal ways, has normal intonation, does not have entirely fixed discourse rules but does use formulae, although not in a very concentrated fashion. The events of the race as it happens are related by race commentators in play-by-play mode. Play-by-play mode involves relaying abnormally fluently, although not necessarily rapidly, the events which the commentator is seeing. Play-by-play commentary is a formulaic genre while colour commentary is not.

Recall that callers watch the race through powerful field glasses while they call the race. The commentary begins twice, in that for radio listeners the commentator comes on before the race and talks about the field, the odds, and how the starters are lining up at the barrier. As the starter's flag is raised, the commentary proper begins and is switched on over the public address system at the course. The commentary always begins with a formula such as *away and racing now*. This formula announces that the circumnavigation of the track by horses and riders is beginning. From that point on what has been placed at risk is truly at stake.[7]

Starting formulae

and there they go
and they're away and racing
they're off and racing now
they're off and running now
they're on their way
they're off and away

The caller then usually describes the horses who started well or badly. Seen from the perspective of fortune's wheel the best starters are at an advantage while the slow starters are not. In accord with the dictates of fortune's wheel, the good starters are mentioned in preference to the poor starters.

Good start formulae

one of the best out was X
X away fairly well
X making a pretty good beginning
X began well

Thereafter the caller relates the progress of the horses around the track. He does this by beginning with the leading horse and moving through the field of runners until he reaches the last one. For every horse he provides its name and its location in two possible dimensions. These are its position relative to the horses in front of it and how far out from the rail it is. Both these are relevant to the horse's current and future fortune and consequently the fortunes of its connections and the punters who have wagered on it. The closer to the leaders a horse is, the more its chances are currently to be seen as being at the top of fortune's wheel and conversely, the further back it is in the field, the lower it is on fortune's wheel. Horses which are on the rail have a shorter distance to run and are therefore in a better position to win while those further out have a longer race to run and are therefore potentially disadvantaged.

Linear order formulae

X trails the leader
right behind the leader is X
running second is X
X came next
in the trail
a length further back then is X
X by a neck from Y
X has got back

Distance out from the rail formulae

on the rail
on the inside rail
on the inside of X
closer in to X
on the outside
wide out
X numeral wide

Linear and distance-out formulae

followed on the inside by X
back on the inside
down on the inner
next along the rail then to X
in the one one

The formulae listed above often show dimensions within which the place on fortune's wheel is to be calibrated. Since linear sequence is primary, a horse's place in the linear sequence is calibrated in terms of lengths, half lengths, necks and noses, the measure of a horse. Perceptually, linear order is more salient since linear order determines the sequence in which horses pass the winning post. Beside these body-oriented calibrations are places in the sequence such as *next, behind*. Distances out from the rail are in different dimensions. Here the body width of a horse plays a role but not the only role. Horses are *on the rail, one out* from it or *two wide, further out*. Calibration is not therefore in terms of the horse's cross-sectional size but how many horses are between it and the rail. This demonstrates that the distance from the rail is not as significant as distance in front or behind.[8]

Special attention is given to the leader(s), those currently highest on fortune's wheel, and to tail-enders, currently lowest on fortune's wheel.

Leader formulae

X has made it into the lead
X in the lead
X the (clear) leader
X in front now
X in the front
X putting his nose in front
X take over the running

Tail-ender formulae

X who's at the back of the field
X the tail-ender
X at the tail end of the field
last is X
X drops out to last
X the last to go by
last of all now is X

Having reached the end of the field, the caller then returns to locating the leader(s). He does this by way of loop formulae which locate where the field as a whole is in the progress of the race. Again this is intimately connected with the cycle of the race. At the commencement of the race, not so much hangs on where the individual horses are in the field. Towards the end, much does. Loop formulae indicate where on the physical track the field is and where in the progress of the race the field is.

Track location formulae

around the northern turn
they gallop down the back
off the back they come
into the back straight they go
they work around across the top

Race location formulae

numeral metres left to go
numeral metres left to run
they come past the numeral

The calling of the sequence of horses is cyclical and proceeds as many times as the caller can cover the field in the time of the race.

At the finishing post, the caller must indicate clearly where the horses came in order since it is at this point that the beneficence of fortune is (temporarily) determined. Also at this point, whether a horse was further out from the rail or not becomes irrelevant and is not mentioned.

Finishing formulae

they go to the post
they pass the judge
as they went across the line
X goes to the pole to win it
X has got up to win it
X has got the last say
X goes away to win it
X has won the money
followed in by X
followed home by X
last home is X

Occasionally this predictable ritual is punctuated by life-threatening events when horses and riders fall or 'go down'. Here too there are formulae which relay such events. Since these events have a serious impact on the progress of fortune's wheel, they are worthy of being lexicalized.

Potentially life-threatening event formulae

X broke up[9]
X broke in the running
X went down

Mastery over the horse, as indicated earlier, is exercised symbolically and actually by means of the whip in both harness racing and gallops, and by spurring hard in the case of gallops.

Mastery formulae

go for the stick on X
X (is) hard ridden

All these formulae are specialized for their one task and each task is part of the way in which the racing ritual is realized in speech and the lexicon. This rich taxonomy of formulae is thus intimately linked to events of horse racing. But not to all the events. The fact that the wind is blowing, the riders' colours are fluttering, the horses are frothing at the mouth, the sound of the horses' hooves as they drum past the stands, have no lexicalized form. They are plain for all at the races to see and hear but they do not form part of the phrasal lexicon. This is because they are not central to the cyclic nature of racing explored earlier.

2.4 The significance of race calling

Can we take this analysis further? Are there further significant links between the inner and outer form of the race calling genre? First a cautionary note. Such meta-cultural analysis is beset with danger. The major danger is to reduce the fine-grained nature of the analysis to broad and relatively unsustainable generalization. But some remarks are in order. New Zealand is a post-colonial country and the racing ritual was imported from the United Kingdom along with Gilbert and Sullivan operettas, brass bands and cat fancy.[10] In the colonial period, New Zealand had a rurally-based economy which was heavily reliant on horses for transport and motive power on farms. Racing dates from this period and its celebration of the association of human and horse can be linked to this period.

But the goddess Fortuna and her wheel date from well before this time. What gives her currency now? The weight of cultural continuity is one factor which should not be overlooked. So much of what happens in a culture happens because that is the way things are done, as shown in the case of religions of practice (Staal, 1990). Lexical items like formulae have the same tendency to persist. The ritual nature of races has apparently not changed greatly since the rules of racing were codified by the Jockey Club. But Fortuna has held sway through pagan and Christian times perhaps because of the way the human condition is perceived in many Western cultures. The heroic code of pre-Christian Icelanders, as indicated earlier, would have been in accord with the view that one was a slave to fortune and that the virtuous thing to do was grin and bear it.

In contemporary New Zealand society, risk-aversion is a dominant impulse. There is a belief that, with proper management, risks can be avoided. We take out insurance and believe that what is left of the welfare state will take care of things to minimize risk. Unlike the heroes of the sagas, we hope we will not die, at least not yet. Risk-aversion manifests itself in many ways, a typical one being the holding of inquiries after major or minor tragedies in the hope that such tragedies will not be repeated in the future. Legislative controls of all kinds are imposed or tightened to prevent what is believed to be preventable. In such a context, the rhythms of the racetrack with its partly ritualized risk-taking are symbolic and attractive. Humans have always lived with risk and yet tried to avoid it. At the track this rhythm is given form and constraint. That form is, in part, codified in the formulae of the race caller. In this way, racing has elements of Bakhtinian carnival (Bakhtin, 1973) overturning the mundane normative conventions of risk-aversion into their opposite: the embracing of risk. The carnival is also a liminal period, a time out, for the overturning of the conventional mundane social order by a heightened, emotionally charged enjoyment of a ritual antistructure. For at the races, instead of the linearity of the mundane day, of growing older and dying, there is asserted its complementary: the cycles which also govern human existence. Cyclical patterns of days and seasons, lifecycles and religious rituals provide mute testimony to the pervasiveness of the circle in human culture. As racing acts out its cycles, it provides a ritual embodiment of the promise that the cycle will bring us back, not withstanding its attendant risks, to where we can try again. It is thus an embodiment of hope, and of the possible triumph of hope over despair, as it is of the vagaries of fortune which, not withstanding our best efforts, can bring us down.

These conclusions suggest that a humble genre like race calling exists in a social order which is not just local. Beyond it are wider social perspectives which make sense of it. To do it justice requires these wider perspectives to be noted.

2.5 Methodological epilogue: participant observation and sampling

At various points in this book I thought it worthwhile to provide a non-technical account of the methodology used in the studies being presented. Since many of my methodologies are praxis-based and have evolved over a thirty-year period, these sections will put them on record. This should help students of formulaic genres to engage in their own studies of similar genres. As with the text itself, these sections are informal. Formal methodologies may be obtained elsewhere. The methodology that I have employed in the study of race calling and racing is not restricted to the study of racing and race calling. I have employed it in a number of other studies of formulaic genres and their performance.[11]

Any study of a genre supposes that the genre sits at the intersection of the situational parameters which give rise to the variety. My approach to the study of situation is informed by anthropological traditions. I believe one needs to come to an awareness of a culture and its rituals by being a participant observer. This is both easier and harder in one's own culture that in another. It is easier because one has an intuitive (native) understanding of the culture which one does not have of a culture in which one has *not* been brought up. It is harder in that these intuitions must be made overt. One must try to understand what it is that makes this situation work the way it does. When that knowledge is native, it is sometimes harder to make it overt. If one wishes to understand auctioning, then one must go to auctions and understand how these fit in the market models which prevail in one's society and how they operate as vernacular public rituals. If one wishes to understand racing, then the same objectives hold. One must go to the races, participate both as a native and also as a dispassionate observer. The understandings must then be given a form which other natives can understand since one is trying to uncover the tacit understandings that natives share about these events. (See Cassidy, 2002 for an exemplary study of racing.)

The other element of the study of a formulaic genre is provided by linguistic analysis, in the case of race calling, discussed in section 2.3 of this chapter. That involves recording and transcribing texts. In the case of the genre of auctioneering documented in Kuiper & Haggo (1984) it involved carrying around a portable tape-recorder and a directional microphone and pretending, at least some of the time, to be an interested sound man from the media. Being thus equipped does not enable one easily to operate as a participant observer. However in the case of racing, soundtrack is available directly from radio, where race commentary is broadcast. So recordings can be made off-air while one can peacefully attend the race meeting trying to look like everyone else.

After beginning the recording and transcription process, it is worth asking how much data is enough, i.e when should one stop.[12] There is an assumption behind such a question. It is that there is a representative sample that provides a reliable snapshot of the whole genre. Several important considerations follow. First, since all formulaic genres are variable and context-dependent, only some features are characteristic of the genre in the abstract. When one abstracts away from the local, there is a cost in the loss of immediacy. There is a gain in that this is the only way to discover what the traditional elements of the genre are. These are the properties of the genre that are passed from one native in the genre to the next novice. The inner text type features of a genre can often be seen in a relatively small sample, since once one has seen a relatively small number of instances it is likely that there will be relatively little novelty. In the case of *Times*-style engagement notices, it is clear after seeing twenty or thirty of such notices that the chances of a new form being seen in the next case are low. However, in other genres like race calls one might find that such a point of diminishing novelty comes later.

It is also difficult at the beginning to know whether a new formal feature is original or part of the genre. One auctioneer whom I recorded asked at the beginning of an auction for an item to be held up. He looked at it intently and said, *Oh, it's a beauty*. Without further recording, it would have been impossible to decide whether this was a formula or not. By the time I had heard it a number of times from the same auctioneer I knew it was not an original sentence but a formula. Once heard in the performances of other auctioneers one knows it is not just an idiolectal formula but a genre-specific formula. In the case of *Oh, it's a beauty.* this did not happen so this formula remains idiolectal.

Some corpus linguists take frequency criteria as central to determining whether a phrase is lexicalized, e.g. Moon (1998). For them the larger the corpus the more likely one is to get reliable frequency evidence for the existence of a particular phrasal lexical item. However, frequency is a manifestation of native-speaker knowledge of phrasal lexical items. The absence of a significant frequency count for a particular expression does not provide evidence against it existing. It may be that the contexts in which the data are gathered will not be such that a particular item is to be found in them. We saw in chapter 1 that many formulae are genre-specific. Think again, for example, of the kinds of formulae that are said in prayers in church, such as *Glory be to the Father, the Son and the Holy Ghost*. Unless texts from that genre are in the data, then one will not find such a formula. Ice hockey commentaries will, likely, not be in the major databases which are searched by corpus linguists, so the formula *They hold on for the face-off* will have a frequency of zero in a search of such a corpus.

The same can be said for discourse rules. One must collect enough data to be able to tell what is central to the discourse as a genre, what is idiosyncratic, i.e. idiolectal, and what is original, i.e. non-formulaic free-form text. Again there are no fixed corpus sizes for this kind of judgement because it is a judgement. One stops collecting when it seems that one has enough data to say that there is little likelihood that more data will turn up further general features of the genre. As far as the ethnographic analysis goes, again one must go to enough race meetings to feel that one has become as familiar as one can reasonably be with what goes on there. There comes a point when nothing new seems to be happening. But one needs to know that jockeys fall, that horses are put down after breaking limbs. These are recurrent significant events even if they are relatively infrequent. Finally it needs to be noted that certainty is not a hallmark of scientific enquiry. One can and often is mistaken. Further data collection may reveal further properties of the genre which one hadn't noted previously. That is not a failure; it is a success. All scientists (and all humans) share this capacity for fallibility. You must not set out to be wrong but you must be ready to be wrong and to find ways to find out if you are wrong. Social scientists sometimes forget this in a fruitless quest for certainty, seeing it, for example, in statistical significance.

3
Forecasting the Weather[1]

Everywhere you go, you always take the weather with you.
Crowded House *'Weather with you'*

3.1 Introduction

The previous chapter described the spoken genre of race calling and placed it culturally in a context of ritual social action and individual social motivation. This chapter deals with a genre which is also formulaic but is written to be spoken, i.e. it is about the writing of scripts. The genre of the previous chapter was comparatively simple whereas its social context was comparatively complex. The written genre of weather forecasting, by contrast, is formally complex while socially it is comparatively simple. We listen to the weather forecast to find out what the weather is likely to be today or tomorrow. The forecasts are produced by professionals who have their own way of talking about weather to each other but have other ways of talking about the weather to us through the media. In the place of the confined context of race days and their minority of initiated racing aficionados, the scripts of this chapter were written for a whole nation of radio listeners and TV viewers. Its context is institutional since these forecasts are the work of a public body. The genre is also remarkable, in that, when this study was written, the scripts produced by the weather forecasters at the New Zealand Meteorological Office provided the sole source genre for all other weather forecasts broadcast in New Zealand. Since then, however, a number of different forecasters have provided services to media. Consequently the uniformity of the genre has changed. The Met. Office, too, has moved with the times and provides tailor-made forecasts for individual presenters as part of its service.[2]

In the 'classical' period when forecasting was the sole preserve of the Met. Office, the New Zealand Meteorological Office forecast was broadcast through the National Radio Programme stations. In the wider study, of which this smaller one is a part, Hickey (1991) looks at the way the weather was forecast in New Zealand in 1990. Thirty-nine weather forecasts from a variety of radio and television stations were recorded. The period of time over which they were recorded allowed for some variation in the type of weather conditions presented in the forecasts, but was not long enough to include major seasonal changes. In addition to the broadcast forecasts, one forecast was taken from the Meteorological Service's automatic telephone forecast for the Christchurch district. Five National Radio Programme broadcast forecasts from the Met. Office form the database from which the analysis below is drawn, although many more were listened to. This may seem a small sample. However, as indicated in chapter 1, large corpora usually yield little more than comparatively small corpora, given how stereotyped the formulaic genres such as weather forecasts are.

The Meteorological Office which produced the texts on which this analysis is based, is a state-funded organization set up to forecast the weather. Forecasts prepared by the Met. Office were, in 1990, either broadcast directly from the office or were repackaged by the media into a form styled for their viewers or listeners (Bell, 1991).

This is a study of a formulaic genre which is also an occupational register. Doctors have routines for interviewing patients (Coulthard & Ashby, 1975), defendants for pleas in mitigation before sentencing (Gruber, 2007). The genre to be examined in this chapter is so stereotypical that Goldberg, Driedger, & Kittredge (1995) show how a machine-based speech production system can produce weather forecasts while Mitkov (1991) provides a machine-based system for translating weather forecasts in a multilingual society.

3.2 Structural properties of Met. Office forecasts

In 1990, the National Radio network forecasts for the entire country were broadcast after the news bulletins at 5.30, 6.30, 7.30 and 8.30 am and 10 pm. The morning forecasts described the expected weather situation until midnight of the same day, while the evening forecast was until midnight of the next day. An extended-range forecast for the next five days was broadcast at 12.30 pm. In addition to these forecasts, short forecasts, coastal forecasts and mountain forecasts were also broadcast throughout the day. The broadcast voices giving the forecasts on the National Radio Programme belong to meteorologists at the Met. Office.

Suppose that we are listening to one of these forecasts. After the introduction from the news presenter, the weather presenter begins his forecast with a greeting to the listeners and news presenter.[3] Depending on the time of day, this will be *good morning, good afternoon* or *good evening*. These are the only greetings used. The less formal *hello* is never used. There are two possible reasons for this situation. First, it might be that *hello* is proscribed by the Met. Office Guidelines (hereafter MOG). These guidelines prescribe certain terms and proscribe others for public broadcast forecasts. For example, forecasters were not to use the modal auxiliary *will* because it suggested certainty nor were they to use the words *chance* or *risk* because of their 'unflattering connotation'. Instead terms such as *possible* and *may* were to be used. The MOG is therefore rather like the editorial assistant at *The Times* who ensures that all engagement advertisements in the *Times* conform to *Times* style. Second it is possible that the proscription of *hello* is traditional.

As it happens, instructions for commencing the forecast with a greeting were not included in the MOG. Instead, the choice of these formal greetings reflects the formality of the weather forecast on National Radio, *hello* being excluded by convention rather than proscription. The forecast begins immediately after the greeting. Met. Office forecasts come in five distinct sections which can be represented by the following discourse structure rule:

> R1. Forecast → greeting + synoptic situation + district forecasts + long-range forecast + close[4]

The rule can be read as indicating that the forecast has hierarchical structure where the whole forecast has five parts which come after the arrow and are linked by the plus signs indicating their order. Each of the constituents of the forecast will be examined in turn and we will find that each itself consists of further structured sequences.

3.2.1 Synoptic situation

The synoptic situation describes the state of the pressure and frontal systems over and surrounding New Zealand, and in some forecasts the expected effect of these on the weather. There is no variation to be found in the sequence in which the subject matter of the synoptic situation is dealt with. Subbiah (1989) divides this section into Pressure, Winds and

Rain, but does not account for any repetition that can occur, nor for the fact that the synoptic situation is actually divided into two sections according, primarily, to the kind of detail which is to be found in these sections. The synoptic situation can be represented as follows:

> R2. Synoptic situation → general synopsis + (specific synopsis)

The general synopsis occurs first. Any information given is of the most general nature possible, in that it covers a large geographic region and goes into little detail about the weather conditions there, with the language used reflecting this. The content and order of the elements in this section can be represented as follows:

> R3. General Synopsis → \pressure system + verb of motion + location \ + (direction moving from + \ area affected by system\ + effect on weather + location of affected weather + \ length of time forecast weather expected to persist\)

The term 'direction' refers to any of the eight main compass directions. Although much of the information in this section of the forecast is optional, the order in which it is presented is never varied. The variety which is apparent in this section between forecasts is thus due to the amount of optional information which has been included, rather than to individual forecasters inventing their own methods of ordering information.

An analysis of the content of each of the constituents above reinforces the finding of Subbiah (1989) that the language of weather forecasts is highly formulaic. Given the sample of forecasts on which this study is based, the formulae we give as examples do not constitute an exhaustive list but they are representative.

> Pressure system formulae include: *a ridge of high pressure, a (shallow) trough of low pressure, a stationary anti-cyclone, a slow moving front, a depression.* Location formulae include: *(just to the) 'direction' of New Zealand, (just to the) 'direction' of the Chatham Islands, across New Zealand, over (central) New Zealand, on to New Zealand.*

This section of the synoptic situation uses the most general descriptions possible when describing the location of weather phenomena. Modifiers are used if a more precise location is required, but this does not seem to be common practice. The names of districts are never mentioned at this point. The way that the location is described is only partially in keeping with the instructions given in MOG (B 3.3.5.1), in that while the location is given in terms of well-known places, it does not give their distance from such places in kilometres but instead uses less precise modifiers. Given that MOG are so general about locating pressure systems, it is interesting that more exact locations are not given by the use of well-known place names such as *Otago*. This reinforces the hypothesis that this part of the forecast is designed to be as general as possible.

In the discourse structure rule, pressure system and location appear in slashes because it is possible for an anti-cyclone in one area to produce a ridge of high pressure in another area which itself affects the weather. Both pressure systems and locations are mentioned at this point in the forecast. As shown in the rule, it is also possible for a general synopsis to consist entirely of descriptions of various pressure systems and their locations without giving any information about their effect on the weather. However, as shown in the rule, no more than three locations or pressure systems are mentioned in any of these situations. The constituent relating to the direction of movement is instantiated by the formula *from the 'direction'* (which was used once only in the data). Effect-on-weather formulae include: *bring(ing) fine weather, bring(ing) (continuing) dry, settled weather, with (continuing) dry, settled weather*.

The forecast weather is described by the use of adjectives modifying the noun *weather*, rather than by detailing separate components of the weather. Its description is also limited by the fact that precipitation is the only weather condition which may be described in the effect-on-weather section of the general synopsis.

Settled according to MOG (C 2.2) refers to weather which is expected to continue for a number of days so this part of the forecast is general enough to remain valid for a number of days.

The location of affected weather is given by the formula *most districts*. This description of the location appeared in all forecasts giving location and is indicative of the fact that this part of the forecast aims to give information which is relevant to as much of the country as possible while not including that which is relevant only to small areas.

The length of time for the forecast weather is typically given by the following formulae: *over the weekend, for the next day or two, through 'day'*. The forecasters are able to describe the time span either in terms of the number of days or with reference to a part of the week. The general synopsis refers to the prevailing conditions no more than two days ahead.

Although there is a choice of phrases available for use in many sections of the general synopsis, this choice is not large and in most cases the general synopsis makes up only one sentence of the synoptic situation. After this initial sentence, the optional second part of the synoptic situation, the specific synopsis, begins. Although it contains much the same sort of information, this information is of a more detailed nature than that of the general synopsis. Its discourse structure is thus somewhat different from that of the general synopsis.

R4. Specific Synopsis → \ { type of air flow / pressure system } + location + (effect on weather + location of affected weather + time of forecast weather)\

This entire section appears in slashes because, as will be seen, it is concerned with smaller parts of the country and the same type of information can be repeated for each area up to three times. The categories from 'effect on weather' to 'time of forecast weather' appear in brackets because it is possible that this section can consist entirely of information about pressure systems and their location without describing the effects on the weather.

Each constituent is implemented by formulaic phrases. But the content of the phrases is somewhat different from that of the general synopsis. Each category will be examined in turn. The type-of-air-flow formula is *a 'direction' flow*. Pressure system formulae include *a (weakening) trough of low pressure* and *a ridge of high pressure*. While the only information given here which is different from that in the general synopsis is about air flows, this appears to be significant since air flows are never mentioned in the general synopsis. This is thus an example of the type of extra detail found in this section. Location formulae include: *(over) 'direction' (of) the Tasman Sea, 'direction' New Zealand, (across) 'direction' of North Island*. Location appears to be optional in this part of the forecast only when a flow is being described. In all other cases the location of the pressure system is given. Modifiers are used more frequently to indicate a more exact location than in the general synopsis. But the locations are still very general. Effect-on-weather formulae include: *a few showers, some drizzle, showers, a 'direction' change*. The information given in this section is of a more specific nature than that in the general synopsis and refers not to the weather in general, but to various elements of it.

When more than one type of weather is forecast for one area, the wind conditions always precede precipitation. This can be represented as:

R5. Effect on weather → (wind) + precipitation

The phrases listed above can be divided into two groups, depending on which constituent they refer to: wind-conditions formula, *a 'direction' change*, precipitation formulae: *a few showers, some drizzle, showers*. If the effect on the weather constituent is selected, then precipitation is always mentioned while wind conditions are optional and appear to be mentioned only if a change in wind conditions is expected.

Effect-on-the-weather and the location are usually repeated for various areas of the country so that more than one of the conditions can apply in a single forecast. Location-of-affected-weather formulae include: *'direction' of the country, 'direction' coast of North Island, (far) 'direction' of North Island (areas), Cook Strait*. Detail is given by reference to the islands of New Zealand and even to areas within those islands. The use of *coast*, *far* and *areas* allows the forecaster to direct the listener's attention to more specific areas in New Zealand. Referring to Cook Strait is a specific and economical way of indicating that parts of both the North and South Island may be affected. The way that location is described in this part of the synoptic situation is indicative of the fact that this section is less general and provides forecasts for smaller areas of the country, in particular the separate islands.

Time-of-expected-weather is given by formulae such as: *in the 'time of day', later tomorrow*, which appears only in this second part of the synoptic situation. Thus, while the general synopsis gives a general forecast for all parts of the country, the specific synopsis gives a more detailed account of changes to the weather that are expected to occur in smaller areas of the country. Just as the location of the weather and its nature are described in more detail in this section, so is the time scale. While the general synopsis describes time in terms of days, this section further divides the days into parts.

In summary, the synoptic situation of National Radio forecasts is made up of two distinctive sections, each structured by its own rules and having its own characteristic formulae.

3.2.2 District forecasts

The district forecasts begin with an introductory formula which can be represented as in figure 3.1.[5] The version of this sentence which uses

Forecasting the Weather 49

```
START ⇢ Now ⇢ the ⇢ forecasts ⇢ to midnight ⇢ tomorrow ⇢ STOP
        ↗ Here are ↗    ↗ district ↗       ↗ up ↗        ↗ 'day' ↗
```

Figure 3.1 The opening formula of a National Radio forecast

the name of a day is used only in the five-day forecasts. It has specified the time which the district forecasts are valid for, with the result that unlike the synoptic section, time need not be mentioned for the remainder of this part of the forecast. In keeping with the much more specific and detailed amount of information which will be included in this section of the forecast, this amount of time is more specific than that described in the synoptic section.

For weather forecasting, there are thirteen districts in New Zealand, including the Chatham Islands. The descriptions always begin at the top of the North Island, working down the East Coast of the North Island, across the centre of the North Island from east to west and then down to the southern-most tip of the North Island. Progress then is north to south down the West Coast of the South Island then north to south down the East Coast before the forecast for the Chatham Islands is given (Subbiah 1989:11). Subbiah points out that this pattern of regions is convenient for the forecaster in terms of preparation, and convenient for the audience in terms of assimilation of information. The size of these regions is also convenient for the giving of detailed information, in that they are relatively small but there are not so many of them that this information takes an overly long time to present. This should ensure that people listening for a region near the end of the forecast are still concentrating when their region is reached. This way of putting regions in a predictable order may seem the natural way to proceed but Wray (2002:81) reports that BBC4 has a weather-led format where the order of regions in the forecasts is determined by the major weather systems. That order can therefore change from day to day depending on where the pressure systems and fronts are located over the UK.

MOG (B 2.1) give the following as possible elements for forecasts for the public: (a) synoptic situation, (b) wind, (c) type of weather, (d) temperature, (e) precipitation, (f) state of cloud cover, (g) humidity, (h) time. Not all of these elements are included in any forecast. According to MOG (B 2.1.1), most forecasts consist of (b), (d), (e), and/or (f). National Radio forecasts consist of some or all of these elements, depending on the expected weather and who the forecaster is. In addition, (a) synoptic situation and (h) time always appear. The remaining elements are dealt with in detail in the district forecasts. They are described for each district or area in turn and may be mentioned more than once in each district if a change in the weather is expected or if the area is being further broken up into smaller sections for the forecast. The order of these elements is not fixed, but varies depending on who the presenter is. However there are some patterns that appear to be followed to a greater or lesser degree. Oliver Druce, one of the forecasters in our sample, always presents these elements in a set order:

> R6: Druce district forecast → \(cloud cover)\ + \(temperature)\ + \(precipitation)\ +\(wind)\.

Temperature is seldom included in his forecasts. Depending on the weather situation, some of these elements may not be mentioned or may be mentioned more than once, but never more than three times in a single district. If there appears to be some variation from this order, this is due to the introduction of a new part of the district into the forecast or the forecasting of a change in the weather some time in the future. An example of this is the sequence:

> *For Wellington and Wairarapa, fine in the morning with moderate northerlies. Southerlies freshening in the afternoon with some cloudy periods and possibly a few showers.*

Within the area described, the order of elements is:

> R7. Cloud cover + wind + cloud cover + precipitation.

However within the two times mentioned, morning and afternoon, the order is:

> R8. Morning → cloud cover + wind
> R9. Afternoon → cloud cover + precipitation.

This is in keeping with the Druce district forecast discourse structure. The southerlies mentioned at the start of the afternoon section can be accounted for as being part of the wind section of the morning forecast, providing a convenient bridge from morning to afternoon weather.

Another forecaster, Bob Lake, uses a different order which is:

R10. Lake district forecast → \(cloud cover)\ + \(precipitation)\ + \(wind)\ + \(temperature)\.

Other forecasters have no order that they favour, but there is a tendency among those who refer to temperature to forecast this last in each section. The difference of order and elements emphasizes that even among National Radio forecasters there is variation in the forecasting style used.

Each constituent element of a district forecast has associated formulae. For example, the constituent 'cloud cover' has the following structure:

R11. Cloud cover → $\left(\left\{\begin{array}{l}\text{extent1}\\\text{change1}\end{array}\right\}\right)$ + type of cloud cover + $\left(\left\{\begin{array}{l}\text{extent 2 + duration}\\\text{duration}\\\text{change 2}\end{array}\right\}\right)$

Type of cloud cover may be expressed by the following formulae:

cloudy, fine $\left(\left\{\begin{array}{l}\text{*weather}\\\text{and sunny}\end{array}\right\}\right)$, *high clouds*.

While there is a large selection of phrases which describe cloud cover in MOG (C 2.5), only two are found in the forecasts. Although there are no instructions given on combining elements from this section, the combination *fine and sunny* is a popular formula with forecasters. *Mainly* is used to give more detail. The use of *high*, as in *high cloud*, seems to serve the same purpose, and is in keeping with the hypothesis that forecasters will use non-MOG phrases in the interests of providing as accurate a forecast as possible.

The extent constituent (R11) may be realized as:

(a few) cloudy areas, *some (coastal) cloud*, *areas of* $\left(\left\{\begin{array}{l}\text{high}\\\text{low}\end{array}\right\}\right)$ *cloud*, + *cloudy patches*, + *cloud (and mist) patches*.

None of these formulae come directly from MOG. However most of them are used by the majority of the forecasters, so it is likely that they were learned tacitly or were passed on explicitly during training. The use of both *cloud* and *cloudy* in these phrases allows some degree of variation during the forecasts.

Duration is expressed by formulae such as: *cloudy at times, cloudy *night and morning, *often cloudy, *mostly cloudy, fine in the *morning, *(some) fine intervals, *mostly fine, *mainly fine, sunny this *afternoon.*

These descriptions are not restricted to one kind of weather, but are used in the same way as phrases taken from MOG. For example, *mostly* is used with both *fine* and *cloudy*, but the term *cloud* is not used when describing duration and although the phrases *cloud night and morning* and *a few periods of cloud* are possible they are never used, while *cloudy night and morning* and *a few cloudy periods* are, again showing the arbitrary nature of the formulaic inventory.

The change constituent (R.11) can be expressed by: *becoming cloudy, *cloud increasing, fine at first*; and although there are seven ways to indicate change given in MOG (C 2.8.4), only three are used. The structure of the section dealing with precipitation in the district forecasts can be represented as follows:

$$\text{R12. Precipitation} \rightarrow \left(\begin{Bmatrix} \text{intensity} \\ \text{duration 1} \\ \text{extent 1} \end{Bmatrix} \right) + \text{type of precipitation} \\ + (\text{change}) + (\text{extent2}) + (\text{duration2})$$

These categories are the same as those used for cloud cover, with the addition of intensity. But there are differences. Type of precipitation is expressed by the following words: *showers, rain, drizzle, *falls*. The intensity of precipitation is given in formulae such as *light showers*; its duration by:

$$a\ few\ \begin{Bmatrix} showers \\ drizzle\ patches \end{Bmatrix}$$

$$*some\ \begin{Bmatrix} showers \\ rain \\ drizzle \end{Bmatrix}$$

$$*occasional\ \begin{Bmatrix} showers \\ rain \end{Bmatrix}$$

showers in the afternoon;

its extent by: *areas of drizzle, *drizzle areas, scattered rain, rain becoming widespread, isolated showers. The term areas, although not found in MOG, is used of both cloud cover and precipitation. *Drizzle areas* follows the trend of modifying existing duration phrases. The other phrases, unlike those for cloud cover, are all taken from MOG (C 2.8.3). If there is to be change in precipitation then formulae such as the following are used: *showers developing, rain developing, rain becoming widespread*. These phrases are taken from MOG (C 2.8.4).

As has been shown, at least one presenter treats temperature as a less important element of the district forecasts. Other presenters, although not excluding temperature completely from all forecasts, do often exclude it. Because of the nature of temperature, only the categories of air temperature and time are included in forecasts.

R13. Temperature → air temperature + (time)

The following phrases are used: *warm (*weather), cool*. These indications of temperature both come from MOG, and are based on the average temperature in the district being forecast for at the particular time of year. Forecasters could give the temperature in degrees but this never occurs on National Radio. *Temperature* is used of weather only when temperature is directly preceded by cloud cover.

Time formulae include: **by day, in the afternoon*. The phrase *by day* is often used when describing the temperature and implies a difference between day-time and night-time temperature, without specific detail being given. *In the afternoon* is a more detailed indication of time.

Wind can be represented as follows:

R14. Winds of 11 knots or more → $\left(\left\{\begin{array}{l}\text{speed}\\ \text{temperature}\\ \text{(speed) + variable}\end{array}\right\}\right)$ + (direction) + ('winds') + (change)

Of these constituents either or both 'winds' and direction must be included in each description of wind.

R15. Winds of less than 11 knots → $\left\{\begin{array}{l}\text{speed}\\ \text{(intensity) + (sea)breeze(s) + (location)}\end{array}\right\}$ + (wind(s)) + (change)

Either *breeze* or *wind*, but not both, must be used in each description of wind. Terms used for wind speed include: *light, moderate, fresh, strong*. Terms for wind temperature include: **cool, *cooler, *warm*. The entire category of 'temperature' with reference to wind is absent from MOG. Terms for wind direction include: *northerly, *northerlies, southerly, *southerlies, *southwest, sou'westerly, *northeast, *northwest, *northeasterlies, *easterlies, *east, *westerlies* with MOG (B 3.4.3.1) stating that direction must be given by reference to one of the eight points of the compass. Nouns such as *southerlies* are not included in MOG, but these and adjectives without the *-ly* suffix are used by all presenters.

The term *winds* is not present in MOG, but is compulsory after all adjectives in this category. It also appears alone. Thus *winds* must follow all adjectives of direction in the 'wind' category while the term *variable* is used when no definite wind direction is maintained for any length of time. *Variable* also does not appear in MOG even though it describes a possible wind condition for which no other term is suggested. The terms *breezes* and *sea breezes* are used only of winds of less than 11 knots. These terms also do not appear in MOG but are used by all forecasters. (Knots are approximately nautical miles and as a measure of speed are understood as nautical miles per hour.)

Formulae expressing change of wind include: *winds becoming variable, northerlies freshening, winds *tending sou'westerly*. Intensity of the wind is given by formulae such as: **little wind, *gentle winds*, another category also absent from MOG but which is used by all forecasters. Wind location formulae which include **along the coast, *by the coast, *in coastal areas*, are given only when breezes are described and seem to describe the type of wind that comes off the sea. This is another category absent from MOG but used by all forecasters.

While there is a strict structure to the forecasts of winds under 11 knots in these forecasts, MOG offers little information on how to describe them. In fact, the guidelines suggest the use of the phrase *not much wind* (B 3.4.2.2) for winds of this nature. The detail in which they are described in these forecasts suggests that the forecasters consider these winds to be important and have evolved their own ways of forecasting them.

The long-range forecast, which follows the district forecasts, likewise consists of a set of discourse structure rules and formulae. These will not be discussed since their character is identical to that which we have already exemplified in the discussion so far. After the long-range forecast, the whole forecast finishes with the formula *and that is the end of/ends the weather forecast*.

3.2.3 Summary – National Radio forecasts

All forecasts on National Radio follow a strict discourse structure and utilize formulae, thus constituting a formulaic genre. The genre is written and acquired in two ways: explicitly through training and by reference to the MOG, or implicitly by reference to earlier forecasts. For instance, although the structure for forecasts is not given in MOG, it is adhered to by all forecasters. Each constituent of the forecast consists of a number of possible weather conditions. Although forecasters include the same conditions in their forecasts, the order in which they do so varies from forecaster to forecaster. However the structure within each weather condition is the same for all forecasters, as is the choice of formulaic phrases for each constituent. Thus, the only level at which individual forecasters style their forecasts is in the order in which they mention weather conditions. A limited vocabulary is given in MOG, and most of the terms in these forecasts are either part of this vocabulary or derived from it. When non-MOG terms are used they are also technical in nature. Where the MOG makes no reference to groups of terms such as geographical terms or verbs, forecasters again use the same or similar terms as one another. Indications of the type of vocabulary which is suitable must be passed on during training and through MOG. This, too, is a characteristic of this tradition.

The rules we have proposed to account for much of the content of these forecasts are indicative of the high degree of uniformity among forecasts. Styling by individual forecasters is minimal. The style of these forecasts in general varies little from that of MOG. They are characterized by their technicality and lack of superfluous material. National Radio weather forecasts contain only the facts about the weather, and information about which part of the forecast is being given.

3.3 Weather forecasting as a scripted formulaic genre

The forecasters whose forecasts we have analysed manifestly use a highly structured form of speech. They also use a restricted set of formulae and technical terminology with special conditions of use and meaning. Individual forecasters have a few personal idiosyncrasies and all of them are not bound in everything they say by the Met. Office Guidelines. There are thus uncodified traditional elements to their speech.

To understand how forecasters from the Met. Office come to speak as they do we need to look at their training. Met. Office forecasters are trained meteorologists who receive formal training in preparing forecasts for public broadcast. This training takes the form of reading a number of forecasts produced by other forecasters and becoming acquainted with the MOG. After spending some time studying these items, the trainee forecaster practises producing forecasts with the raw data available to the Meteorological Service. These are checked by qualified colleagues and compared to other forecasts. The trainee is free to seek advice on how to produce forecasts and the qualified forecaster offers instruction at this point. This process continues until the Meteorological Service is happy with the standard being produced. The trainee has then become qualified to produce forecasts for the general public.

Like many recently qualified apprentices, a forecaster, when he begins producing his own forecasts, refers closely to the forecasts produced most recently before the one on which he is working. These completed forecasts act as a style reference, with phrases and even whole sections being taken from these forecasts if they are applicable to the forecast in production. The characteristic prosodics of these forecasts are passed on by a combination of consultation with trained forecasters, training by Radio New Zealand, listening to broadcast forecasts, and instructions in MOG. The learning of these prosodics is thus a conscious activity.[6]

The training of a forecaster differs from that of performers in oral traditions in a number of ways. Many oral performers have neither a written version of their text nor a set of guidelines on how to produce similar texts to refer to during or after their training. Finnegan (1981) in her research on praise singers, notes that some oral performers do have written forms of their work produced after they have composed it, and refer to these scripts prior to performance. Even in these cases the transmission of the techniques of oral poetry and the stories of the tradition is carried out orally. Furthermore, performers in these traditions receive no formal training in their skill but learn it by exposure to other performers, or one performer in particular, over a period of years (Edwards & Sienkewicz, 1990). In short, many formulaic genre traditions are largely transmitted orally. Since it is largely a scripting tradition, weather forecasting is not.

So why do weather forecasters use a formulaic genre to provide forecasts? Kane believes that:

> formulaic structure is adopted by the weather report to organize the random nature of the weather and to group the weather forms into perceptual units for ease of listener consumption (Kane, 1987:15).

In summary, written scripts determine the way in which forecasters are trained. Forecasts are the result of a tradition, albeit a written one. That they are part of a tradition is shown by the static nature of the forecasts produced by the Meteorological Service. The existence of guidelines to aid in their production, and the nature of the training, indicate that there is a standard form that forecasts must take and that this form can only be altered by intervention. The unpredictable weather is thus counterpointed by the dependable predictability of its forecast.

3.4 General conclusion

Broadcast weather forecasts arise from the interplay of a number of factors. The first is the current and past weather data on which the forecast is developed, about which nothing is said in the forecast but which is material to making the forecast. Then there is the weather yet to come in all its aspects. The Met. Office Guidelines play a role in constraining what may be put into the scripted forecast but do not constrain it entirely since traditional and idiolectal elements to the forecast also play a role. The resulting discourse rules and formulaic inventory makes scripted weather forecasts a formulaic genre of considerable complexity. We are now a long way from the simplicity of *Times* engagement notices.

4
Polite Genres in a Multilingual Community: Greeting and Eating in Singapore[1]

> *Underlying systems of politeness are cultural values associated with perceptions of* face.
>
> Blum-Kulka (1997:143)

4.1 Introduction

The previous chapters have examined formulaic genres in a largely monolingual community. But what happens in a bi- or multi-lingual community? Specifically, what happens when that community's speakers who are multilingual use a formulaic genre? Do they experience and learn a different set of formulaic genres for each of their languages or is there overlap? Singapore provides one suitable site for answering these questions. Singapore is a multilingual and multicultural community. Its resident population is ethnically Chinese, Indian and Malay. English is the language of public administration, so many people in Singapore grow up bi- and multi-lingual and you might therefore be tempted to think, bi- and multi-cultural (Fraser Gupta, 1998; Platt, Weber & Ho, 1983).

The dialectal character of the English spoken by Singaporeans is the subject of debate. Official institutions such as the National University of Singapore support a policy promoting standard English (actively discouraging 'Singlish', Singapore English) while the unofficial situation is of a wide range of dialectal uses of English. Scholarly opinion differs as to how best to account for the diversity of English in Singapore. Earlier John Platt proposed that a lectal continuum existed from pidgin-like basilectal forms through mesolectal forms to acrolectal forms, the latter being little different from British Standard English (Platt, 1975). More recently this has been seen in terms of the high to low levels of a diglossic speech community (Bao, 2003:25).

This chapter looks at members of the Hokkien-speaking community in Singapore who are bilingual to some degree in both English and Hokkien, the degree in the case of English being largely a function of education. It is an interesting question, therefore, what cultural content prevails in the formulaic genres that members of this community are native speakers of. Two situations in which small polite formulaic interactional genres are normally used are the focus of attention. They are chance encounters and meal times. Why choose politeness genres? Whereas the previous chapters examined domain-specific genres, some of the least domain-specific formulaic genres in most cultures are in its general interpersonal domains. It is not by accident that early studies of formulaic genres in English were in this area (Coulmas, 1981; Ferguson, 1976). A major corpus study of formulaic utterances (K. Aijmer, 1996) also examines this domain. It has also been a major domain for studies in cross-cultural pragmatics, e.g. Blum-Kulka, House & Kasper (1989). Greeting people, thanking them, making requests and apologizing are central to social life and thus common speech acts. But not all societies use identical performative formulae and strategies to perform such speech acts. A request in a Chinese culture, for example, may be initiated by what looks like an apology in English. Nor need it be expected that what happens during casual encounters and at meal times will necessarily generalize to other situations.

Why is this? Humans are a social species. They live in groups and what they do and are permitted to do, and how they are perceived by themselves and other members of the species play a significant role in social life. It follows that every member of the species, in so far as they are socialized, must hold certain assumptions about who they are socially and what their compass of socially sanctioned action is.

These two factors in individual social life are conventionally subsumed under Goffman's concept of face. Goffman's familiar (1967:5) definition of face is as follows:

> The term *face* may be defined as the positive social value a person effectively claims for himself (sic.) by the line others assume he (sic.) has taken during a particular contact.

Brown and Levinson (1978:67), again as is well known, define face in two ways; in terms of positive and negative face:

> negative face: the want of every 'competent adult member' that his (sic.) actions be unimpeded by others.

positive face: the want of every member that his (sic.) wants to be desirable to at least some others.

A distinction between positive and negative face can therefore be drawn as follows. Positive face is the desire of the individual to have a recognized value within the society in which they live. You need to know about your standing in relation to others, including, for instance, others' opinion of you, and your relative status to others. The derivative needs of this general desire are the need to be liked, to have your needs appreciated, to have your value ranked as highly as socially possible. Suppose that the positive politeness parameter is a kind of self-image arising out of social interaction. At one end of the parameter, the positive end, you will suppose that everyone loves you, giving you a positive self-image, and at the other end that everyone hates you, giving you a negative self-image. This is a clear simplification of the complexities of human senses of self-worth but it will do for our purposes and may not be too far off the mark in many cases.

Negative face constitutes the other element of the desire for a place in society. Here the desire is for an imposition-free space wherein you can maintain freedom of action within the boundaries set by society. You need to be able to assess your freedom to act or to refrain from acting, depending on preference, responsibility or external constraint. Derivative needs include the desire to be free from coercion, imposition and constraint within the space you claim for yourself, or that society allows. Let us suppose that negative face is a kind of personal action parameter at one end of which you feel you are free to do anything you wish and at the other end that you are entirely constrained and can do nothing on your own cognizance.

Adjustment for different cultural contexts must be made and it is here that this chapter's case study will focus. Politeness formulae of Singapore English, it will be shown, are dependent on a background of Singapore Chinese culture and thus that the culture-specific features of face work in Singapore English are those of Singapore Chinese culture. This is to be expected. Though traces of non-Chinese indigenous influences are obvious in some forms of Singapore English, 'strong reinforcement from Chinese' is to be expected. The Chinese background of the majority population gives some support to this view (Platt, 1984:106).

4.2 Meeting and eating in Singapore Hokkien and Singapore English

Native-like negotiation of meeting and eating involves a cultural matrix which can be presented in an analysis of the conditions of use of the politeness formulae belonging to the genre. This analysis constitutes the genre's cultural context. If we were writing a dictionary of these formulae then this description would constitute for each formula its codified conditions of use. The text-type side of the genre will be illustrated by means of lists of formulaic expressions from both Singapore English and Singapore Hokkien. These formulae are arranged to show the whole lectal continuum. Each Singapore Hokkien formula is given in a literal translation which, by comparison with the Singapore English version, documents the prevalence of loan translation when the translation is compared with the English equivalent. Each formula is also given a gloss.

4.2.1 Chance encounter greetings

Chance encounter greetings might be exchanged between any two speakers. In English you might say, *How are you doing?* and the reply might be, *Fine thanks*. In New Zealand, if you don't know the other person, you might say, *Gidday*, while the other nods their head in response. Such dyads are stock in trade for discourse analysts (Schegloff, 1972). In Singapore a number of factors play a part in whether and how people address each other in a situation where they happen to meet. Seniority affects the choice of stylistically relevant greeting and any decision as to who should initiate these greetings. Speakers who are greatly different in social rank would be unlikely to use such greetings, at least the ones mentioned here. However, someone with high power may use certain greetings with juniors, as a friendly or condescending gesture: *Had your lunch/break?* or *Just back from lunch?* A junior has no choice but must provide a greeting to a superior.

Familiarity is an important variable. If you meet a total stranger, then you normally would not greet them. Familiarity and power interact. If you are a senior member of an organization but work closely with a junior member, then you would expect to receive a greeting from a junior colleague. It is more usual for juniors to greet seniors first and some degree of familiarity must exist between them. For instance, a very junior employee would not use these formulae with the company chairman.

Familiarity also affects the choice of stylistic-cum-face variant. Speakers of an acrolect may use an acrolectal greeting with a basilectal speaker if they are not well acquainted and have no high regard for the other person's face needs. Normally you should reply to a greeting, though a friendly nod and smile may be enough response to a greeting. Stylistic homogeneity is usually maintained. A basilectal speaker expects a doctor or a teacher to talk as befits their position and, though a basilectal speaker might be assured and perhaps flattered by any stylistic (and face) adjustments, i.e. accommodation, made by the speaker, respect for the speaker may be reduced. You may choose, however, not to maintain stylistic homogeneity, in order to create a humorous effect. An acrolect speaker may greet a fellow speaker of the acrolect with a greeting in the basilect. This narrows the intimacy gap, besides creating a humorous effect enjoyed by both. If you greet a basilect speaker in a basilect form, any further conversation is unlikely to be in the acrolect. With a greeting in the acrolect, you would not expect further exchanges to be conducted in the basilect.

With all these sets of politeness formulae, variants of the Singapore English greeting formulae have corresponding forms in Singapore Hokkien (or, in terms of the direction of influence, vice versa). The formulae belong to four groups illustrated below in section 4.2.1.1. The cultural concern with food is reflected in the greeting formulae found in **(a)**. The formulae centre around various aspects of the meal – whether or not it has been taken, when and where it is (usually) taken. In **(b)**, formulaic greetings centre on three aspects of the addressee's particular outing – the fact that the addressee is going to a particular place (say, the market), to some unspecified place, or to some unclear destination which prompts the speaker's question of, *Go where?* No personal interest is taken in the replies as these formulae are just culturally acceptable ways of greeting each other. In **(c)** the speaker comments on the addressee's appearance of busyness – the addressee appears busy, appears busy with something, or appears busy most of the time. The speaker shows a friendly but not a personal interest when making these comments. In the last group of data **(d)**, the speaker makes reference to the time gap since the last meeting. That is followed by enquiries into the addressee's well-being. Greetings relevant to this last case may be more elaborate in form. The speaker might phrase their greetings thus: *Haven't seen you for a long while. How's life? Still busy? So, where are you going now?*

Interpreting these greetings in Brown and Levinson's terms it seems that the speaker aims to narrow the intimacy gap with friendly enquiries. The speaker attends to the addressee's interests, asking questions about meal-time interests, destination, appearance of being busy and the addressee's well-being after a long separation. The speaker also expresses feelings of sympathy or approval: *Every time see you so busy (one). (Have to) do everything yourself ah?, Busy (h)or? This time of the year, Busy with your children ah? Look after them not easy.., Wah, you so busy. Always see you go somewhere.* These suggest Brown and Levinson's strategy 15 is being used in which the speaker gives the addressee the gifts of 'sympathy, understanding, cooperation' and approval (Brown and Levinson 1978:134).[2] The addressee's response may be no more than a smile and a nod but that in itself shows acknowledgement. However, a verbal response is more common. The addressee is likely to repeat some part of the speaker's greeting formulae. Mutual attendance to face is thus observed.

4.2.1.1 Chance encounter greetings in Singapore Hokkien

(a)

Literal Translation (LT): *X, eat already ah?*
Idiomatic Sense (IS): X, you've had your meal?
Parentheses surround possible expansions of the formula.
Braces surround alternatives separated by a '/'.
Ah, *wah*, and *(h)or* are pragmatic particles.

LT: *Eat full not yet?*
IS: Had your meal?

LT: *Go out eat ah?*
IS: Going out for your lunch/dinner?

LT: *Go out buy/eat ah?*
IS: Buying something for your lunch/dinner?

LT: *Eat full already ah?*
IS: You've had your lunch/dinner?

LT: *Want with us together eat or not?*
IS: Care to join us for the meal?

LT: *Every time see you this time go out eat.*
IS: This is your regular lunch/dinner hour?

(b)

LT: *(You) go where?*
IS: Where are you going?

LT: Board bus ah? Go where? / (You) sit go where?...I also want to go there.
IS: You are taking the bus? Where to?...Actually, I'm going the same way.

LT: Take your children go where?
IS: Where are you taking your kids?

LT: Go shopping ah?
IS: Shopping?

LT: Go market ah?
IS: Going to the market?

LT: Take children study books ah?
IS: Taking your kids to school?

LT: You also come this place jalan jalan ah? Walk walk also good.
IS: You've come here {to 'window-shop'? / for leisurely walk?} A leisurely stroll does one good.

(c)

LT: Every time see you so busy one.
IS: You seem so busy all the time.

LT: Busy ah?
IS: Take it that you are busy.

LT: I every time see you so busy one.
IS: I can't help noticing that you are {quite a busy person / always busy with something.}

LT: Children make you busy (h)or? Look after them not easy.
IS: The children keep you busy, eh? They are quite a handful these kids.

LT: Wah, you every time so busy. Very hard find you.
IS: It's hard to find you in. You are always out somewhere, busy with something.

(d)

LT: Very long no see you (h)or? (You) Good or not?
IS: Haven't seen you for quite some time. How are you?

4.2.1.2 Chance encounter greetings in Singapore English

(a)

Eat already (ah)?
Makan already? [*Makanan* is a Malay word for 'eat', 'meal', 'food'.]

Lunchtime {already ah? / ah?, / already?}{Lunch time, is it? / I see it's lunch-
   time already! / You having your lunch now, are you?}
I just had lunch/dinner. What about you?
Want to join me for lunch/dinner?
Join us for lunch/dinner?
You always have (your) lunch/dinner at this time ah?
Wah, everybody {seems to like this place so much. Lunch-time always so
   crowded, ((h)or?) / like to eat here}
You like coming here, do you? I rather like this place myself. Food is cheap.
   Service is good. Environment is clean. Worth the money you pay for, eh?
Do you always come here? You don't mind the crowd.
Seems that we both like this food-centre. Otherwise we won't keep bumping
   into each other.
I come here whenever I can. It's not so crowded. What about you? What do
   you think of this food-centre?

(b)

Go where?
Go somewhere ah?
Take bus ah? Go where?...{I also want to go there / I am also going there, /
   I am also going the same way.}
Take your children go somewhere ah?
Come here do/for what?
Going shopping?
(Window-)shopping (ah)?
Going (to) market?
Going out with your children ah?
You also come here jalan jalan ah? Go out once in a while also good (h)or?
   [jalan jalan = stroll, window-shopping; go out = an outing of some
   sort.]
Take your children to the funfair ah?
Hi! Where are you going?
In a hurry to go somewhere?
Where are you heading?...Actually, {I'm going the same way / I just came
   from that place.}
What are you doing here? (Don't expect to see you here.) Going somewhere
   (ah)?
...So, where are you going now?
Going the same way, are we?
You are going which way?
Which way are you going?
Going to X place?

Are you going to X place? {Just been there myself / Just going there myself.}
...So, you are going to X place.
Going to X? Ya, one needs some relaxation.

(c)

Every time see you so busy (one). (Have to do everything yourself, (is it ah?)
[busy = preoccupied with one thing or another – doing the daily/weekly marketing, taking the children to school, getting to work on time etc.]
So / very busy, is it?
Busy (h)or? This time of the year.
This time of the year very busy (h)or?
So busy for what? Every time see you so busy.
Busy shopping ah?
Busy? Shopping? {We just came back. / We are also going there. / We are heading the same way.}
You are always busy on X days ah? Always don't see you on these days.
Busy with your children ah? Look(ing) after them not easy (h)or?...
Busy?/Working? Where you work?
This time of the year keeps you busy, doesn't it?
So busy these days, are you? Don't see you around.
You are always up to something. So active. (Seldom find you at home.)
[No negative implications intended here.]

(d)

Long time no see you. So busy ah? How are you now?
So long haven't see(n) you. {Good or not? / How? / How are you now?}
Long time no see! {How are you?, / How's life? / How's life been treating you? / How are things? / Where are you working now? / Still working in that office, are you?}
Haven't seen you for a long time. How are you?
Have lost touch with you. How are things?

4.2.2 Before-meal formulae

The second example of a Singaporean formulaic genre involves a dyadic exchange before meals. Such meal openers are common in many cultures. In the Netherlands a meal begins with *Eet smakelijk* or *Smakelijk eten* in France with *Bon appetit* in Japan with *Itodakimasu*. In Singapore there is traditionally an opening and reply. The genre in Singapore is different from the European meal openers in that it rests on the necessity in Chinese culture for younger members of the family to defer to older relatives and other older people. Thus the following people will be addressed using before-meal formulae of this type: older relatives, parents of friends and friends of parents. If the participants are extremely familiar, then this tends to discourage the use of some of the formulae below. It is consequently less common now to use before-meal formulae with one's parents and older siblings. The familiarity gained through a working relationship with an older colleague, however, does not create a strong obligation to use before-meal formulae since these formulae are essentially family-based.

The formulae are expected to be used before the meal commences and are usually used in the home although they are not uncommon in restaurants. The person being deferred to is expected to reply with a formulaic acknowledgement. In replying, the older relative will often point to or nod towards the meal, motioning for the original speaker to commence.

The Chinese concern with respectful address to elders and hosts is detectable in both Singapore Hokkien and Singapore English. You must not begin a meal without first paying an acknowledging address to elders and hosts. It shows respect to your elders and/or acknowledges debt. In the former instance, it simply means 'I'm about to start on the meal'. A possible accompanying meaning invites the addressee to join the speaker in the meal but the respect motive is stronger. If the hostess is busy elsewhere, participants would resort to using a different type of before-meal formula, one which specifically invites the hostess to join the speaker in the meal. Hence, they might say, *Join me, X?, X, want to join me?* or *X, you are not eating?*. Some informants who use the 'higher' lectal forms claim not to have used before-meal formulae. They would say nothing but simply wait for the hostess to start the meal. For other speakers of this category, i.e. users of higher lectal forms, if they use the before-meal formula it would be one made in Singapore Hokkien or some other Chinese dialect.

This aversion to using a Singapore English version of a before-meal formula is attributable to the thinking that it sounds jarringly basilectal – no educated speaker would make such direct loan translation from Chinese to Singapore English, only the Chinese-educated or the lowly-educated would use before-meal formulae, because their mastery of English is far from adequate. There is some truth in this. However, some educated speakers (those with at least a secondary education in the English medium) do use before-meal formulae. For these, perhaps the cultural compulsion to use it is too great. Certain families are more insistent than others on using the culturally accepted forms. Then, too, it could be that preserving appropriate usage is more important than sounding 'prestigiously' mesolectal or acrolectal. It could also be a matter of habit. Situational cues have their effect too – in the presence of other educated speakers a speaker may be more reluctant to use before-meal formulae; conversely, the absence of these speakers make the use of the formula less face-damaging; then again the speaker may have a high regard for the addressee's face needs (assuming the addressee speaks the basilect) and therefore tries to speak on a level with them.

Employing before-meal formulae is part of deference behaviour. The speaker uses Brown and Levinson's negative politeness strategy 5 to redress possible damage to the addressee's negative face.[3] The addressee may be the hostess, an elderly or senior guest. According to Brown and Levinson, negative politeness strategies redress particular face-threatening acts. But this is not necessarily so here. The addressee may be an older guest at your home. In this case the addressee is the debtor, especially if they have been invited to join the family for a meal. Nevertheless, it is necessary to pay respect to the addressee's negative face. The respect motive is obvious here. In showing deference, the speaker satisfies 'hearer's want to be treated as superior' (Brown and Levinson 1978:183).

In such situations, the greater the seniority of the addressee, the greater damage to the addressee's negative face in not treating them with respect. The cultural obligation to use this respectful mode of address is quite strong with relatives, and friends of parents and parents of friends. Here the social distance between the participants may be small. People in this category include parents-in-law, grandparents, aunties and uncles, older cousins and perhaps parents. In contemporary Singapore, the latter are not likely to be included. This reflects a trend away from traditional practices. So if the speaker's regard for the addressee's negative face (for example, being the parent of a friend) is high, they will show deference by using a before-meal formula. But if the speaker gives priority to their own face needs (say, the want not to appear an uneducated speaker in the presence of acrolect speakers), they will say nothing, use a different before-meal formula instead, or a Chinese version of a before-meal formula. If the addressee is a parent-in-law or grandparent-in-law, the speaker may have little option but to use a before-meal formula in Singaporean English if they are English-speaking and if the speaker prefers to speak in that language.

4.2.2.1 Before-meal formulae in Singapore Hokkien

LT: Auntie, (I) eat/drink.
IS: (Auntie, Mrs X) I'm about to start on the meal. (Care to join us?)

LT: *To your mother say I eat/drink (h)or.*
IS: Please let your mum know that {I'll be starting on the meal soon. / I'm eating now.}

Parents to their children:
LT: *You no call auntie eat/drink ah?*
IS: You haven't made your address to auntie?
LT: *{Got call or not? / Got call auntie (eat/drink) or not?}*
IS: Have you made your address to auntie?
LT: *Call already ah?*
IS: So, you have made your address. (Am I right in making this assumption?)
LT: *Must call ah. Cannot so no manners.*
IS: You really must address your elders. It is most rude not to do so.
LT: *Must call ah. No call cannot eat.*
IS: Address your elders or else no dinner for you.
LT: *Have you call auntie?*
IS: Have you paid your respects?

4.2.2.2 Before-meal formulae in Singapore English

Auntie, (I) eat/drink.
Drink/eat, Auntie.
(Please) tell your mother I'm going to eat now. [If friend's mother is busy elsewhere.]
(Please) let your mum know I'm going to eat/makan now.

Parents to their children (depending on their age):

(How come / Why) you no/don't call auntie eat/drink?
You no call auntie eat/drink ah?
Got call auntie (eat) or not?
Call already ah?
Call auntie eat/drink?
Say to auntie, 'Auntie, eat.' 'Come join me.'
You haven't call auntie (eat/drink).
Must call auntie (first). Don't call cannot eat.
Must call first.
[I'm not letting you have your meal unless you make the necessary address first.]
Have you call auntie (eat/drink)?
Have you {addressed / call} your grandparents? Must call. Don't call very rude.
  {Must let them know you are eating / going to eat.}

4.2.3 Reply formulae to before-meal formulae

The use of before-meal formulae obliges the addressee to reply. Thus seniors use these replies to acknowledge deference behaviour shown by juniors. The situational context for the use of these reply formulae is thus identical to that of the initiating formula. As an accompaniment, head nods and pointing gestures by the speaker are common. They encourage the speaker to begin the meal right away.

Acknowledging a before-meal formula comes in various forms – the addressee advises the speaker to eat quickly (before the food becomes cold) or slowly (taking her time with it); bids the speaker to help herself to the food; explains that she will have her meal later; presses the speaker to start eating/drinking (this is common to all forms of redressive replies). The addressee may choose to use all these forms. In this context, the addressee would have been a senior hostess. If the addressee is an elderly guest at the speaker's home, all would expect juniors to address the guest with a before-meal formula (never mind that the addressee is the debtor in this instance) and the addressee to give an appropriate reply in turn. But now the reply simply tells juniors to begin the meal.

Variants of reply formulae are few in number and most are used interchangeably.

4.2.3.1 Reply formulae in Singapore Hokkien

LT: *Yes, yes, eat/drink / (H)or*
IS: Yes, {go ahead / carry on}

LT: *(H)or quickly eat/drink. Otherwise cold.*
IS: Yes, eat/drink quickly, before it gets cold.

LT: *(H)or eat/drink. Slowly, slowly come/eat/drink.*
IS: Yes, just go ahead. Take your time.

LT: *(H)or you eat first.*
IS: Yes, just carry on.

LT: *(H)or you eat. I eat already.*
IS: Yes, carry on. I've taken mine.

LT: *(H)or you go eat. I no so early eat.*
IS: Yes, do carry on. I don't usually have mine till later.

4.2.3.2 Reply formulae in Singapore English

Eat, eat, eat/drink, drink.
(H)or (H)or go ahead. Better eat quickly. (Otherwise) Will get cold.

H(or) / Yes, carry on. Eat slowly. Take your time.
H(or) / Yes, eat while it's hot.
H(or) / Yes, go ahead. (Don't wait for me).
H(or) / Yeah, you go ahead. {We('ll) eat later / We('ll) have ours later}.
(H)or just make yourself at home.

4.3 Politeness strategies in Singapore

What kind of general cultural background lies behind the use of these two Hokkien and English formulaic genres? It appears that Singapore is neither a predominantly negative-politeness culture nor a predominantly positive-politeness culture. Singapore culture occupies a middle ground, showing excesses in neither deference nor comradely behaviour. The idea of incurring debt is culturally perceived to be obnoxious. Brown and Levinson (1978:252) mention a problematical dimension. Whose face should have precedence in the protection of face? Singapore Chinese society clearly allows the addressee's face to take precedence but the underlying assumption is that the addressee would reciprocate in the same way. The result is mutual respect for each other's face. If the addressee fails to respond in the manner expected, if they choose to break culturally accepted behavioural norms, smooth interaction will be impossible. The speaker may sustain some damage to their own face since their effort at face redress is not reciprocated. This destroys interactional ease between parties. Some cultures differ in the degree to which the wants of others are allowed to supersede face wants. Efficiency and/or the power may take precedence over face needs (Brown and Levinson, 1978:254). This applies to Singapore, too, but to a lesser extent than in some Western cultures. A culturally-sensitized awareness of the other's face needs as well as those of your own requires there to be some regard for face.

The want to be sincere is another area of difference. In many Western societies 'blunt sincerity' may not necessarily be seen as face-threatening. It is therefore allowed to oust face-regard as a factor in politeness behaviour. On the whole, society in Singapore does not share this normative preference. Sincerity is not of prime importance, at least not when face is threatened. Some show of sincerity is enough. Both Singapore Hokkien and Singapore English share this cultural leaning towards face-regard, a societal norm that is Singaporean as well as Chinese. As will be seen in chapter 9, these normative preferences were overturned during the Cultural Revolution in mainland China.

The conclusion which may be drawn is that, in so far as cultural import is concerned, the speaker of Singapore English is speaking

Hokkien but with English-like words and syntax. A basilect speaker would suggest this even more strongly. Loan translations, as the selection above shows, abound in the formulae of Singapore English.

This situation has two sets of consequences: one for the native speaker of Singapore English who tries to use their English outside Singapore and another for the native speaker of some other English who tries to use their English in Singapore. It is clear that the formulae listed above can be deceptive. A number of them sound just like formulae in other Englishes. For example, enquiries about whether a person has eaten may be made in the UK and USA. But there they are not chance encounter greetings but enquiries about whether one has eaten. When, as a non-Singaporean, you join a family for a meal, however, you may occasionally find formulae being used which are not necessarily paralleled in other English-speaking cultures, just as you will not necessarily know that when the head of a fish in a fish dish is pointing at you when it is served, you are an honoured guest and should take the first helping.

Thus a speaker of Singapore English will have acquired a native variety of English which is not fully transferable to another English-speaking society. Singapore Chinese culture is different from the culture of Australia, New Zealand, the UK and the US. Fluent native speakers of Singapore English may therefore have to learn some elements of English all over again if they move to another English-speaking country. This time the linguistic aspects of the language can be transferred to the task of learning the new language but the cultural aspects will not be able to be transferred. These cultural aspects perhaps are of more weight than the linguistic aspects. Equivalent difficulties in language learning, of course, await the speaker of some other English who hopes to speak English as a native in Singapore. Speakers of acrolectal Singapore English will be at the greatest disadvantage since they have reason to suspect from the linguistic character of their knowledge of English that it is transportable, just as speakers of formal varieties of other Englishes will be most deceived by speakers of acrolectal Singapore English.

Native-like competence in a language is, it seems, only possible if it is accompanied by the acquisition of an appropriate native culture. This follows for every formulaic genre, since every genre has is own cultural niche within a matrix of larger cultural predispositions and practices. Furthermore, speaking a language is, as suggested in chapter 1, in itself no guarantee that you can function natively in all the places where that language is spoken. Even being bilingual does not guarantee that you will be bicultural. The formulaic genres of a speech community will testify to that.

4.4 Methodological epilogue: the enculturated native speaker as researcher and co-researcher

The fieldwork for this chapter was conducted by Daphne Tan, as she was called in her English incarnation, and Tan Gek Lin, as she was called in her Singapore Hokkien incarnation. The fieldwork she did could only have been done by someone with her native appreciation and understanding of the Singaporean community of which she was a native and with the help of her friends and relations who provided data and commentary.

Many of the chapters of this book are based on research conducted by and with natives in this way. In some cases, such as reporting on the races and auctions, the native was me. In others it was a student or colleague. The research reported in chapter 6 would not have been possible without the native understanding of Marie Flindall who was a checkout supervisor when the research was carried out and who provided an entrée to the supermarket in which she worked. The work on the Cultural Revolution reported in chapter 9 could not have been done without Ji Fengyuan and Shu Xiaogu both of whom had lived through and participated in the Cultural Revolution. The work on pump aerobics was done in consultation with Michele Lodge who had been attending pump aerobics classes for a number of years, and the work on dance callers required guidance from George Slade who has been a life-long square dancer. Work on the history of tobacco auction chants would not have been possible without Frederic Tillis's intimate knowledge of black folk musical traditions. Frederick Tillis is an African-American composer and musicologist.

The requirement that one needs to have native-like command of a genre in order to be able to study it effectively would be no news to an anthropologist. It is, however, not always a practice in sociolinguistics where variationist paradigms may make it seem that native-like communicative competence of a variety of a language is not necessary. There are thus two avenues to studying formulaic genres. One is to become native-like in the genre oneself. This includes being only passively competent. The other is to work with someone who has native-like fluency in the genre. The studies in this book have used both options. The former option has one drawback. It is time-consuming. It took me at least five years to become thoroughly familiar with one formulaic auctioning genre, that of the livestock auctioneers in my province. My colleague Geoffrey Miller spent years studying the musical traditions of auctioneers in the north-eastern USA. So data collection, if by data we mean linguistic texts, is not enough. Being thoroughly familiar with the cultural niche in which texts are created is also necessary. Experience is the only way to gain such familiarity. It must either be one's own experience, or that of a consultant.

5
Playing a False Part: Projecting and Perceiving Fraudulent Identities on the Internet[1]

> *Successful staging involves the use of real techniques – the same techniques by which persons sustain their real social situations.*
> Goffman (1969:247)

5.1 Introduction

This chapter takes a more wide-angled image of formulaic language, demonstrating that formulaic genres incorporate other linguistic elements alongside phrasal lexical items with socially prescribed conditions of use and with relatively fixed discourse structure. In the texts to be discussed in this chapter, linguistic formulae work in consort with these other elements, as they do in most other formulaic genres, to create a complex whole. The texts are e-mail spam letters by authors purporting to come from non-English-speaking backgrounds. As such they exhibit non-native selection in their use of formulae and in other features of English. The chapter will first consider letters as a genre and then the way in which a particular sub-genre, business letters, is being used to attempt fraud; next how foreignness is projected 'through non-native errors' and, finally, how these documents are perceived by naïve recipients.

5.2 The play

5.2.1 Introduction

The history of letter transmission over the past century provides a clear chronicle of the way in which the technologies which are used to produce and transmit letters have created a communication revolution.

In the not-so-mythical past, letters came from various parts of the world with stamps and postmarks on them providing mute testimony to their exotic origins. They travelled the globe in ships and trains, and later in planes. They took less and less time to reach us. The world was shrinking and it was doing so by means of globalizing technologies. Now many of the world's letters are in digital form and reach their destinations in (split)seconds. In doing so they apparently obliterate barriers of time and space; but not of culture. In so many ways cultural norms still assert themselves in letters. The new technologies also provide previously unavailable opportunities for subversion. Because we can communicate with people to whom we would previously never have written letters and who inhabit other cultural spaces, we can become involved in new and exciting ways to present ourselves on the international stage as personae of our own creation, since many of those who receive our letters may know nothing of us except what we provide for them to read.

The letters which form the data for this study are familiar to anyone who receives e-mail on the internet. They propose a lucrative arrangement for the recipient of the letter if he or she is willing to be involved in getting money out of Africa. Generally, the letters purport to come from a person who is either a relative of a significant African resident, such as a Head of State, or a state or corporate official of high rank, such as a bank manager. Generally, the message is that an African person, now deceased, has deposited a large amount of money in an account or with a security firm. Either a relative of the person concerned, or an official who has discovered the existence of the deposit, wishes to engage the cooperation of the recipient of the e-mail in uplifting the money in order to get it out of Africa. A high fee is promised in return for this service. The proposal involves a multiple fraud. First, it is clear, in most cases, that the large sum of money which is 'on deposit' has been fraudulently acquired by the deceased (or occasionally still live) person. Second, it is also clear, in most cases, that the writer of the e-mail is not legally entitled to the money (though they may claim the contrary). Third, the mechanism proposed for getting the money out of Africa is illegal.

A small corpus of such letters is analysed in this chapter to investigate their character and that of their writers. The analysis will show that how writers of such letters present themselves, and their 'foreignness', involves multiply-layered linguistic fraud. To do this will involve examining the formulae used in the letters followed by a general error analysis, suggesting that a writer's errors allow them to be evaluated as a persona. The letters demonstrate a complex interplay between many linguistic devices, including formulae, providing a good indication of the letters' idiolectal and dialectal fraudulence.

The leading hypothesis is that the attempted fraud on the recipient of the e-mail letters is only possible through the use of a combination of idiolectal, text type, and dialectal features which are subversive. For the partnership between writer and reader to be attractive, writers must present themselves as non–native speakers of English, specifically as African. They must also present themselves as competent to a degree in the ways of banking and the law, since they have devised a plan involving banking and legal issues. But they must not present themselves as overly competent since that might suggest to the reader that he or she could be the victim of a capable and possibly ruthless party. This suggests that a particular Goffmanian persona in the form of a maybe partly naïve, semi-competent African is to be presented in the e-mail. The tools at the disposal of the author (the agent who created the writer of these e-mails) to attain this end are the focus of this study.

5.2.2 The cast

A corpus of 21 letters provided the initial data. The cast of letter writers was as in table 5.1. This is the cast list. In the case of this cast it need not be supposed that the characters are playing themselves. The writers of these letters are 'playing a false part'. They are engaged in, and proposing further to engage in, fraud. So it may be that the parts are being played by others who are not Jeff Savimbi or Jewel Taylor. The distinction here is between the ostensible writer of the letter, the son of Jonas Savimbi, the wife of President Mobutu Sese Seko, and the author of the letter. Suppose, therefore, that, most likely, these purported writers have not written the letters in question but that they have been written by authors who are able to manipulate the linguistic resources at their disposal for particular effects (Kuiper & Small, 1986). The more plausibly they are able to do so, the more plausible the persona of the writer of the letter will be.

If that is the case, then the e-mails ostensibly written by the above characters are akin to fictional letters such as those in the eighteenth-century novel *Pamela,* with the difference that these e-mails are intended to deceive the recipient as to their provenance. They are e-mails in the real world, not letters in a possible world. This becomes a significant consideration when the language of the e-mails is examined. The letters must be persuasive enough for a perhaps naïve recipient to suppose that the character who is stated as having written them

Table 5.1 Writers of fraud letters

Text	Letter writer	Position	Significant deceased/financial source	Position
1	Zuma Ibrahim	Senior employee, The South African Ministry of Energy and Mineral Resources	Mr Robinson Moore	Free State Consolidated Mining Corporation
2	Amed Toffa	Manager of Bill and Exchange of the Foreign Operations Department, Union Bank of Nigeria	Foreign customer	No details, Nigeria
3	Jeff Savimbi	Son of Jonas Savimbi	Jonas Savimbi	Angolan Unita rebel leader, Angola
4	Mariam Bobiladawa Verisa Sese-Seko	Widow of President Mobutu Sese-Seko	President Mobutu Sese-Seko	President of D.R. Congo
5	Elisabeth Lamine	Wife of Dr Maxwell Lamine	Dr Maxwell Lamine	King of (Kanema tribe) of Federal Republic of Sierra Leone
6	Dr Victor Aduba	Branch Manager, United Bank of Africa, Lagos, Nigeria	Anonymous foreigner (Turkish)	Contractor with one of the Government Parastatals, Nigeria
7	Anonymous	Senior official of The Federal Government of Nigeria's Contracts Review Panel	None. Live foreign national	Nigerian government officials
8	Gideon Akinremi	Highly placed official in, the Federal Ministry of Petroleum & Mineral Resources, Nigeria	None. Petroleum Trust Fund	None given

9	Mariam Sese-Seko	Widow of President Mobutu Sese-Seko	President Mobutu Sese-Seko	Present of D.R. Congo
10	Broose Rothrock	Auditor General of a bank in Africa	Phillip Morris	Manager, Morris & Morris Coy.(pty). SA.
11	Anthony Rulanga	Son of Dr Christopher Rulanga	Dr Christopher Rulanga	Black Zimbabwean opposition party rich farmer
12	Barrister Yusuf Ibrahim	Personal attorney to an employee of Shell Development Company, Nigeria	Anonymous	Employee of Shell Development Company, Nigeria
13	J. Mobutu	Son of President Mobutu Sese-Seko	President Mobutu Sese-Seko	President of D.R. Congo
14	Mrs S.A William	Wife of Mr A. William	Mr A. William	Well-known farmer, Zimbabwe
15	Joseph Nkono	Eldest child of Engr. David Nkono	Engr. David Nkono	No position given
16	Youweri Bedie	Son of His Excellency Henri Konan Bedie	His Excellency Henri Konan Bedie	President, Cote d' Ivoire
17	Sesay Massaquoe	(By inference) former Head of State, Sierra Leone	None	
18	Samuel Savimbi	Son of Jonas Savimbi	Jonas Savimbi	Angolan Unita rebel leader
19	Youssouf Amin Geui	Son of General Robert Geui	General Robert Geui	President, Ivory Coast
20	Arnold Frank	Director of Delivery/Operations, security company, South Africa	President Mobutu Sese-Seko	President of D.R. Congo
21	Jewel Taylor	Wife to Charles Taylor	(Not deceased) Charles Taylor	Ex-President of Liberia

actually did. For that to happen their author must create an artefact of enough sophistication to make it appear that the writer whom a reader infers to have written the letter actually did write the letter. The letters might, for instance, arouse a reader's suspicion as to the authenticity of authorship if the competence in English which might be inferred for at least some of the writers is not what would be expected. Senior officials and political leaders in Africa might be expected to have high levels of English competence at least in the writing of business letters, which these e-mails purport to be. However, they may plausibly exhibit some interference effects of the other languages which they most probably also speak and write, and of the local varieties of English which obtain in their country of origin. Business letters are a narrowly circumscribed genre and people of the seniority of some of the writers of these e-mails would have had many years of experience reading and writing such letters (Dwyer, 2000). A reader might also expect that, for example, the offspring of billionaire potentates would have had an overseas university education and thus ought not to make elementary spelling and punctuation errors. Yet even the most proficient of these letters deviate in elementary ways from the expected standard for the writing of such letters. Many also show competencies in the writing of letters which are at odds with the expressed position of their 'writers'.

Another ground for suspicion is that these are e-mail letters. Normally a business letter containing such a weighty matter as the transfer of millions of dollars would be on paper. We are therefore dealing with a disjunction of media. We would expect paper but receive electrons.

A countervailing consideration has already been hinted at. The recipients of these letters must believe that the writers are foreign, rich and partly naïve or stupid. Otherwise why should they be writing to you and me asking for our help? So we can ask how do these writers present themselves linguistically and how are they perceived by people who might typically receive such e-mails?

5.2.3 The scene

The African countries from which the cash mentioned in the e-mails purports to come are significant:

West Africa: Liberia, Nigeria, Sierra Leone, Ivory Coast
Central Africa: Congo
South-west Africa: Angola
East Africa: Zimbabwe
Southern Africa: South Africa

All these countries have been in the news as places where a number of the following socio-political factors are alleged to be present: corruption, extreme wealth, particularly among the political elite, civil war, political assassination, gold, diamond and petroleum extraction. These factors are material considerations when one is contemplating a proposal of the kind outlined above.

The African nations also have indigenous languages and introduced languages, the latter either as a result of a colonial past or, in the case of Liberia, as a result of it being populated by American slaves:

Francophone Africa: Congo, Ivory Coast
Portuguese-speaking Africa: Angola
Anglophone Africa: Sierra Leone, Liberia, Nigeria, Zimbabwe, South Africa

All the letters provide evidence for forms of English-as-a-foreign-language competence on the part of their writers, some of it possibly traceable to the colonial language of the purported country of origin of the letter. There lies behind these e-mails a presupposition of colonial exploitation. The recipients of the e-mails in 'the West' can presuppose that there is great wealth in Africa, that colonial rule has left a legacy of Western-educated but corrupt officials, generations of corrupt despots, civil strife, and thus the possibility of easy pickings. These e-mails bank on neo-colonial exploitative presuppositions on the part of the recipients in order to overturn them. They attempt this by, in turn, attempting to gain access to the bank accounts of Western recipients of the e-mails and reversing the colonial cash flow.

5.2.4 The script

The e-mails can be seen as Goffmanian scripts of considerable sophistication. They rely on a background knowledge of the genre of business letters such as one might find being taught in a course on business communication (Chase *et al.*, 1998; Dwyer, 2000). They are formally letters of request. They also rely on the much less circumscribed genre of e-mail. This makes them a hybrid genre. On the one hand, proposals for business partnerships are normally formal, highly stereotyped and emanate from companies. On the other hand, e-mail is normally informal and used for conducting person-to-person communication of less significant import.

Business formulae, one may suppose, can therefore be used as diagnostic data for an analysis of the projection (by the author) of the writer's persona.

5.2.4.1 Formulae

Over 400 phrasal lexical items were initially extracted from the letters. There are chance factors in such data collection, specifically as to identifying formulae in the first place. These factors are well-known (Moon, 1998; Wray, 2002). Let us take it that the selection is large enough to be representative, since there are around 20 formulae per letter on average. The diagnostic technique to find these items was to use native intuition, particularly in the case of restricted collocations where these were idiomatic. Prepositions and verbs and their syntactic complements are well-known for their potential arbitrariness of collocation. For example, payments are made *in* someone's favour, items are stored *for* safe-keeping, one *deposits* money *in* a bank account, one *freezes* assets, one *disburses* revenues. Many attributive adjective–noun combinations are also collocationally restricted. For example, one has *close* relatives, *late* husbands, uses *diplomatic* channels.

The formulae were classified as to their level of formality. The categorization was intentionally coarse. The categories were: hyperformal, formal, semi-formal and informal. We can suppose that, given that the letters are business letters of request, formal formulae will be the norm. Where e-mail conventions are used, such as at the beginning and end of the letters, less formal formulae might be found. Where there are alternative formulae available we would expect, following a norm that stylistic homogeneity is to be maintained in business letters, that a formal formula will be used rather than a less formal one. The formulae were coded for hyperformality where the expression was more formal or archaic than would be considered appropriate in a formal business letter

Table 5.2 Examples of formality level of formulae

Formality level	Examples
Hyperformal PLIs	*all this while, repose one's confidence in someone, of blessed memory*
Formal PLIs	*by virtue of, to this effect, prompted me to*
Semi-formal PLIs	*what I want you to do, going through some old files, let someone down*
Informal PLIs	*so keep it secret, get back to me, put someone in the picture, lay low*

Table 5.3 Examples of domain-related formulae

Domain	Examples
Commerce	*incur expenses, maturity of a contract, deposit the sum of, freeze assets*
Law	*next of kin, attest to the claim, hold in trust, executed under...*

of request (see table 5.2 for examples). Formulae which were specifically from the domains of law and commerce were coded since the letters were offers of engagement in a commercial transaction (see table 5.3 for some examples). Lastly formulae were coded for any collocational errors.

5.3 Foreigner talk: formula analysis

The corpus of formulae was then subjected to three different hypothesis-driven analyses. The first hypothesis was that, to be persuasive in their attempted fraud, the letters would differentially utilize linguistic parameters such as those outlined. Some authors would wish their writers to appear highly competent and knowledgeable while others would want their writers to appear to be friendly, informal, muddling people. Letters which were stylistically homogeneous would contain almost all formal and semi-formal formulae whilst those writers who were less homogeneous would appear foreign and possibly less competent.

Table 5.4 shows some letters are stylistically completely homogeneous, i.e. they could have been written by a native speaker as regards this aspect of their phraseology. But in other letters only two-thirds of the phraseology is consistent with a business letter of offer. Writers of the letters are thus able to present themselves as competent near-natives where their letters exhibit high degrees of stylistic homogeneity. They can present themselves as more personal, idiosyncratic and less competent by using a number of informal formulae. They can also present themselves as non-native by the use of hyperformal formulae.

Second, one would expect letters of offer inviting the recipient of the letter to join a partnership to contain at least some formulae from the domains of business and commercial law. Letters differ sharply as to their proportion of such formulae. Where letters utilized high proportions of domain-specific phrases, they project the persona of a competent professional in the area of banking and finance whereas if their letters contained a low proportion of such

84 Formulaic Genres

Table 5.4 Stylistic homogeneity levels in fraud letters

Text	Style homogeneity %	Text	Style homogeneity %
1	100	12	100
2	89	13	82
3	78	14	79
4	78	15	100
5	80	16	96
6	64	17	80
7	92	18	91
8	96	19	88
9	91	20	96
10	91	21	100
11	93		

Table 5.5 Domain specificity of formulae in fraud letters

Text	Domain specificity %	Text	Domain specificity %
1	26	12	53
2	15	13	36
3	11	14	7
4	33	15	12
5	18	16	21
6	20	17	10
7	36	18	48
8	56	19	15
9	25	20	19
10	26	21	0
11	13		

domain-specific formulae, they would be seen as not highly competent in these areas.

Table 5.5 shows that some letters have half their phrasal lexical items coming from the field of business, while some have none. The writers are thus able to, and do, present themselves as being either highly professionally competent or not, through their selection of phrasal vocabulary.

Third, we would expect non-standard collocations. Collocational errors are common in non-native speaker writing, e.g. *be honest to me*

Table 5.6 Error rates in fraud letters

Text	CE rate %	Text	CE rate %
1	16	12	15
2	30	13	27
3	22	14	14
4	19	15	19
5	30	16	20
6	13	17	15
7	24	18	10
8	17	19	25
9	8	20	19
10	18	21	6
11	33		

vs *be honest with me*, *seeking for your assistance* vs *seeking your assistance*. To be convincing non-native writers, we would expect the writers of these letters to produce such errors.

Table 5.6 shows that no writer is error-free and that there is a sizable error range from 6% to 33%. Again it seems that writers may present themselves as near native in their use of restricted collocations or much less so, but no writer presents themselves as native.

Looking at these three parameters of linguistic selection, it might be the case that individual texts vary from one another as to the extent to which these parameters range. We therefore subjected the three sets of data above to statistical analysis to see whether they were related in a statistically significant manner. As might be expected, stylistic homogeneity and the collocational error rate were strongly related (Wilcoxon $W = 231$, $p <= 3.133e\text{-}08$). (The Wilcoxon test used here gives an indication of the statistical significance of the relationship between paired sets of data.) Both these sets of data are measures of native-like command of the language. Stylistic homogeneity was also significantly related to the degree of domain specificity of the formulae (also Wilcoxon $W = 231$, $p <= 3.133e\text{-}08$). Since many domain-specific formulae are formal or semi-formal, this is again not surprising. However the collocational error rate was not significantly related with the domain specificity of the formulae (Wilcoxon $W = 422.5$, $p <= 0.4734$). This plausibly suggests that even if a writer uses a great many domain-specific formulae, (s)he may still make collocational errors in using them.

5.4 Foreigner talk: general error analysis[2]

What of general non-native features in the letters? Looking at these features enables the letters to be read as examples of the use of English as a foreign language. For this part of the study the sample of writers was reduced to six. They were selected through a ranking process in which six colleagues ordered the letters in terms of 'nativelikeness' (Pawley & Syder, 1983). Two letters were selected from the top of the order, two from the middle and two from the bottom. The order of the letters was virtually identical for all respondents with only the occasional exchange of order for the middle two letters.

An analysis was conducted based on an error correction system from the field of English for Speakers of Other Languages pedagogy. Here it was supposed that foreignness could be presented through foreigner errors. This was an essential requirement in the presentation of the writer as a non-native speaker.

Each of these letters provided a certain level of grammatical and lexical non-standard features. The six letters chosen represented the range of such features, from a level of language capacity somewhere between Low Intermediate and Advanced or (very) High Intermediate (in English as a Foreign Language terms). Table 5.7 shows the proportion of errors to word count provided by each writer.

Note the rank ordering of the letters on the basis of this analysis is in line with the way in which the letters were perceived by the respondents in the selection process by which the 6 letters were chosen from the set of 21 which were used for examining the phrasal vocabulary of the writers. Table 5.8 shows the types of error which were found.

Table 5.7 Error rates in selected fraud letters

Letter number	Writer	Errors/words	Error %	Purported major languages
1	Zuma Ibrahim	21 / 437	4.8	S.Africa + English
7	CRP	37 / 568	6.5	W.African + English
4	Mrs Mobutu Sese-Seko	47 / 460	10.2	Swahili? + French
5	Mrs Lamine	83 / 564	14.7	W.African + French
18	Youssouf Amin Geui	67 / 362	18.5	W.African + French
3	Jeff Savimbi	47 / 199	23.6	W.African + Portuguese
	Total		302	Excludes alternative analyses

Table 5.8 Error type by standard ESL criteria (Note: The errors have been calculated as the number of errors divided by the number of words in each letter. The number and type of errors in the selection of six letters assessed by the survey respondents. Capitalisation is relevant only in letters 3, 5 and 7.)

Letter no.	Error (example)	Correction	Error type	Count
18-Youssouf	as the beneficiary waiting	as the beneficiary, waiting	P	92
18-Youssouf	sequel	following	Voc	43
18-Youssouf	go through	read through	WC	37
18-Youssouf	an advise	some advice	Sp	35
3-Jeff	the government	government	xArt	31
4-Mrs Mobutu	taking	is taking	VF (aux)	13
1-Zuma	Africa	African	Gr	12
3-Jeff	keeper	keepers	Agr-PL	9
18-Youssouf	contact of	contact details for	OMIS-N	9
1-Zuma	Be rest	rest	Rep	6
4-Mrs Mobutu	was	is	T	5
1-Zuma	Moore leased	Moore and leased	OMIS-Lin	4
3-Jeff	abidjan west	on the west	OMIS-Prep	4
18-Youssouf	waiting to hear	I'll be	OMIS-V(P)	4
3-Jeff	Base on this	?	Irrel / Mng?	3
5-Mrs Lamine	even we	we even	WO	3
			Total:	310

KEY: − = type; , = and; / = or.
P: punctuation; VOC: vocabulary; WC: word choice (Collocation); SP: spelling; Art: article problem; VF: verb form; Gr: general grammar error; Agr: agreement (plural or 3rd person singular); OMIS: omission − N: noun, Lin: link word, Prep: preposition, V(P): verb (phrase); Rep: repetition; T: tense; Irrel / Mng: irrelevant or meaning unclear; WO: word order incorrect.

5.5 Perception

Having explored some of the linguistic means by which a persona can be projected in fraud letters, we now turn to the question of how such a persona is perceived. To do this, a line of enquiry pursued by folk-linguistic researchers and social psychologists was employed. Six of the letters which were analysed in detail were used as stimulus material, removing from them all identifiable reference to persons and places. The 21 respondents, all students in courses in sociolinguistics, were asked to indicate what they thought of the writers. Most of the students had heard of Goffman's social psychological theories as contained in *The Presentation of Self in Everyday Life* (Goffman, 1969). A standard set of questions used by Bayard and his associates was employed since these had been trialled previously (Bayard & Green, 2005) as well as some additional questions relating to the writers' places of origin.

Figure 5.1 shows the readers' preferences as to the provenance of the writers. It appears that the error rate of the writers reflects their

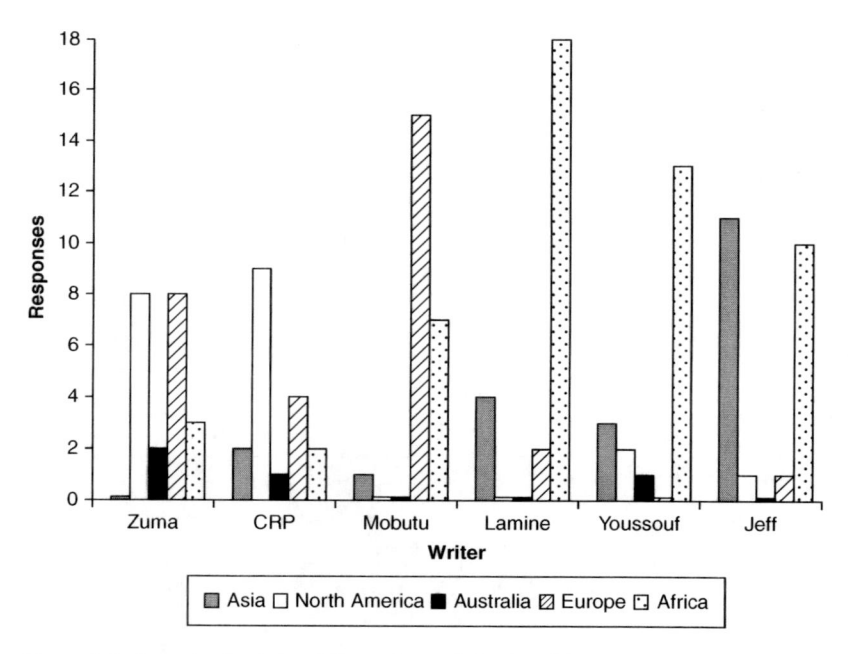

Figure 5.1 Perceived origin of the writers of the fraud letter

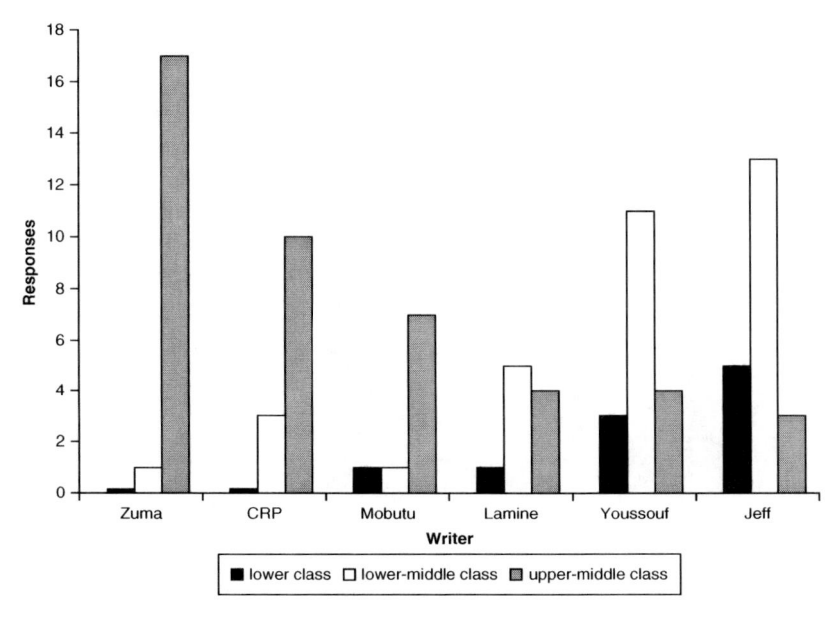

Figure 5.2 Impression of the writers' social class

continent of origin. Those with more foreigner-talk features are more likely to be regarded as African, those with fewer errors more like to be regarded as being from North America or Europe where, presumably, more native-like English can be expected. The other impressions generated by these letters follow a similar pattern. Those with lower error rates are regarded as higher in socio-economic status and more educated: see figures 5.2 and 5.3.

The writers' style is also a reflex of their error rate since, on all the style parameters, the trend line is downward from writers with the lower error rates to those with the higher rates, as is shown in figure 5.4. Error rates are also a good predictor of the vital matter of confidence, those with lower error rates scoring higher on confidence variables than those with higher error rates. Those personality traits which might lead one to trust a writer in a financial transaction are therefore strongly correlated with their low error rate, as is shown in figure 5.5. Unfortunately for the authors, reliability scored significantly lower than other relevant personality traits.

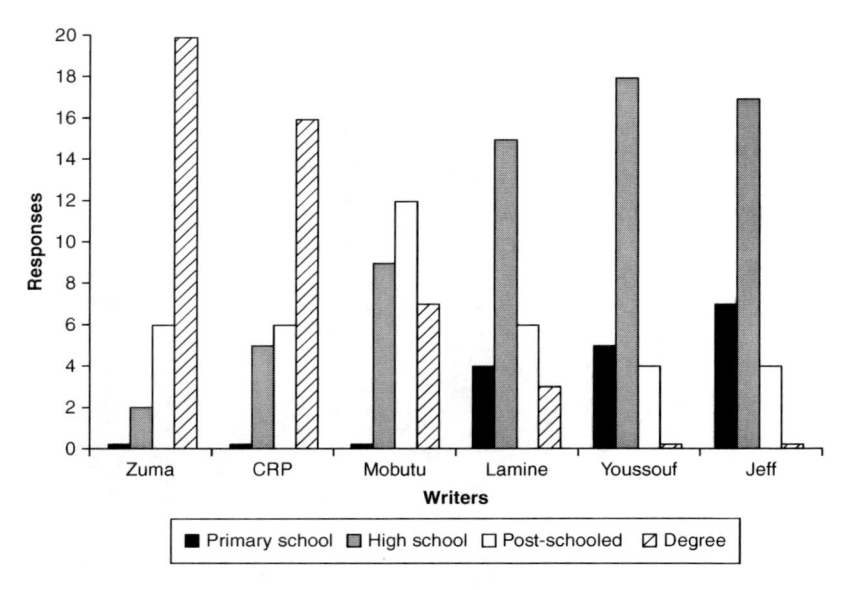

Figure 5.3 Impressions of the writers' educational level

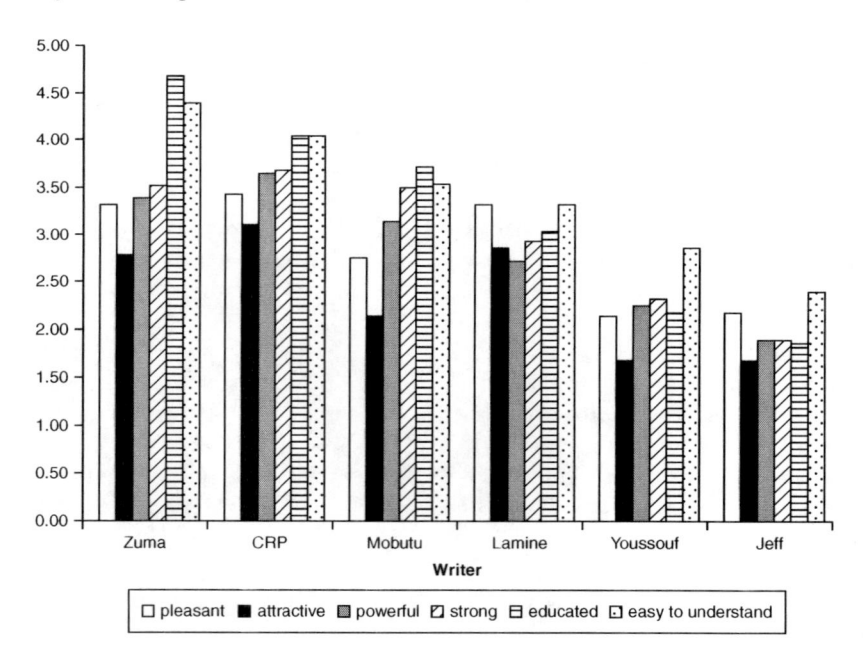

Figure 5.4 Impressions of the writers' style

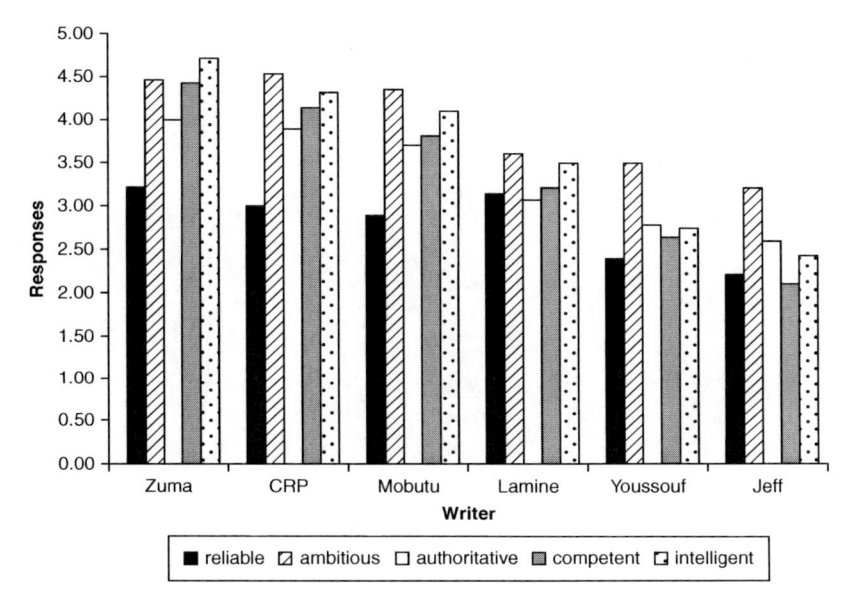

Figure 5.5 Impressions of writers' personality traits

5.6 Conclusion

English has in the last few decades become the language of international commerce, as evidenced by the fact that English business communication texts are studied in all parts of the world. With globalizing technologies, e-mail has allowed English to function increasingly as an electronic lingua franca, not only for informal communication but also for business. This chapter has shown how knowledge of English can be used to attempt business fraud by trading on the foreignness markers available through the phrasal lexicon and in EFL errors. In both these, a large set of linguistic means exists by which authors can attract readers to form impressions of the writer's (foreign) persona. Such personae themselves become globalized. Millions have received letters from Mrs Sese-Seko and formed an opinion of her as a character in a global drama, albeit that she might well be a creation of some author whose existence her letters' recipients infer. These inferred personae appear to be related to the errors the writers make. We have also seen how the genre of business letters can become a hybrid form when transferred from its normal paper medium to e-mail, and how the formal features of such letters, including the phraseology of the genre, can take their place in the hybrid form, leading to new ways of attempting to make money.

Part II
Genrelects

6
Idiolectal Variation: Ritual Talk at the Supermarket Checkout[1]

> Be not afeared; the isle is full of noises, sounds and sweet airs, that give delight and hurt not.
> William Shakespeare, *The Tempest* (III, ii, 135–6)

6.1 Introduction

Although we have already seen something of genre variation in the earlier chapters of this book, in the following chapters the central focus will be on genre variation and change. Other theorists have also explored genre from a variationist perspective. Biber and his associates (Biber, 1988, 1995; Biber, Conrad & Reppen, 1998), for instance, employ a set of general variational parameters such as clause type (Biber, Conrad & Reppen, 1998:139–143) and apply these to large corpora to identify and correlate with a broad variety of text types used in setting up a corpus. These text types are distinguished by Biber from genres which he sees as being a function of external factors (Biber, 1989:39). Recall that I have also used Biber's distinction. Systemic linguistics also employs variationist approaches to genre. Nesbitt & Plum (1988), for example, use parameters made available by the grammar itself.

My approach is to pre-select both the genre features and the relevant text type features and then explore how they vary. While other approaches may suffice for larger and more heterogeneous corpora, in the following chapters, as in the previous ones, you can be fairly certain from the outset what the relevant parameters of variation are because the text type is tightly constrained internally and in its social context.

This chapter continues the exploration of greeting rituals begun in chapter 4 and adds to them parting rituals. The speakers here are supermarket checkout operators performing rituals of encounter

(Firth, 1972; Laver, 1981; Salmond, 1976) in the form of service encounters (Goffman, 1969; Merritt, 1976, 1977).

By a service encounter I mean an instance of face-to-face interaction between a server who is 'officially posted' in some service area and a customer who is present in that service area, that interaction being oriented to the satisfaction of the customer's presumed desire for service and the server's obligation to provide that service (Merritt, 1976:321).

The encounter ritual takes the linguistic form of a set of opening and closing moves, and the central section involves a set of moves for payment to be made by the client. Since these service encounters are in the nature of 'ritual interchanges' (Goffman, 1967), it is not unexpected, given the case made in previous chapters, that checkout operators utilize a formulaic genre for them.

Previous chapters have shown that central to any formulaic genre are discourse structure rules and an inventory of formulae. We have already seen in the fraud letters of chapter 5, authors using a formulaic genre to create Goffmanian personae. In this case study, the analysis will be more detailed and will use a more formal approach. First the genre will be documented and then the individual linguistic personae of its users, i.e. their personal genrelects, will be explored. In this case, the genrelects are those of a group of supermarket checkout operators at two supermarkets in Christchurch, New Zealand.[2]

In New Zealand, checkout operators can and do build on the opening routine which is discussed later, to begin a rather more free form of talk about matters which have nothing to do with the functions they are performing, namely checking out items through the barcode scanner, accepting payment for goods and so on. They can talk, for example, about the weather, their clients' pets, or what they hope to do at the weekend. When this happens we have a form of institutional talk which is not, at least directly, relevant to the task at hand.

This kind of interchange might be seen as 'small talk', namely:

> discourse operating in a limited domain and dislocated from practical action and what Malinowski thought of as 'purposive activities' which include hunting, tilling the soil, and war in 'primitive' societies (Coupland, Coupland & Robinson, 1992:208).

At the supermarket checkout, talk about the weather or one's weekend activities has no direct practical use other than as a form of social intercourse.

The encounter's openings and closings can also be viewed as a kind of small talk since only the exchange section dealing with payment for groceries is fully functional. There are other societies where verbal greetings and partings at the supermarket are much rarer than they are in New Zealand. For example, in the Netherlands in one supermarket I frequented for a period, the only thing normally said by the checkout operators was the formula, *Spaart u airmiles?*, 'Are you saving air miles?' The rest of the transaction was accomplished in silence.

There will be more said later in this chapter on just what the purposes of these openings and closings are and how 'genuine' they are.

6.2 Setting the empirical scene

6.2.1 Macro socio-cultural aspects

In supermarkets the grocer has been replaced by a number of more specialized employees who perform the tasks which grocers used to do by themselves or along with an assistant or two. The checkout operator is one of these more specialized staff. Checkout operators perform the following routine tasks: they tally the prices of the items selected by the customer and accept payment for the goods and also, in many cases, pack the goods. This specialization involves a transfer of labour costs from the retailer to the consumer. First the consumer selects the goods rather than asking the retailer to select them. The consumer places the goods on the 'counter'. This leaves much less time for speech than the protracted interaction between the old-time grocers and their customers who had time to talk over the merits of various products, not to mention local news. The action at the checkout is reduced to a Fordist routine. However, in New Zealand it is normally accompanied by a minimal amount of talk dealing with payment for the goods. Whenever you make face-to-face payments, the ritual of exchange functions as the topic of such talk, the checkout operator being the agent for the retailer in accepting payment for goods and services purchased.[3]

Those who perform the tasks of checkout operator require training to handle the mechanics of the checkout such as the use of the cash register, the microphone used to call for assistance, the cash card machine if there is one, and the barcode scanner which is now ubiquitous at (or more literally in) checkouts. Such training is usually very brief, being of the order of an hour or two and a period of supervision thereafter. The interactions with clients are also brief, being of the order of a few minutes with most clients being strangers.

In New Zealand the great majority of checkout operators are women, many of them young, many of them working part-time. They are not infrequently either in secondary or tertiary education.

6.2.2 Micro socio-cultural aspects

So what happens at the checkout? A small queue of shoppers is lined up at the checkout. As you enter the checkout lane, you come potentially within view of the checkout operator behind the counter. Usually an earlier client is being served at the time when you begin to place your prospective purchases on a moving belt or on a counter. Normally the checkout operator does not acknowledge your presence until having farewelled the previous client. Then they will make eye contact, however briefly, with you and greet you; the opening linguistic move in the service encounter.

The actions which the checkout operators perform are almost entirely rule-governed. They begin by scanning each item on the checkout slide. Occasionally items refuse to scan and are manually entered into the cash register using the barcode number wherever possible.[4] Items which are not barcoded have their price entered. Once all the items have been scanned the total is tallied by the cash register and the total is conveyed to the customer. The customer then pays in one of a number of ways; the goods are packed if they have not yet been packed and the customer leaves with his or her purchases.

A number of conditional steps have been left out of this description. For example, at most supermarkets in New Zealand cigarettes must be purchased at the checkout because of restrictions on their sale to minors. So, if the customer wants to purchase cigarettes the checkout operator has a sub-routine to get them. Many supermarkets in NZ now sell alcoholic beverages. Again these cannot be sold to minors and so in some supermarkets the checkout operator must signal to the supervisor to gain approval to sell such products. Again this is a conditional sub-routine of the kind that says 'if reading a bottle or carton of alcoholic beverage into the barcode scanner, call for supervisor'. The various ways of exchanging money are also each governed by sub-routines. The checkout operator must find out if the customer wishes to pay by cash, cheque or plastic card. For each there is a specific routine to transact. At some supermarkets customers pack their own goods and they have three ways of doing so: they can use either boxes which are on a bench away from the checkout, or they can use plastic bags which the checkout operator provides, or their own eco-friendly bags. Again there is a choice point here and a sub-routine to accompany it.

Besides this major routine and its many possible sub-routines, another routine is being transacted, a speech routine. The checkout operator and the customer meet each other at the checkout and after a short period of time take leave of each other. This routine has a beginning, middle and end like a conversation (Schegloff, 1972; Schegloff & Sacks, 1973). The beginning and end of conversations have a strong tendency to be formulaic because what needs to be done in them is a matter of social ritual.

We therefore have, at the checkout, people performing physical routines in the way they perform their checkout tasks and potentially, linguistic rituals in conducting talk with the supermarket's customers (Coulmas, 1981). This context for talk therefore again provides a good testing ground for the prediction that routine actions which require accompanying routine speech tasks will have that speech performed primarily using formulaic genres.

6.3 Methodology

This study was undertaken in 1991 at two supermarkets from two different supermarket chains, in two different suburbs of Christchurch, New Zealand over a period of about a month. One was in a lower socio-economic suburb, the other in a higher socio-economic suburb. About two hundred interactions were collected as follows.[5] Nine checkout operators were recorded, two male and seven female. Not all are represented by the same number of interactions since our aim was to look mainly at the ritual elements of checkout speech.[6] Customers were informed of the project by a large notice at the beginning of the checkout aisle and informed that the other aisles were not fitted with recording equipment. After the recording sessions, the taped interactions were transcribed onto cards and thence onto computer. Given the aims of the study there was no attempt to control for social variables such as the age, socio-economic status or gender of the clients. Clients were recorded at random as they came through the checkout. We were interested in the formulaic inventory and discourse structure used by checkout operators, and recorded the clients to see how they contributed to the interaction, i.e. we were interested in the ritual aspects of the interactions rather than the sociolinguistic variables which accompanied them.

As usual in such circumstances the normal caveat about the effects of microphones on people who are being recorded may be entered. They are manifest in one or two interactions where the operator and customer discuss the business of being recorded, and in one case, how it is better to say as little as possible.

6.4 What happens at the checkout: the tradition

As will be clear to all denizens of the supermarket, the events at the checkout for any normal transaction constitute a finite system. Only certain things can happen and they happen in certain sequences and not others. That is not to say that unusual things cannot happen. It is just that they are not part of the routine. For example, an armed hold-up is not part of the routine but asking a checkout operator for a product you have not been able to find is a routine event although not one that occurs with great frequency.

Talk at a Christchurch checkout normally begins with a greeting from the operator to the customer or, occasionally, with a greeting to the operator from the customer. The only times when greetings are omitted are when the customer pre-empts the greeting with a question. For example:

Transcript 6.1[7]
Customer: *Do you have today's paper?*
Operator: *No. We don't sell the paper. Sorry.*

Not infrequently even when the customer has pre-empted the greeting the operator will return to it after the pre-emptive question has been dealt with.

Transcript 6.2
Customer: *Doing a swap?*
Operator: *Yes.*
Operator: *How are you?*

In this latter extract the customer's first utterance is an enquiry about the operator taking over from another who has gone for a break. But the operator still greets the client with *How are you?* after having answered

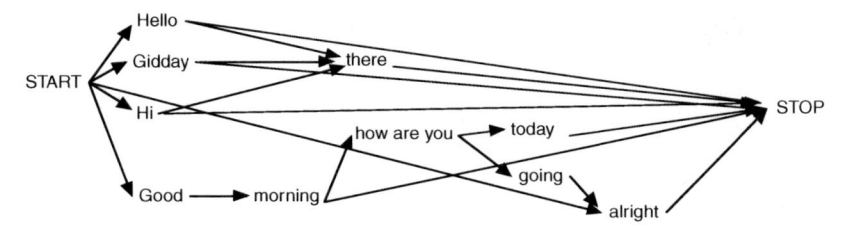

Figure 6.1 Greetings (starts plus information elicitation)

the inquiry. Some customers, often older ones, like to 'get in first' so as to indicate their preparedness to enter into a small talk phase as soon as possible. Notwithstanding such pre-emptive moves by clients, the data suggest that the greeting by the operator is virtually obligatory.

More remarkable is the highly formulaic nature of these opening moves with 88% (176/200) being generable by a single finite state system shown in figure 6.1.[8] The greetings follow the rules for opening conversations of Schegloff (1972) and Smith (1991).[9] In many circumstances, such as the telephone conversations used by Schegloff (1972), interlocutors must identify one another. At a checkout, participants omit identifying each other because their identities, in so far as they have a bearing on the checkout conversation, are implicit. Operators wear name badges with their given names on them. Customers are seldom known to the operators and even when they are it is often not by name. Operators do not have to identify customers by name, as they would on the phone, since the person is standing in front of them. It also appears to be a convention of service encounters that one does not, as client, identify oneself or be asked to do so by the person who is serving you.

'Once participants have identified each other, they must signal the start of the conversation' (Smith 1991:50). This is often done by exchanging greetings. The typical opening words of supermarket greetings are words such as *Hi, Hello, Gidday, Good morning* which are typical start formulae. Their function is to be the opening round in a verbal interaction and they are often one of an adjacency pair in symmetrical conversations. However, supermarket interchanges are not normally ones between equals and so, in the majority of cases where the start is uttered by the operator, the customer gives no reply.

The start phase of a checkout interaction may be followed by a formula which is ambiguous. In some cases it is taken to be an information elicitation formula which aims 'to elicit information from the addressee'

(Smith 1991:64) and in other cases a formula elicitation formula in that it elicits not information but a formula in turn. In a majority of cases at the checkout there is one and only one such formula and it is *How are you (today)?* As Smith (1991:64–5) indicates, following Firth (1972:110) and Coupland *et al.* (1992) '[i]t is well-known to New Zealand speakers (and a source of confusion to non-native English speakers) that a response... may not be needed and, in fact, not even desired.' That certainly seems to be the case for some customers at the checkout since only some customers reply to the operator's information elicitation formula (if there is one) at all. Of the 128 information elicitation formulae, only 89 received replies. This is an unusual situation in that normally such formulae are part of an adjacency pair, as Coupland *et al.* (1992) show.

There is a tendency in some cultures to feel that what is said by service staff during a 'start' phase of the kind of service encounter one has at the supermarket is insincere. At Disneyland, the smiling faces which constantly ask you how you are seem to be being friendly because Disneyland is a happy kingdom which trains all its staff (on pain of firing) to be ever-cheerful. Certainly staff in many service situations are enjoined by the management to be friendly, cheerful and ever-polite. It does not follow that all checkout operators are necessarily being insincere when they greet clients. It seems genuine in two ways. It is an opportunity for the operator to be positively polite and also creates an opportunity for the client to begin a genuine conversation. If the formula *How are you (today)?* was generally perceived as insincere, then it would be regarded as semantically empty having only pragmatic value as a move in a ritual. However, that it is not parsed as a semantically empty ritual move can be inferred from its capacity to function as the introductory move in a small talk interaction where the client responds to the inquiry as an information elicitation, i.e. by taking it literally.

At this point it is useful to distinguish between two kinds of talk that go on at the checkout: the matrix interchange which is obligatory, consisting of an opening, an exchange section and optionally a close, and the overlay small talk which has the same opening but expands as the response to an information elicitation. Many supermarket conversations have just a matrix interaction which is more or less functional and whose centre is transactional, having to do with payment. However, if a reply to the information elicitation formula is forthcoming from the customer, it frequently signals that there will be overlay small talk as well. Of the 89 conversations in which the information elicitation received a reply 70 led to overlay talk. Thus only 19 elicited merely a formula by way of reply. There were only three overlay interchanges begun from a customer's initiative.

A reply by the customer to an information elicitation by the operator indicates that the customer is prepared for there to be more than a matrix interchange. It does not signal what the content of the overlay conversation will be, as the following examples show:

Transcript 6.3
O: Hi.
C: Morning.
O: How are you today?
 You had a good week?
C: Yeh, very good, thank you.

Transcript 6.4
O: And how are you today?
C: Good thanks. It's nice and quiet this morning.
O: Yeah it is.
C: Well, I s'pose it might not be for you.

Transcript 6.5
O: And how are you?
C: Good.
O: It's nice, that low salt margarine, isn't it? Have you tried it?
C: ...low salt. I just picked it up...
O: It's very – it's very nice.

There are a small number of checkout operators who go to more trouble to elicit an overlay conversation. One in particular has a series of formulae which she uses to break though to an unresponsive customer and she is frequently rewarded. She uses formulae such as *Have you had a good week?*, *How's your day been?* and *Glad for the change in the weather?* These information elicitations usually follow the more conventional *How are you (today)?* By their greater specificity and lesser conventionality they appear more genuine and spontaneous to the customer who is therefore under greater pressure to reply.

The topics for overlay talk, if there is any, tend to be selected from a small range, the weather being the most frequent. Other topics include: one of the customer's purchases which may be singled out for approbation, what the customer is going to do the rest of the day or weekend, what the operator is going to do the rest of the day. They are characteristically phatic (Malinowski, 1922) and thus contrast with the matrix interchange which is functional in that its central content section deals with the exchange of money for goods purchased. Typical examples of overlay small talk are interchanges such as the following:

Transcript 6.6
O: Hello. How are you?
C: Good, thanks. I've got all the goodies in there.
O: Oh, what've you got there? Fattening foods?
C: Yes, fattening foods.

Transcript 6.7
O: Hi. How are you?
    You had a good week?
C: S'pose so. Been all right. Glad the weather's come right.
O: Yeah, 'bout time it did.
C: You're not wrong.

Transcript 6.8
O: Hi, how are you today?
C: Good.
O: Have you had a good week?
C: Yep.
O: Survived the bad weather?
C: At least it's fine now; get the washing dry and the rest of it.
O: Yeah.

Transcript 6.9
O: Doing anything special for Easter?
C: No.
O: No.
C: You?
O: No – we've got friends coming from the North Island – so – keep us pretty busy. Yes.

The overlay interchange, if there is one, normally occurs in the period between the time the operator starts checking the goods through the barcode reader until that is completed at which point the exchange section of the matrix conversation must take place. In the absence of an overlay period of small talk, everyone keeps silent until the exchange section of the interchange. On other occasions a short overlay conversation is followed by a period of silence until the barcode scanning is complete.

However, sometimes the overlay chat continues beyond the exchange section:

Transcript 6.10
O: Hi, how are you?
   Lovely day today.
C: Yes... you should be busy today.
O: Yes.
C: There's so many other shops open, though.
O: We were, um, very busy during the week.
C: Yes - oh, I think you'll always be busy... people still eat, don't they?
O: Yes.
C: No matter what... what they still... taste food.
O: 's twenty-eight dollars eighty-five thanks
   Doing anything special for Easter?
C: No, no...
O: No
C: ...caravan. but... expensive...
O: Yeah, yeah. Twenty-eight, twenty-nine and one's thirty
C: ...Doing up... house, fixing up the garden and things, you know.
O: Okay, well have a good weekend. Thank you.

Not all the overlay small talk is on a single topic, as extract 6.10 shows with its four topics: a start on the weather, the business of the day for the checkout operator, the fact that people have to eat, and then what the customer is going to do for the Easter weekend.

The start of the exchange section of the matrix interchange is sometimes signalled by a formula such as *Will that be all?* which indicates that the operator has tallied all the goods on the slide. Such formulae are also indirect requests for the customer to indicate whether they wish to purchase cigarettes. Occasionally the opening of this section may be signalled by a formula which merely indicates that the exchange section is about to start. For example, an operator might say *There we are* or *There we go*. One operator uses both as can be seen in figure 6.2.

The obligatory constituent of the exchange section is the operator's indication to the customer of the total value of the customer's purchases.

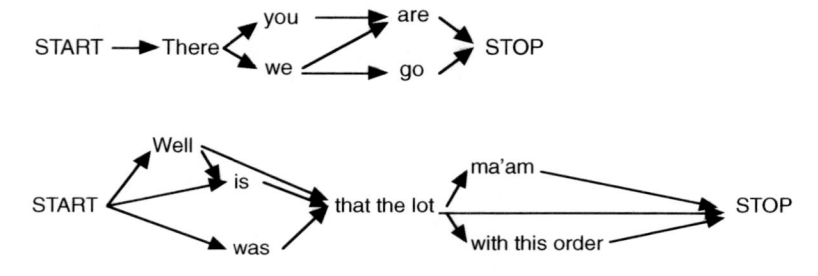

Figure 6.2 Introduction to exchange section formulae

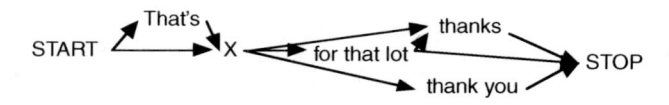

Figure 6.3 Cash call formula

This is always indicated by a formula: see figure 6.3. The customer does not respond verbally to the cash call but provides payment in some form or other and the operator usually thanks the customer for it, again with a formula. If the customer uses a cash card, the operator often asks whether the customer wishes to have any cash from the till along with paying for their purchases. Again this is done using a formula such as *Would you like any cash with that?* The finite state system which generates almost all the receipt of cash formulae is found in figure 6.4. If there is change to be counted out, the operator often signals this with a formula as in figure 6.5. The operator then counts out the change and often again thanks the customer and again with a formula as in figure 6.6.

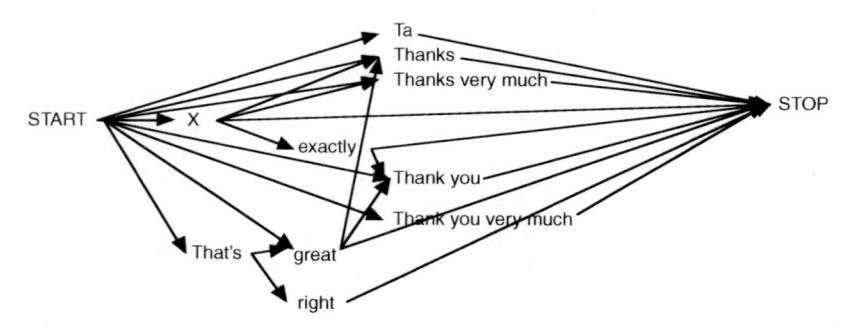

Figure 6.4 Receipt of cash formula

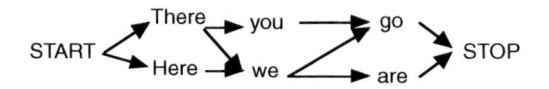

Figure 6.5 Introduction to change counting formula

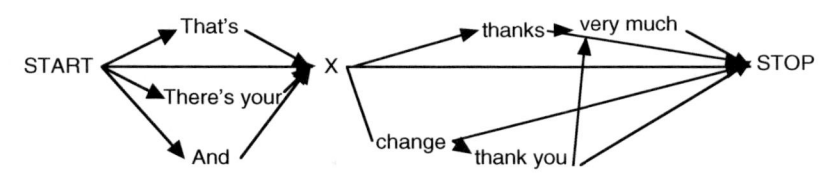

Figure 6.6 Change counting formula

The exchange section is then complete and the customer leaves. But, following Schegloff & Sacks (1973), Smith (1991) suggests that departure also has a set of discourse constituents. Endings or leave-takings may start with back references to what has taken place earlier in the body of the interchange. Back references are normally 'thank you' formulae thanking the customer not for their money but for the whole transaction. They may also indicate that the transaction is complete by a formula such as *There you are*. This can mean that the operator thanks the customer four times; once when giving the total from the cash register, once when receiving the cash or card, once when counting out the change and a last *thank you* as a back reference to the whole transaction. There are times when the exchange section passes without a single reply from the customer as in the following interchange:

Transcript 6.11
O: *Is that the lot?*
   Twelve dollars fifteen, thank you.
   Thank you very much.
   There we are; seven dollars eighty-five change. Thank you.
   There we go, thank you.

This may again exemplify the strategy of not completing the adjacency pair which we saw earlier as a feature of some New Zealand English varieties, or it may reflect the service role of the operator and thus the client's sense that speakers in such roles do not need always to be treated to bilateral courtesies, as is shown in figure 6.7.

108 *Formulaic Genres*

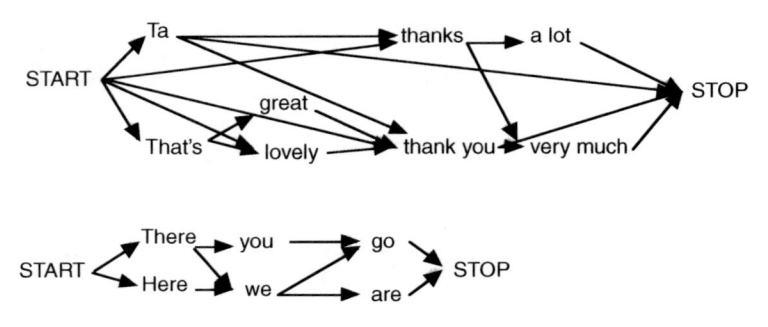

Figure 6.7 Back reference formulae

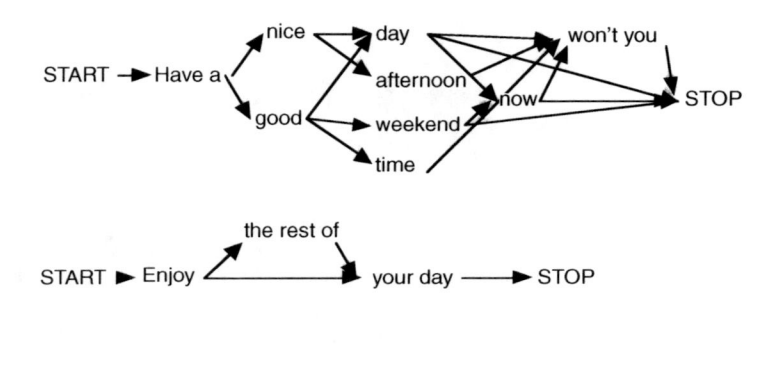

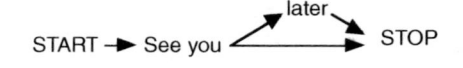

Figure 6.8 Positive face stroke formulae

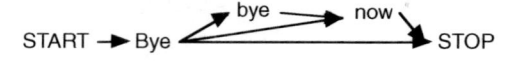

Figure 6.9 Termination formula

A farewell may also contain positive face strokes (Brown & Levinson, 1978) in which the operator wishes the customer well or, much less frequently, the customer wishes the operator well. *Have a nice day* is a typical version of such a formula (see figure 6.8). Then, at the extreme end of the conversation, there may be a termination to parallel the introduction. *Bye*, or *bye, bye* are typical examples of such terminations (see figure 6.9).

It appears then that checkout operators avail themselves of a particular discourse structure for their matrix interchanges. This can be represented by a set of context-free rewrite rules (Scherzer, 1974; Salmond, 1976).[10]

Discourse structure of matrix conversation

Matrix interchange → Opening + Exchange + Close
Opening → (Start) + (Info./formula elicitation)
Exchange → Total + (Receipt) + (Change)
Close → (Back ref.) + (Positive face stroke) + (Termination)

These rewrite rules generate, i.e. provide an explicit account of, how checkout speech formulae are used at each point in the discourse by indicating where the formulae may be used. Another way to see the rules is therefore as providing indices attached to each formula restricting where in a discourse sequence a formula may be used.

6.5 Checkout operator tradition and individual speech

The typical interchanges between customers and checkout operators look, on the face of it, as though they have little room for an individual operator to be different from others, in that they are highly formulaic and the discourse structure of the matrix interchange is highly restrictive. In fact this is not the case. In checkout operator speech there is both a tradition and room for individual utilization of that tradition. None of the operators uses every possible route through the greeting system. Each has their own preferred routes. It may be that these are a result of the relatively small sample but they are strongly suggestive of individuality. The finite state diagrams in figure 6.10 are the greeting routines of three different operators. To understand these diagrams one should compare the range of the possible formulae an operator might use and which are part of the checkout operator greeting tradition, as given in figure 6.1, with the range of formulae the particular operator uses, as given in figure 6.10. This kind of filtering out of individual utilization of the tradition can be repeated for each phase of the matrix interchange. The above examples are indicative of how this can be done.

There are routes through the system in figure 6.1 which do not appear in the data. For example, *Gidday, how are you today?* and *Good morning.* do not appear in the sample. However it can be predicted that operators can and will use such forms because that is the tradition on which they

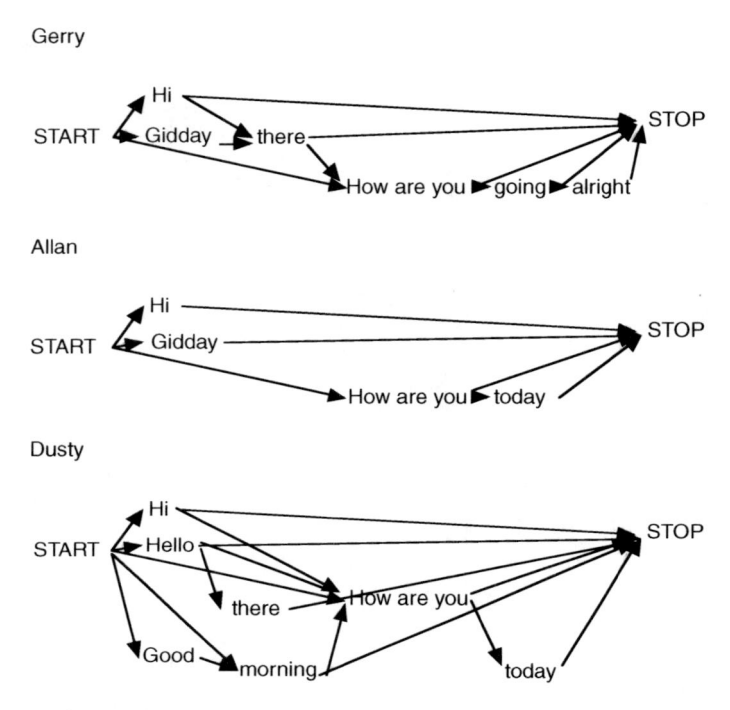

Figure 6.10 Greeting formulae of individual checkout operators

draw. It is likely that the only reason why these are not present in the data is that there is not enough data. In previous work on auctions, Kuiper & Haggo (1984) found that subsequent recording 'safaris' usually found the predicted data and, normally, no formulae which were not generated by the finite state diagrams. This is because formulaic genres are highly restricted, speakers utter the prescribed formulae, and little or nothing but the formulae, in many contexts.

Not only that. Operators use particular tracks through their diagram with greater or lesser frequency and this pattern of preference creates an individual style. The frequency count for greetings generated by the finite state diagram in figure 6.1 is given in table 6.1. Similar tables can be constructed for each phase of the conversation. All operators are thus idiosyncratic in a limited kind of way. Many have formulae that they alone use. Some operators are clearly also much more flexible in their use of formulae than others. They use a greater range and they switch more frequently. The most creative in this regard is Dusty (D) who is an experienced operator and from North America. She goes to considerable

Table 6.1 Greeting formulae used by each operator[14]

Greeting	Guy	Allan	Dusty	Leeanne	Gay	Elsie	Di	Shelly	Kris	Totals
How are you?	1:11%	5:31%	12:32%	5:38%	2:9%		1:5%	1:6%	2:9%	29
How are you today?		5:31%	5:13%		11:48%	4:24%	3:14%	1:6%	1:5%	30
How are you going?	1:11%									1
How are you going, alright?	1:11%									1
Alright?										1
Hello.			2:5%	4:31%	6:26%	1:6%	1:5%		3:14%	16
Hello there.			1:3%							1
Hello. How are you?			1:3%	1:8%			1:5%		3:14%	5
Hello. How are you today?										1
Gidday		1:6%								1
Gidday. How are you?							1:5%			1
Gidday there. How are you going?	1:11%									1
Good morning. How are you?			4:11%							4
Hi	1:11%	5:31%	5:13%	3:23%	2:9%		1:5%	1:6%		15
Hi there.	4:44%									4
Hi. How are you?			5:13%		2:9%	11:65%	13:59%	8:50%	13:59%	55
Hi. How are you today?						1:6%	1:5%	4:25%		6
Morning.			3:8%							3
Morning. How are you today?								1:6%		1
Totals	9	16	38	13	23	17	22	16	22	176

lengths to farewell her customers, sometimes using all three closing constituents such as *Thank you. Have a nice day. Bye bye.* at the conclusion of a single interchange. She is also able to interpolate overlay small talk into a variety of niches. In one case, after a customer had found the supermarket to be out of her cat's favourite cat food, during and after the exchange section Dusty finishes with an enquiry about the cat, as a palliative to the customer's possible ill-will at not having been able to purchase her cat's favourite cat food.

Transcript 6.12
O: *Good morning.*
C: *Morning.*
O: *How are you?*
C: *I'm fine, thanks.*
O: *You look well. You look nice.*[11]
C: *... had - had ten days in hospital.*
O: *Oh did you? You feeling better?*
C: *I've had a new hip put in.*
O: *Oh, well good for you. As - is - you going well with it?*
C: *Yep.*
O: *Super.*
C: *Down to – ah – one crutch.*
O: *Good for you.*
C: *On my right side. Tell me, the Sheba pet food. You've got beef cuts, beef and kidney, but no turkey in. Turkey's the popular one.*
O: *Let me ask Murray for it - 'scuse me, Murray - in the Sheba line of cat food will we be getting turkey?*
M: *We'd like to think so ... problems with the shipping ... from America.*
C: *I see you've got beef and kidney.*
M: *It's just come in - it was it's just come in ...*
C: *Well it must have, cos I didn't see it on Friday.*
M: *No ... only just arrived. In fact I didn't even realize that myself.*
C: *Yeah well ...*
   So I wanted to buy turkey.
O: *Yeah. Should be coming in very shortly. I'll know on Tuesday.*
C: *Okay, I'll go home and tell him.*
O: *Four dollars fifty, thanks.*
   Thanks.
C: *Sorry.*
   ... been out a lot ...

O: That's your cat's favourite, is it?
C: Yes.
O: They all have their favourites.
C: ... might be other cats also like it.
O: That's why - we're out.
C: Yeah. Thank you.
O: Okay.

The least flexible of the operators is Elsie (E) who had only been a checkout operator for a few days. Her small greeting range is matched by small ranges of formulae in every other part of the discourse structure of the checkout routine.

Most operators have strong modal preferences for a particular form and only use other tracks through their system occasionally. Allan and Guy occasionally use the stereotypically male greeting *Gidday.* whereas only one of the women operators uses it and then only on a single occasion.[12] Each operator has the equivalent of a signature in the tracks through the general formulae of the tradition each chooses to use and the frequency with which they use a given track. This signature is an index of their operator persona. This persona no doubt evolves differently over time so that some operators are more conservative, maintaining their signature for long periods, whereas other operators are more flexible.

The tradition which we have mapped as a set of discourse-indexed formulae, and which operators draw on and utilize individually, are not unique to supermarkets. The start formulae and information elicitation formulae which form the opening are all used more widely than in supermarkets, and for the same purpose, namely meeting and parting. In the exchange section, all the formulae are used in retailing in general and all operators at checkouts will have had ample opportunity to absorb them as passive recipients in their role as clients in retail transactions. The same is true for the close components of the matrix interchange which are used elsewhere for partings. They are in general use for the purpose for which they are employed in supermarket checkout interchanges or they are used in other retail settings. The formulae are therefore discourse-function specific but not specific to a supermarket checkout tradition. There is only one exception and this is the addition to the bag or box formula used chiefly by one checkout operator, *Do you want bags with that or are you going to box it?* She appears to have constructed this addition herself since none of her colleagues uses it in quite this form.[13]

6.6 Conclusion

Supermarket checkout operators again corroborate the hypothesis that where routine actions are accompanied by routine speech, such speech tends to be by means of formulaic genres. It is also clear that speakers will borrow appropriate formulae from elsewhere in their speech repertoire to perform the necessary functions in a formulaic genre and that, even within such a tightly constrained environment as that which the routine actions and speech of checkout operators imposes, there is room for individuality, idiosyncrasy and even for a small measure of creativity.

The techniques we have used to map both the tradition itself in terms of its discourse structure rules and its formulae as discourse-indexed finite state diagrams, allow other traditions to be modelled in the same way. It allows the performance of individual performers in the tradition to be modelled by looking at which formulae they use, which tracks through the formulae diagrams they select and the frequency with which they select them. This methodology can be used diachronically to see how an individual oral formulaic persona evolves.

What of the overlay conversations which constitute examples of small talk in the way it is defined by Coupland *et al.* (1992:208)? Small talk at the checkout is framed by the formulaic rituals of greeting and leave-taking on the one hand (as it often is elsewhere) and the exchange section of the matrix interchange on the other. Small talk fills the otherwise silent interstices with inconsequential talk, some of it formulaic itself; inconsequential in the sense that nothing practical generally follows from it. Socially, however, each instance finds common ground between speakers, server and served, on subjects which are as uncontentious as possible: the weather, cat food and generalizations about one's weekend activities.

6.7 Methodological epilogue: working with consultants

Consultants (native informants) are the people you record, talk to or quiz about their lives and their use of language, in order to understand what it is they know and do when they operate as natives in and with the genre you are trying to understand. All the case studies in this book have required at least some reference to live people who were interviewed. In every case study, the relationship with consultants was different, and different relationships require different approaches. The checkout operators were all given new names to protect their anonymity and the clients' names were not recorded. However the auctioneers and race callers who feature in other chapters were happy to be named since they felt that their work was in the public domain. I interviewed, casually, Reon Murtha, the chief race caller in the province of Canterbury, on a number of occasions, asking about various aspects of his craft and racing in general that perplexed me. He also provided tapes of earlier callers because he thought I might be interested. He was happy to be quoted on record.

Human ethics protocols are involved in all studies involving human subjects and these protocols have evolved to become more restrictive over the last two decades. Anyone undertaking studies such as those whose outcomes are outlined in this book needs to clear the study with a university human ethics committee. However it is important first to look at the objectives of the study and see the involvement of the subjects as much as possible from their point of view. The primary concern is that one's consultants should not be harmed by their involvement in the study. They are also entitled to know what the study is about. They are entitled to anonymity if that is what they want. They are entitled to withdraw from the study. Such issues come under informed-consent provisions and there is much written on that subject. I touch upon it here just to make the reader aware that such issues exist and must be dealt with as part of a research project. I should also note that different agencies involved in research have different approaches and different clerical procedures for dealing with human ethics issues. So it is important to see what these are in every case when you are thinking of conducting a study of a formulaic genre.

7
Genrelects, Gender and Politeness: Form and Function in Controlling the Body

> *The body is evil and must be punished.*
> Chris 'Crispy' Burr (mountain biker)

7.1 Introduction

Most human beings believe that they can alter the views and actions of others by linguistic means. Citing a proverb, for example, can be used to attempt to change the view of another. Shouting the opposition down at political meetings and in parliament is another. The mind-altering properties of language and language use are explored by a number of theoreticians. Sapir (1924) and Whorf (1956), for example, are interested in the proposition that the mind might be influenced in its view of the world by formal features of a language; Klemperer (Klemperer *et al.*, 1995) and Orwell (1953) explore the proposition that language can be manipulated by the powerful to control the powerless. This proposition is explored in chapter 10. However, language can also be used to control the body. Speech act theory (Austin, 1976) posits a class of directives which includes all forms of telling others what they are to do. For example, Vine (2001) examines directives in the workplace. In what follows we will look at directive genres that involve remote control of the body. Controlling the body is a fundamental human need. It is exercised at a basic level in the control of processes of excretion and, at the sublime, in the cult of the hero or heroine who has control over the body exercised by supernatural powers (Kuiper, 1998). Motivations for wishing to control the body are many, ranging from the desire to control it because it is inherently evil (possibly a form of Gnosticism), through functional motivations such as controlling it to perform particular tasks,

Genrelects, Gender and Politeness 117

such as having it become a weapon, through to controlling it so that it becomes a beautiful artefact. This chapter looks at directives on the parade ground, in the gym, and at a dance club where, in all three contexts, formulaic genres are used by the speaker to direct the bodies of the hearers.

7.2 On parade

The military parade ground is an archetypal context in which the body of a soldier becomes metaphorically and perhaps even literally a machine operated by their officers. In effect, those who sign up to join the armed services or are conscripted give up their rights over their bodies in certain circumstances to the officers who may command them to perform in a way they might not themselves have wished. The language used to perform such remote control of the body of others can be termed command speech. The particular situation from which the first example is taken is the parade ground at Burnham Military Camp near Christchurch in New Zealand. The sergeant major is directing a group of young people who are in training for a period of weeks as part of a government scheme. They have both volunteered and been selected for this period of training and they will shortly be leaving the camp to return to civilian life. Some hope to join the army. It is Sunday morning and they are practising for their passing out parade. The platoons are marched on to the parade ground, each led by its NCO, and then the sergeant major takes over directing the proceedings.

Here is a short extract from what he says.

Transcript 7.1
don't talk
do not face the calling out
number three company, get on parade
make it three platoons
don't face the calling out
only the markers will move on the command to fall in
fall in
wakey, wakey, three platoon
when you take the paces forward or backward, don't swing the arms
again the calling out is a bit fast
and, at the double, right dress
lower your arms to the side

118 Formulaic Genres

that means put your bloody arm down
put it down
on the command, move, back to your positions
move
listen, and listen carefully
this is the only time I will explain it to you again.
on the command, open on a right dress, come up to attention
front rank, three four centimetre paces forward
rear rank, three four centimetre paces to the rear
head and eyes over the right shoulder
and pick up your dressing
if you don't get it right this time, NCOs take their names and place them on bloody extra drill
in open order, right dress
four platoon, your falling out is too fast
lower your arms to the side.
number two platoon, front rank, stick your head on your right shoulder
don't look around
don't commence your dressing until I've given the order
number three company, stand at ease
company, 'shun
wake up
wake up
stand at ease
company, 'shun
stand at ease.
fall in, the officers
well done, platoon sergeants
good.
(No one else says anything.)

The objective of the 'getting on parade' exercise is to have each platoon move to its assigned position for the purpose of being inspected by an officer. This is achieved by:

1. having the platoon's 'marker' move into position, 'falling in'.
2. Each platoon's three ranks align themselves on the position taken by the marker.
3. They 'right dress' to line themselves up in a straight line on the right-hand member of each of the three ranks.

4. They move to an open formation with the front rank moving forward and the third rank moving back.
5. They 'right dress' again to keep each rank straight, lined up on the right-hand member.
6. They are then told to stand 'at ease'.
7. They are brought 'to attention'.
8. They told to stand 'at ease'.
9. 'to attention'
10. 'at ease'
11. The NCO's are ordered to 'fall in' beside their platoons.

Whatever the function of parade ground drill may be, it is clear that one person is telling other people how to move their bodies. It is also clear that this is done with formulae. Many of these are of considerable antiquity. Many of them are idioms. (Whatever falling in involves, no one falls into anything. Right dressing does not involve clothing.) Each formula plays a fixed part in the routine. There are points where the ranks right dress. There are points where the markers fall in and a point where the NCOs fall in. The places where this can happen are determined by the fixed order of proceedings. So much for the context.

The archetypal construction for directives is the imperative. Imperatives are much in evidence. Most of them are bare verb phrase imperatives such as *wake up*. Bare VP imperatives contain nothing but the directive without modification. Others contain vocatives in the form of the person or persons being addressed, e.g. *Company, 'shun.* and *Fall in, the officers*. Occasionally a directive uses the modal *will* where some future action is being required, as in *Only the markers will move on the command to fall in*. Between the directives there are instructions as to form, i.e. as to how to perform the directive which is about to be given, e.g. *On the command, move, back to your positions*. Some directives tell the hearer(s) what not to do, e.g. *Don't face the calling out*. Very occasionally a comment is made on how things were done rather than how they are to be done, e.g. *Again the calling out is a bit fast*.

The whole of this protocol is aimed at one thing, body control. It is totally formulaic and the genre of parade ground sergeant major talk is justly known for its coercive quality.

I have said nothing so far about the prosodics of the performance. The sergeant major is speaking in a large open-air space. He therefore speaks at the top of his voice in a staccato manner striding up and down before the troops, occasionally turning to one platoon in an aggressive posture to upbraid them.

It may seem curious for human beings to give up control of their bodies to others in the way that those who volunteer for military service do. However it does solve a basic human problem, which is what to do to gain body control. There are, no doubt, other motivations such as the higher good of defending the realm which is purportedly facilitated by placing one's person at the complete disposal of those who serve the realm in military service. But there are also other motivations for placing one's body under orders.

7.3 Pumping

Control of the body may be given up so that the body performs in a desired manner. One way this can be accomplished is by exercising. Exercising can be done in two ways. The first comes as a by-product of activity which is addressed to some other end. For example, most shearers of sheep gain the kind of body control they need just by shearing sheep. The second way involves exercising for no immediate purpose other than exercising. There may be a more distant purpose for this. For example, players of team sports may exercise in order to increase their aerobic fitness or muscle strength in order better to play their team sport. But when they are exercising, they are performing actions whose sole direct purpose is gaining the benefits to be gained by performing the exercise. This can be termed 'solipsistic exercise'. For example, lifting weights in a gym has no function as far as the weights are concerned, whereas lifting building materials on a building site is purposeful beyond the mere lifting of the materials.[1]

In order to gain control over the body through solipsistic exercise, a person may develop their own exercise regime such as going for walks or using an 'abdominizer' or other instruments advertised interminably on television, or they may employ someone else to be their trainer/controller.[2] This other person can control the exercise programme which controls the person who wishes to control their body.

In this case, the metacontroller is in an asymmetric power relationship with their trainee in that they have been appointed, like the sergeant major, to control the person who wishes to control their body (Delin, 2001). They could, at least in theory, go about exercising this control physically and that does happen in some cases; coaches can take the limbs of the people they are training and move them through particular actions as a robot trainer does when using the leading method to program spray-painting robots (MacDonald, 1981). Swimming coaches will occasionally lead the arms of swimmers by physically moving those limbs through the desired movement. Physiotherapists move disfunctional limbs through patterns of motion in order to exercise them. However the more usual way is for the controller/coach/instructor to use directives to instruct the person how they are to control their own body.

Giving directives has interesting consequences. In many circumstances telling someone else what to do involves risks since one is imposing on another. That being so, a variety of strategies can be employed to mitigate the threat posed in giving the directive. The classical account of linguistic politeness (Brown and Levinson, 1978), as we saw in chapter 4, proposes that social beings have two kinds of face needs: positive face needs which have to do with individuals' desire to be thought well of by others, and negative face needs which have to do with their need for imposition-free space. When subject to a face-threatening act which might impact on another's face, speakers often utilize linguistic politeness techniques. You say *I wonder if you would mind closing the window*, rather than *Close the window*. Directives are potentially a threat to negative face and therefore, in giving directives, you are normally required to be polite. Furthermore, much of linguistic politeness is expressed phraseologically (Ferguson, 1976), as the above example shows. The introductory clause *I wonder if you would mind...* is a formula commonly used (and known to be thus used) for the purpose of mitigating face threat. Face threat is a consequential, but itself unintended, effect of imposing in some other way, such as making a request, on another. Face attack, by contrast, is the intended use of various linguistic strategies for the purpose of the coercion and humiliation of the addressee. Being given a directive clearly impacts on an addressee's negative face in that the addressee is constrained in their imposition-free space by being required to do what they are told by the instructor. So it is an interesting question whether the directives issued by an aerobics instructor constitute face-threatening or face-attack acts. That can only be determined by a close examination of the context. Conscripts on a parade ground are frequently the subject of face-attack acts. Recall that the parade ground drill sergeant major above provided the following utterance sequence:

Lower your arms to the side.
That means put your bloody arm down.
Put it down.

Each utterance was shouted directly at each person involved. This appears to be a case of face attack since the utterances impose directly on the hearers' negative face in that they are being required to lower their arms. It imposes on the hearers' positive face in that it may be inferred from what is said that the hearer(s) are so stupid that they cannot understand the first directive since it contains the two-syllable word *lower*, that they need to have it explained in words of one syllable, and need it repeated. It is doubtful that the effect required, that of lowering the arms, required those lowering their arms to be humiliated. Hence a case of face attack.

Unlike conscripted soldiers, aerobics instructees are paying volunteers. There is thus a curious form of coercion. Normally coercion is being forced to do what one does not wish to do. In the gym one does what one wishes to do but at the command of another.[3] You might still suppose, therefore, that, alongside the commands, some politeness would be in evidence.

7.3.1 Pump instructor talk[4]

7.3.1.1 Introduction

The second case study of this chapter looks at the formulaic genre of directives used by pump aerobic instructors and the way instructors utilize politeness strategies, perhaps better termed 'addressee oriented' features (Stubbe and Holmes, 1995).[5]

Aerobics exercise, as performed in a gymnasium, is controlled by two things: the instructor's routine and the music the instructor uses to provide both a rhythmic template for the activity and background music. Performing aerobic exercise in a gym is, for all appearance to the contrary, essentially solitary – rather like ballroom dancing performed by individuals in public parks in China. There are no team members and the activity is not outwardly competitive (although there is an underlying tone of competitiveness as to who is stronger, fitter or has the better body).

The instructor's primary role is to cue the participants through a variety of aerobic or anaerobic moves just as a square dance caller cues the moves in a dance. Aerobics instructors participate in the workout themselves, modelling the exercise(s) while verbally cueing the next move. The next move must be cued before the completion of the move that is currently being modelled.

The second thing an instructor does is motivate the participants in their class. This is achieved in a number of ways. The instructor's own mastery of the routine and consequent mastery over their body can be a motivating factor for those who wish for similar mastery. Tacit competition can also be a motivator, as can various verbal means at the instructor's disposal. These include various forms of face work. Last, the instructor must ensure that participants are maintaining 'correct form', i.e. lifting weights in ways that avoid injury and promote maximum benefit from the exercise. Muscle strain and injuries are often a result of bad lifting technique. Therefore, throughout the workout, the instructor reminds the participants to check their 'form' with comments such as *backs nice and straight, team*.

For each of these functions, there is a certain discourse structure and contained within this structure, a variety of options. These options give room for individuality, although only minimal novelty can be expressed since what is said is almost entirely formulaic.

There are various aerobics instructors' training programmes available in New Zealand. The most common and popular method of training is to attend a course. Such courses contain core-level training which teaches material such as Exercise Science, Nutrition, Injury Prevention and Communication. After the trainee has graduated from this section they learn the techniques involved in instructing. This section is based on practical experience. The trainee is required to write their own choreography and a supervisor attends and evaluates the class. The practical assessment involves the evaluation of the trainee's ability to instruct a safe, enjoyable and effective exercise programme. The instructor is explicitly taught the physical education side of the course. The rest, including the cueing genre, is learnt by watching other instructors and through personal experience. The gym in which this study was performed uses mostly freelance instructors. Such instructors are trained, normally provide their own music and write their own choreography.

The second training method is 'in house'. The instructors in Les Mills' franchised gyms, for example, are supplied with the choreography that they need to use and furthermore, they are explicitly told where to cue and are given suggestions on what to say, rather like the Met. Office Guidelines.[6] This method of training involves the memorization of a text and instructors utilizing it must rely on their ability to recall the written text. Those trained this way use *verbatim recall*. Freelance instructors, by contrast, learn their trade by the acquisition of an oral tradition.

Music plays an integral role in instructing but the choice of music is strictly governed since each move is cued by the tempo of the music. The moves are further cued by a set of discourse structure rules. This discourse structure allows for variation as to how to introduce a new move. However, the choice is relatively strict. For instance, an instructor might say *two up two down* while another instructor might say *two stage upright row now*. See Delin (2001) for a parallel situation relating to step aerobics. Delin also found both freelance and proprietary modes of instructing.

7.3.1.2 Structure of a pump class

The pump class is simply structured. It is divided into exercise sequences which exercise particular muscle groups. The instructors then have the option of the range of exercise movements they will direct towards each muscle group. The pattern is laid out below. Each element in the sequence becomes a discourse structure node:

welcome	
warm up	[all muscle groups that will be used]
squats	[lower body, large muscle group]
chest	[upper body, large muscle group]
dead lifts	[lower and upper body, large muscle group]
biceps	[upper body, small muscle group]
triceps	[upper body, small muscle group]
lunges	[lower body, medium muscle group]

The data reported here comes from tape recordings of four instructors. From each class, the warm up track, the squat track and the dead lift and clean and press track have been transcribed. Each track is an average of five minutes with slight variation in time duration occurring amongst the instructors. The recordings yield between 150 and 220 utterances per track, where an utterance is indicated by pauses. Where incomplete sentences are separated by pauses we have placed them in the same data cell for the purposes of the analysis. Two tracks from each instructor were chosen for detailed analysis: the warm up track and the squat track.[7]

7.3.1.3 Pump discourse structure

The warming up phase will serve as an illustration of how pump classes proceed. Because only about five minutes is available for the warm up, the instructor can only spend around 40–50 seconds on each muscle group. The categories of the warm up are bounded and ordered in a strict sequence although the upright row is optional. The reason for the order is a practical one. Each move gradually builds into another. For instance, the feet in the clean and press remain in the same position for the squat track. The final clean is pushed up and, instead of the bar being brought back down the front again, it is taken behind the head. The instructee then rests the bar on their shoulders and is now in position for the squat track. The instructor's discourse is thus externally driven.

The beginning and end of each muscle group is clearly indicated with the instructor cueing the class that a change in movement is about to take place, for instance: *Feet shoulder width apart, team. We're getting ready for our two stage dead lift.* The instruction *Feet shoulder width apart, team* cues the class that a new move will be introduced and the *two stage dead lift* informs them what the new move is and how many counts are involved. The categories and their sequence are laid out in the first rule of the discourse grammar.

R1. Warm up → shoulder rolls + (upright row) + dead lifts and clean & press + squat + shoulder press +biceps

In each of the immediate constituents of the routine there are again discourse structure rules sequencing what happens. Here are the 'lower' rules for the warm up:

R2. Shoulder rolls → forward × 4 + back × 4
R3. Upright row → singles + two stage + three up, one down
R4. Dead lifts and Clean & press → singles + two stage + three down, one up + clean only + clean single + single clean and press + clean and press × 3
R5. Squat → single + two stage + pulse for three counts + pulse for four counts
R6. Shoulder press → single + two stage
R7. Biceps → singles + two stage

Formulae implement each discourse constituent. Here are some examples taken from the speech of one of the instructors.[8] Each formula occupies one line.

Squat track
Single squat *all right*
              single squat
              here we go
              single squat for [x]
Two stage   *two down two up*
              this time
              two stage
              here we go

	two stage
	half
	and again
Four counts	*down slowly for four*
	move for all four counts
	all right team
	take it down slowly for four
Pulse	*pulse (it) for [x]*
Hold	*hold it there*
	hold it four
	three up slowly
Lower range	*give me the lower range*

<u>Dead lifts</u>
Single	*all right*
	single
	here we go
	single dead lift
	give me [x]
Two stage	*gimme a two stage dead lift*
	two stage this time
	two stage (dead lift)
Dead row	*(all right, give me a)*
	dead row this time
	single dead row
Dead row	*three repeats down*
	dead row
	three repeat
	three row repeat

<u>Clean and press</u>
Clean single	*single clean and press (here)*
	[x] single clean and press
Clean and press	*(now give me a) clean and three*
	take it up
	clean and three
Clean and press	*gimme eight*

7.3.1.4 Form and function in pump aerobics phraseology

Having shown that pump aerobic instructor talk is a formulaic genre in terms of its text type, we can now look at it as an exercise in control, i.e. at its contextual properties. To do that, we will present data on the frequency of both the form of the directives and the function of the utterances of the four instructors. It is important to separate form and function for the reasons suggested in chapter 1. Also, and as is well known, imperative form does not always correlate with directive function. For example, advertising copy frequently contains sentences in imperative mood but the advertiser is not perceived as issuing a directive with any binding illocutionary force. For instance, *See our advertisement in this morning's newspaper* is in the imperative mood but is not usually perceived as a directive.

Figure 7.1 shows the distribution of linguistic forms across the four instructors. The form of the instructors' utterances was classified in four dimensions. Bare verb phrase imperatives are the classic form for directives, e.g. *Eat your porridge!* Such a form consists of an uninflected verb followed by a complement if the verb is strictly subcategorized to take complements, as *eat* is. Truncated imperatives exclude the verb where it can be inferred from the foregoing linguistic or current non-linguistic context, e.g. *Eat your porridge. Now your toast.* Expanded VP imperatives contain more than the bare essentials. For example they might contain a vocative, *Eat your porridge, Jim* or a politeness tag, *Eat your porridge, please.*

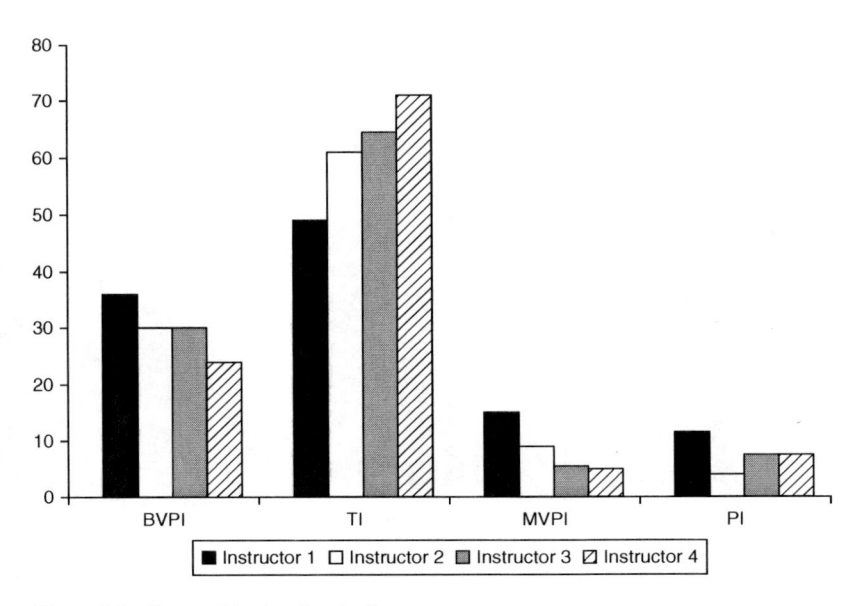

Figure 7.1 Form of instructors' utterances

Imperatives were also classified according to whether they showed any indication of politeness. These were almost invariably modified VP imperatives with a tag of some kind such as the vocative *team* which is a marker of solidarity and thus a positive politeness marker.

Figure 7.2 shows the major functional classification of each utterance. Utterances were classified as either cueing directives, providing directives as to form, utterances which gave a count as to where in a sequence of exercises the exercisees were, interjections, or utterances having a politeness function such as *Great* which, in showing approval of the instructees' efforts, addresses their positive face.

The breakdown of form and function by instructor shows that instructors, like checkout operators, are by no means all the same in the way they instruct. Each has a different persona. This is notable in their use of politeness strategies. In looking at the function of their utterances, instructor 1 is three times more polite than instructor 3. In terms of the function of tags added to imperatives, instructor 1 is also significantly more polite than the other three, three times more polite, for example, than instructor 2. If we look at how these four instructors are perceived, instructor 1 comes across as a team player. Through the use of *we, we're*

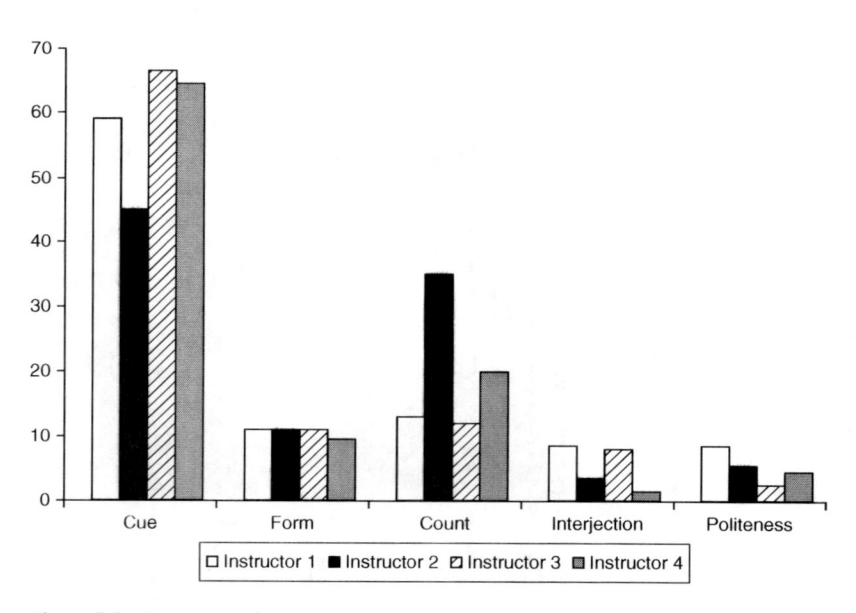

Figure 7.2 Function of instructors' utterances

and *team* in the formulae the instructor aligns with the class. Instructions to the class are often softened with the formulae *all right*, the opening *give me* and the close and opening *ok*, again claiming common ground with the instructees and providing the semblance of tacit agreement. Instructor 3 with the overall lowest proportion of polite utterances, by contrast, normally starts with a few comments on people's form and once everyone is warmed up, begins to challenge them directly. This often takes the form of direct face threat. The class is asked *Can you feel this?* No reply is possible and even if it were, then a reply of *Yes* would involve a loss of face because the reply would show the instructee to be weaker than the other participants. Many instructees find this style aggressive and rude, according to the comments placed in the drop box at the gym. For instance, one class was asked if they were a bunch of chickens. This method of insulting a person's ability in order to make them try harder (to prove that they are not a failure) can be interpreted as face-threatening. The 'hard' approach to motivating people can involve the use of other formulae such as *I want you to get lower* which is a direct challenge as opposed to the softer *Ok team, take it down to the lower range*. However, it seems that while instructor 2's classes are the most physically challenging, many people do not enjoy them because of the instructing style. Again this observation is based on comments in the drop box.

7.3.1.5 Conclusion

The necessity to cue, motivate and ensure participants' safety, puts pressure on the pump instructors to develop a kind of speech which produces maximum physical results for minimum linguistic effort. The range of choice for doing this is limited because there are only a small and select number of ways an instructor can tell the class to perform, for example, a two stage squat. Another important factor is that the class must respond to the cue within a short space of time, normally about two seconds. Therefore the class does not have time to process and respond to a creative, or a longwinded, cue. The short, repetitive nature of cueing and ensuring participant safety is therefore facilitated by two factors: (a) the instructor does not have time to create novel sentences and therefore instructors rely on formulae and (b) the participants do not have time to process novel sentences and they too must rely on memorized formulae. A beginner to pump is always noticeable because they are normally a beat behind the instructor. At this stage, every cue that the instructor makes is novel to them and, in general, the beginner does not have the same ability to process and respond to the cue as quickly as a regular attender of pump classes does. In this sense, the regular attenders to pump classes are also heirs to the formulaic tradition of pump instructors.

The findings regarding the diverse styles of motivation suggest that although there is a variety of ways participants can be motivated, the instructor who attends to the face needs of participants will be perceived as being more approachable and therefore will be more popular than someone who attacks the participants' face (*What are you? A bunch of chickens?*).

7.4 Dance calling

The third case study of directives involves a further change of focus. This time the participants are members of a dance club. They meet weekly and, for them, dancing is primarily a social activity. Members are mainly older. While dancing may keep them fitter and healthier, the aim is not to build the body beautiful. The club has two kinds of dances: square dances and round dances. Square dancing has European folk dance origins but is now globally associated with the American West. Square dancing is highly ritualized to the point where many dancers wear clothing modelled along Western American lines. The music to which the dancers dance is also often Country and Western.

Squares called *sets* consist of eight dancers: four men and four women in pairs. On each side of the square, positions are conventionally held by the man. Each location has a number. Two locations have a name: *heads* and *sides*, heads on one side of the square have their backs to the caller and on the other side face the caller, sides are at right angles to the caller. Square dancers perform set moves in sequence. Moves have names. Square dancing has a caller since callers either make up or recall the sequences of the moves of which all dances consist. Hash calls are original, i.e. the sequence is made up ex tempore, while patter calls are predetermined.

Round dancing is ballroom dancing performed by pairs dancing in a large circle with a cuer. Here too the choreography involves sequencing of set moves. These may be in waltz, foxtrot, quickstep, cha cha and rumba timing. Again all moves have names. Unlike square dancing, no partners are changed during the dance.

As in the parade ground and the gym, external indirect control by the caller or cuer is normally exercised in very much the same way. The dance caller or cuer:

- cues the next move, in effect telling the dancers what they are to do next (but unlike the aerobics instructor without modelling of the move);
- instructs the dancers as to form, that is telling them how the are to perform the move;
- comments on various matters, such as someone getting lost
- motivates the dancers through the presence or absence in the call of polite or 'addressee-oriented' features of speech
- provides interpolations, e.g. *hey*

As with the other directive genres, dance calling is formulaic. Square dancing formulae include, for example:

allemand left that corner
all eight, spin the top
girls, star left one turn

Examples of round dancing formulae include:

crab walks, two measures
cucarachas twice
sliding door over and back

Formulae in dance calling are tightly structured. All square dancing formulae follow the following pattern:

R1. (intro) + (vocative) + move + (resulting position) + (vocative) + (coda)

with the restriction that there may be only a single vocative per formula. (see the examples in table 7.1).

Round dance formula structure is a little simpler. Such formulae conform to the following schema:

R2. (vocative) + move + (resulting position) + (vocative)

again with the restriction of only one vocative per formula (see the examples in table 7.2).

As with the other two directive genres examined earlier, dance calling and cueing formulae are typically in the imperative mood, including the types given for aerobics instructors: bare VP imperatives, e.g. *spin turn. follow your neighbour,* truncated VP imperatives which elide the V when

Table 7.1 Examples of square dance calling formulae

Intro	Vocative	Move	Resulting position	Vocative	Coda
		bus down	to make me a line		
	ladies	chain the cross			
		swing through		fellas	
	boys	explode	and give me lines		
well now	the side pair	up to the middle and back			
	men	back in the left hand star			you know
		extend the tag			

Table 7.2 Examples of round dance cueing formulae

Vocative	Move	Resulting position	Vocative
	part and point		
	spin turn		
	chassee	to banjo	
	two left turns	to face the wall	
lady	roll across		
ladies	travel the door		
	show them		guys

it is clear what that is, e.g. *and a half*. Modification exists in the following forms: vocatives in some cases, e.g. *boys, trade*, other constituents such as adverbials of time, manner etc, and addressee-oriented features, e.g. *well, you go to meet a little lady, bend me a line*.

As with the aerobics instructors, the calls of four callers were transcribed: two square dance callers and two round dance callers. Two hundred directives of each were transcribed and coded for the features of function and structure. The functions were: cue, politeness, form, comment, interpolation. The coding according to form was: bare VP imperative, truncated VP imperative, augmented, or modified VP imperative, utterances with a politeness modification e.g. *let's* or *team*, other.

The differences in formula structure and formula selection between aerobics instructors, square dance callers and round dance callers are, in part, the result of differences in the requirements of the dance and the gym. To cue a lift in pump aerobics, vocatives are always non-essential since everyone is performing the same lifts. For some moves, when the move is called in square dancing, those making the move need to be addressed because not all the members of the square make the move. This explains the need for vocatives, a need which we also saw as necessary on the parade ground. For round dancing, since the moves normally include the dancing pair alone and all dancing pairs, vocatives and resulting configuration are seldom necessary. Looking at figure 7.3, we can see that square dance callers use a very similar proportion of bare VP imperatives but they differ in the number of modified VP imperatives and truncated imperatives they use. Square dance callers need to provide more than just cueing information whereas round dance cuers do not. The latter can and do therefore use more truncated imperatives and fewer augmented imperatives. This set of observations, in part, supports the motivated view of genres proposed by some of the theorists cited in chapter 1, namely that if you know the crucial elements of the external form of the genre then you can predict the inner, text type features of the genre.

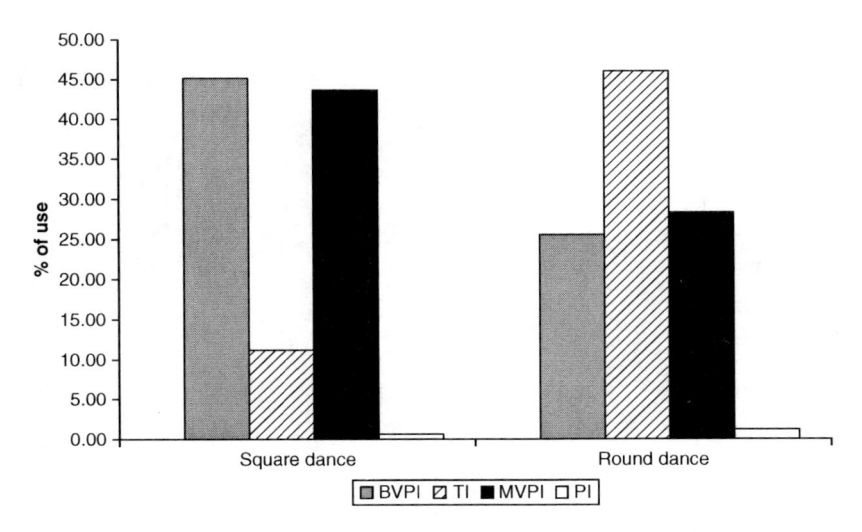

Figure 7.3 Forms in square vs round dance calling

However, if we come to the function of the utterances of dance callers and cuers, then the situation is rather different, as we can see in figure 7.4. Both square and round dance callers' and cuers' utterances are largely devoted to cueing. But the traditions of square dance callers are such that they are expected to provide interpolations such as singing along with the music, some of the time, producing what is termed 'patter'. Round dance calling traditions do not include patter. These differences do not arise from the exigencies of calling but from the way each genre has evolved.

Aggregating the calls of dance callers, although it provides clear differences in both form and function of the two kinds of calls, obscures the fact that, as with pump aerobics instructors and checkout operators, individual differences are also significant. Figures 7.5 and 7.6 show that there is considerable variation in the preferences each caller has for both the form and function of their utterances within the range set by the traditions of each type of call.

Looking again at all four callers, it will be clear that politeness features within formulae and specific utterance are rare. Only one of the callers uses any forms which are explicitly or implicitly polite. But all the callers

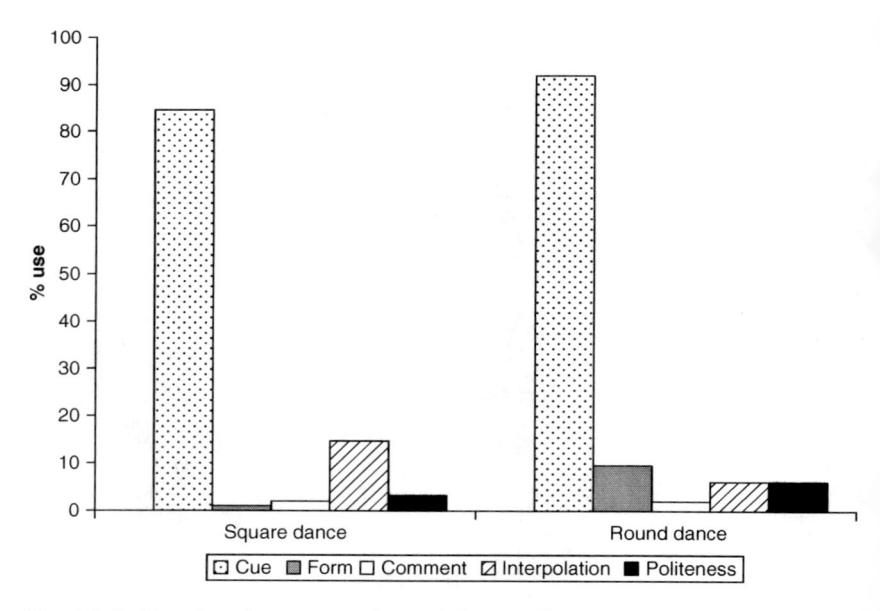

Figure 7.4 Functions in square and round dance calling

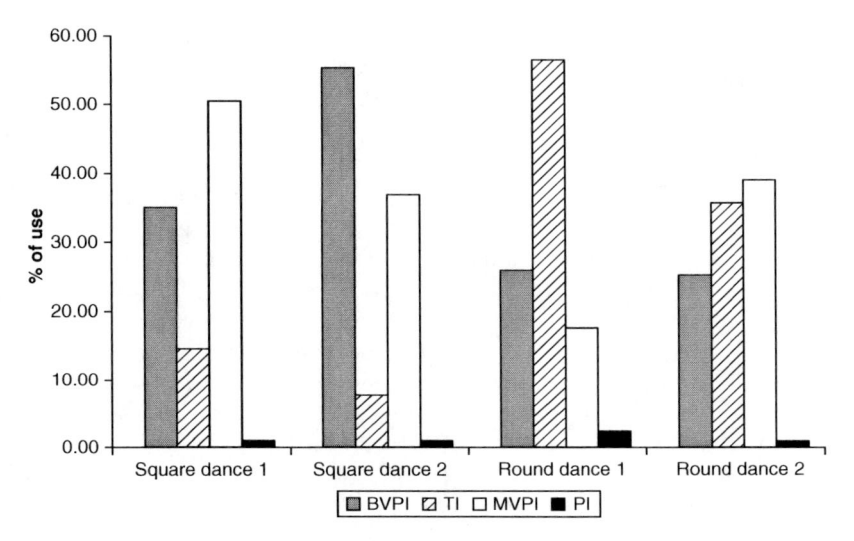

Figure 7.5 Forms of dance callers' utterances

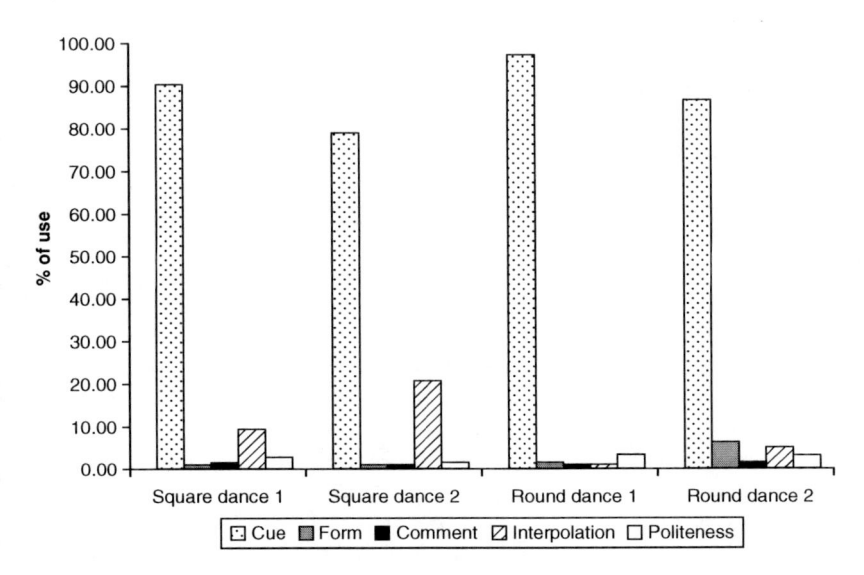

Figure 7.6 Functions of dance callers' utterances

and cuers have an occasional utterance which might be interpreted as polite.

7.5 Directives, gender and politeness

The literature on politeness frequently makes a case that women use forms which have a politeness function more often than men would use them, particularly in mixed company (Holmes, 1994). It might therefore be predicted that of those who issue directives, those showing the higher frequencies of politeness forms and functions are more likely to be women, while those showing lower such frequencies are more likely to be men. The sergeant major who began this chapter was a male. There was certainly no politeness evident in his directives (although he does praise his NCOs at the end of the transcript). As we saw, there was evidence of on-record face attack. We saw that the four aerobics instructors varied in the extent to which they were both positively and negatively polite. All four of these instructors were women and as such, showed a range of frequencies of politeness forms that might otherwise be regarded as gendered. The square dance callers were both men while the round dance cuers were both women. Given the small proportion of utterances which might be interpreted as polite, it is probably not appropriate to infer any effect of gender on the absence of politeness features in these calls.

All this is not to say that the gender effects on the frequency of politeness features in discourse noted in the literature do not occur in other contexts. They clearly do, as Vine's (2001) study of directives in the workplace shows. So why do they not occur in the speech of those who control the bodies of others? To answer speculatively we should again look at the local traditions in each case. There is no reason to suppose that sergeant majors would not get perfectly acceptable performance from troops if they were more polite. However it is traditional that sergeant majors are nasty, noisy and feared. One presumes that woman sergeant majors share these characteristics. Aerobics instructors may appeal to different groups of clients who wish to exercise. Since the formulaic repertoire provided by the aerobics instruction tradition makes available a range of styles, instructors can select a 'softer' or 'harder' persona from amongst those styles. In the case of dance callers, the traditions of dance calling appear not to provide for politeness to play a significant role. Goffman would not be surprised by this finding.

It might be objected that there is not time for politeness to play a role. This is not true. There is time while a move is being performed for those issuing directives to be polite, not expansively so but, as the use of a term like *team* in the utterances of aerobics instructors shows, a split second is enough. I am here making a case for the micro against the macro. Generalization in the human sciences is tempting, but it may be misapplied (Flyvbjerg, 2001).

The above phraseology of body control also suggests that there may be other phraseologies of body control which can be analysed for what they have to tell us ethnographically about cultural dispositions with respect to body control. For example, schoolroom directives issued by teachers have changed radically in the last thirty years. Aerobic exercise, with its mixture of the social and individual and its narcissistic element in creating the body beautiful, has a long history in Western thought and action (Dutton, 1995). Military history is no doubt replete with officer sadists; how this disposition is linguistically expressed may, however, differ from one military culture to the other. Here, as always, phraseological investigation borders on and contributes to cultural analysis (Shilling, 1993).

8
Regional Genrelects in Engagement Notices

> *Marriages to be contracted must be published in the churches by the priests so that, if legitimate impediments exist, they may be made known.*
>
> Fourth Lateran Council, 1215

8.1 Introduction

Chapter 1 suggested that engagement notices have been placed in newspapers for many decades. They are, in the terms of van Gennep (1960), a marker of entry into the liminal stage preceding marriage, although one must currently allow for post-modern convention as the following notice shows:

> *Brown - Smith: Susie and Jim are pleased to announce that after eight years we finally did it! As this took so long, don't expect a wedding!*

The notice functions as a public announcement of the engagement. There may be a number of reasons why such essentially personal matters should be placed in public notices when it is not legally required that this be done. In the case of *The Times* it might be that the public notification of bloodline continuities and discontinuities is a motivation.[1]

Being a written text type with a long history, engagement notices constitute a genre in terms of the external exigencies which give rise to them, and a text type in terms of the internal textual regularities which are manifest in them. This determination is further supported as follows. First, '[i]n the case of newspaper genres ... we find an unmistakable "generic identity"' (Bhatia, 2001:67). Since engagement notices are clearly identifiable in a newspaper, we may assume that they constitute a well-defined genre. Second, engagement notices constitute part of a folk taxonomy of genres relating to rites of passage, and folk taxonomies are generally a reliable way of seeing the external factors of a genre, since '[g]enres are text categories readily distinguished by mature speakers of a language' (Biber, 1989:5) and 'for those who share genre knowledge within a culture, there is generally a shared name' (Johns, 1997:22). The folk taxonomy further includes births, marriages and deaths notices.

Many genres occur in more than one region but their variant forms may, as a result of the way they are transmitted, be specific to a region. For example, tobacco auction speech shares linguistic features with other auctioning varieties but has unique features as well. These unique features are located in the tobacco country of the south-eastern United States (Kuiper & Tillis, 1985).

The humble engagement notice will, in this chapter, yield data which, like the formulae of race calling, can be interpreted to reveal cultural differences. The two cultures involved are those of Australia and New Zealand in which people speak differing geographic dialects of English (Bell & Kuiper, 2000; Blair & Collins, 2001). This investigation thus explores geographic genrelects. Since engagement notices are a written genre, the selection of parameters of variation are restricted to discourse-structural, lexical and syntactic variables. They have been extracted after preliminary analysis in the manner of Labov (1972:44).

In the case of the corpora of engagement notices of this chapter, pre-selected parameters of variation seem appropriate and prove to be satisfactory.

8.2 Methodological remarks

In chapter 1 we looked at the rather rigid form of the genre as contained in *The Times*. In this chapter *The Times* will be used as a benchmark for an account of some of the parameters along which similar notices vary in New Zealand and Australian newspapers. No other inferences about British engagement notices are to be drawn from the *Times* data. For example, it is certain that there are other ways of placing engagement notices in the British press.

8.2.1 Data

Four hundred engagement notices, one hundred from each of three sources, and fifty from two further sources, are the data for this study.[2] The hundred benchmark notices are taken from *The Times* over a period of some weeks in 2002. One hundred New Zealand notices were drawn from the New Zealand Independent Newspapers Limited paper, *The Press* in 2001. A further hundred were drawn from the *New Zealand Herald* and the *Otago Daily Times* also dated in mid 2002. The reason for drawing a double set of data in the case of New Zealand was to investigate stylistic homogeneity and thus exclude the possibility that selection could be a function of editorial house style. The hundred Australian notices were randomly selected from Independent Newspapers Limited papers in Australia, also in mid 2002.

8.2.2 Text type variables

A set of formal variables manifest in the data was selected as follows:

1. Was the formula active or passive? This variable was selected because it is an index of formality.
2. Which of the six formulae conventionally used for engagement notices in the data was selected?
3. Where the formula had variant forms, which variant of the formula was selected? Variants were only coded for formula 3 as that had a significant amount of variation.
4. Where a formula contained an adjective indicating affect, which adjective was selected? In some engagement notices parents are delighted, in others they are merely pleased.
5. In what order are the couple named?
6. How were the parents named?
7. Was the dative formula *to family and friends* used?
8. Was either the man's birth order or the woman's birth order or both mentioned?
9. Was the domicile of the parents mentioned?
10. Was the domicile of their offspring mentioned?
11. Was the location of the engagement mentioned?

These individual parameters can be reduced to the following:

Formula choice: This parameter includes whether the selected formula is in the active or passive voice, whether it is a formula specific to engagement notices or whether it is a more general congratulatory formula. There are two passive formulae and two active formulae specific to engagement notices and two more general formulae manifest in the data. Only the engagement-specific formulae were further analysed.

Formula variation: For most of the formulae, there are variant forms. Those variants which are syntagmatic can be read off the finite state diagrams in figure 8.1. Paradigmatic variation includes who is the subject of the active forms. Sometimes it is announced by the couple, sometimes by them and their parents, sometimes by both sets of parents, sometimes by just one set of parents. The way parents are named is a variable, as are:

a. the adjective choice in one of the active formulae,
b. whether or not the birth order of the engaged couple is mentioned,
c. whether the domicile of the parents or the domicile of the children is mentioned,
d. whether the location of the engagement is mentioned, and its date.

These choices are made in a contingent manner, as can be seen in figure 8.1. The data were coded for the appearance of the variables and then numerically analysed.

8.3 The engagement notice in New Zealand and Australian newspapers

8.3.1 Australian notices

The Australian data shows that Australian engagement notices are considerably more flexible than is *The Times* in terms of what they allow along the parameters of variation outlined earlier. The Australian notices contain few invariant features. Both active (88%) and passive formulae (3%) are used. Only formula 2 (which is rare in the UK data)[3] is not used. For each of the other formulae, various variants are used. Table 8.1 gives the frequency with which particular formulae are used. Note that three notices do not involve the use of engagement formulae but are what might be termed 'creations', e.g. *Smith – Brown: Auds, Den, Mal and Rox are very happy with the engagement of "our" Jimbo to Angie, and welcome with love Angie and Kyllie to our family.*[4]

Unlike the *Times* notices, formula 1 does have variants. One of the three cases has the opening *It is with great pleasure that....* The preposition *of* is used in one case rather than *between*, as in *the engagement is announced of....* In 87% of the notices the woman is mentioned first. This is close to an inversion of *Times* style. Many of the formula 3

Passive formulae:

Formula 1

(It is with great pleasure) the engagement is/was announced (with pleasure) between/of NP

Formula 2

The forthcoming marriage is announced and will take place on NP_1 at NP_2 between NP_3.

Active formulae:

Formula 3

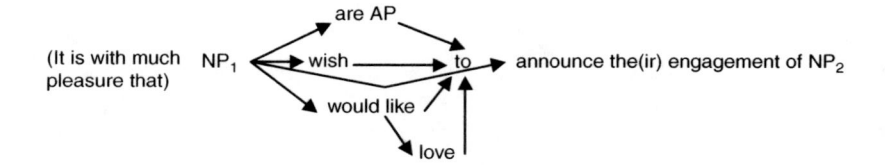

(It is with much pleasure that) NP_1 wish / would like / love / are AP to announce the(ir) engagement of NP_2

Dependencies:

1. *It is with much pleasure* does not co-occur with *are AP*.
2. *Their* only if NP_1 is the engaged couple; otherwise *the*.

Formula 4

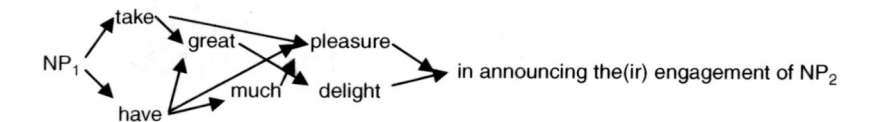

NP_1 take / have great / much / pleasure / delight in announcing the(ir) engagement of NP_2

Formula 5

Congratulations to NP_1 on your/their engagement

Formula 6

NP_1 wish NP_2 ... on your/their engagement

Figure 8.1 Passive and active formulae in engagement notices

Table 8.1 Frequency choice of formula in the Australian engagement notices

none	1	2	3	4	5	6
3%	3%	0%	67%	21%	4%	2%

Table 8.2 Variant forms of formula 3 in the Australian engagement notices

no 'auxiliary' modifiers	are ADJP	wish	would like	would love	It is with great pleasure that
N = 10, 15%	N = 47, 69%	N = 7, 10%	N = 3, 4%	N = 0, 0%	N = 1, 1%

Table 8.3 Adjective phrase selection in the Australian engagement notices

pleased	delighted	happy	thrilled	proud	very happy	pleased and proud
N = 17, 36%	N = 14, 30%	N = 6, 13%	N = 3, 6%	N = 3, 6%	N = 2, 4%	N = 1, 2%

Table 8.4 Distribution of formula 4 variants in the Australian engagement notices

take pleasure	take great pleasure	take great delight	have pleasure	have much pleasure	have great pleasure
N = 3	N = 1	N = 1	N = 7	N = 8	N = 1

variants are used. Table 8.2 shows the frequency distribution of these. Where an adjective phrase is required in the first variant of formula 3, the choice of adjectives is shown in table 8.3. Note that this set of possibilities only occurs if the variant requiring an adjective phrase is selected from the available set of variants in the first place. Such an obligatory contingency is typical of syntactic variation in formulae.

In cases where there is no auxiliary modifier and the formula reads *NP announce(s)...*, adverbials are frequently inserted. There are ten such cases and *happily* is used in five cases while *with (great) pleasure* is used in two. Formula 4 also has variant forms distributed as in table 8.4.

144 Formulaic Genres

Table 8.5 Who announces the engagement in the Australian engagement notice?

Couple	Couple and parents	Both sets of parents	One set of parent(s)
N = 18, 19%	N = 1, 1%	N = 33, 35%	N = 41, 44%

Table 8.6 Forms of address in the Australian engagement notices

Title initials surname	Title given and surnames	Given and surnames	Given names only	Title and name
N = 1, 1%	N = 3, 4%	N = 34, 41%	N = 44, 54%	N = 0

Since the great majority of notices in the Australian data are in active form, it is possible to note who is announcing the engagement. The possibilities are: the engaged couple, the engaged couple and their parents, the two sets of parents only or one set of parents.[5] Note again, this syntactic possibility for paradigmatic variation is obligatorily contingent, i.e. it only arises if one of the active formulae is selected. The frequencies with which these variants are chosen are given in table 8.5. Modes of address for parents have a frequency distribution different from *Times* style. The modal preference for *Times* style is: titles of husband and wife, given name of husband and surname of husband. Australian style preferences can be seen in table 8.6.

8.3.2 Stylistic homogeneity in New Zealand engagement notices

While it is clear that *Times* style is a house style, the Australian data show that all engagement notices are subject to similarly rigid style requirements. The Australian data was based on a chronologically continuous sample of one hundred notices taken from a number of INL newspapers. However, we might still be dealing with house style in the case of the New Zealand notices rather than a geographic genrelect, since initially all 100 NZ notices were taken from *The Press* of Christchurch. In order to make a case for engagement notices having geographic dialect distribution, we first analysed the 100 *Press* notices from the INL newspaper stable. We then compared the distribution of its variants with those in a mixed corpus of a further 100 notices, with 50 drawn from *The New Zealand Herald* (Wilson and Horton) and 50 from the *Otago Daily Times* (Allied Press Limited), the assumption being that, if the distributions in the two corpora were significantly similar, then this would be a function not of house style but of the stylistic preferences of New Zealand communities of practice in the placing of engagement notices. Furthermore, if the distribution of variants in Australian notices randomly selected was significantly different from the commonalities of the New Zealand distribution, then that could be attributed to geo-cultural factors.

To establish stylistic homogeneity a set of correlations was made between the *Press* data and the *Herald/ODT* data using those variables in which there occurred a parameter with a significant number of variables, specifically the selection of formulae, the selection of adjectives in formula 3 and the naming of parents in formulae 3 and 4. We also selected a further set of variables which returned only binary values, for their rank order again comparing the *Press* and *Herald/ODT* corpora. We supposed that if the correlations were high and positive then we were measuring variable choices which were reliably correlated as between the two data sets. Results were as in tables 8.7–8.10. Not all variables

Table 8.7 Formula selection in New Zealand engagement notices

Formula	Press	Herald/ODT
Non-formulaic	0	7
The engagement is announced...	9	5
The forthcoming marriage is announced...	0	0
Someone is adj to announce...	81	76
Someone takes great adj in announcing	10	12
Correlation coefficient of formula choice	1	

Table 8.8 Adjective choice in New Zealand engagement notices

	Press	Herald/ODT
proud	1	1
pleased	22	31
excited	1	1
delighted	40	57
thrilled	16	23
happy	12	17
very happy	4	6
rapt	1	1
pleased and proud	1	1
Correlation coefficient	1	

146 Formulaic Genres

Table 8.9 Parental naming in New Zealand engagement notices

Naming practice	Press	Herald/ODT
Parents not mentioned	20	24
title plus initials plus surname	2	2
title plus given and surname names	2	1
given and surnames	42	41
given name only	34	30
other, e.g. *Count Benckendorff*	0	1
Correlation coefficient	0.99	

Table 8.10 'To family and friends' and other binary variables in New Zealand engagement notices

	Press	Herald/ODT
'to family & friends'	43	31
man's birth order	10	5
woman's birth order	18	23
parents' abode	55	42
children's abode	2	13
place of engagement	16	13
addendum	21	31
Correlation coefficient	0.87	

Table 8.11 Subject of active formulae in New Zealand engagement notices

	Press	Herald/ODT
passives	9	12
engaged couple	30	22
couple and parents	33	16
all parents	9	17
one set of parents	19	33
Correlation coefficient	0.21	

were as definitive. The subject of the active formulae parameter correlated positively but with a relatively low correlation coefficient: see table 8.11. On the basis of these correlations, we may suppose that the New Zealand data is relatively homogeneous. But there also exists a basis for leaving the subject of the active formulae parameter out of further consideration, given that it appears to be a much less regular feature of New

Zealand engagement notices. On the basis of the demonstrated homogeneity, the *Press* data set was used for comparison with the Australian data set.

8.3.3 Australia and New Zealand style choices

So what were the major differences both between the Australian and New Zealand notices and between them and *Times* style? The selection of a formula for an engagement notice begins with the selection of a specific engagement formula or a general congratulatory one, then, for the genre-specific cases, either an active or passive form, and then within each of these there is a choice of two different formulae. The way these choices have been made can be read off figure 8.1 which shows formula choice. It can be seen that New Zealanders use passive formulae about twice as often as Australians and that Australians use non-genre-specific formulae and completely novel creations – whereas New Zealanders do not. This suggests a greater trend towards informality as one moves from *Times* style, to New Zealand style, to Australian style. This finding is

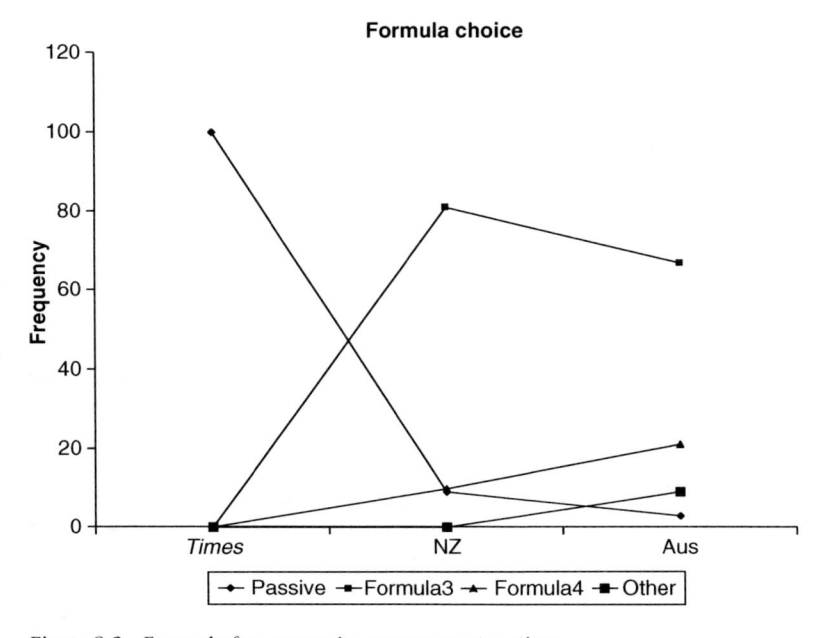

Figure 8.2 Formula frequency in engagement notices

Domicile of parents

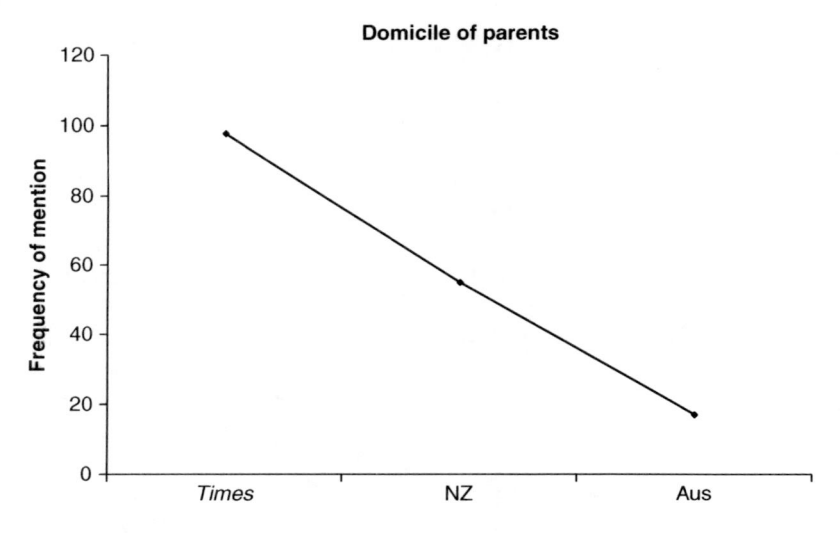

Figure 8.3 Frequency of mention of parents' domicile

supported by the inclusion of the domicile of the parents where again New Zealand style is between *Times* style and Australian style, as figure 8.3 shows, and the order of mention of the engaged couple, as figure 8.4 shows.

Formula 3 is the most common selection for both Australians and New Zealanders. In both Australian and New Zealand style, a bare form of formula 3 such as *Jo and John Smith announce the engagement of...* is available. This form is selected in about twice as many Australian as NZ cases. In most such cases there is a form of adverbial modification such as the word *happily* included.

The most frequently selected variant of formula 3 is... *are ADJP to announce...* form. This again leads to further possible paradigmatic variation in the choice of adjective phrase. If adjectives are grouped as showing a higher degree of positive affective involvement (*thrilled, delighted*) as opposed to a moderate degree of positive affective involvement (*pleased, happy*) then this selection is shown in figure 8.5.[6] New Zealanders appear to be more affectively effusive in their selection of adjectives, preferring *delighted* and *thrilled* about twice as often as Australians (56%:36%). The conclusion to be drawn from these two sets of selectional data are thus that Australians have a modal preference for greater informality and more affective restraint than New Zealanders.

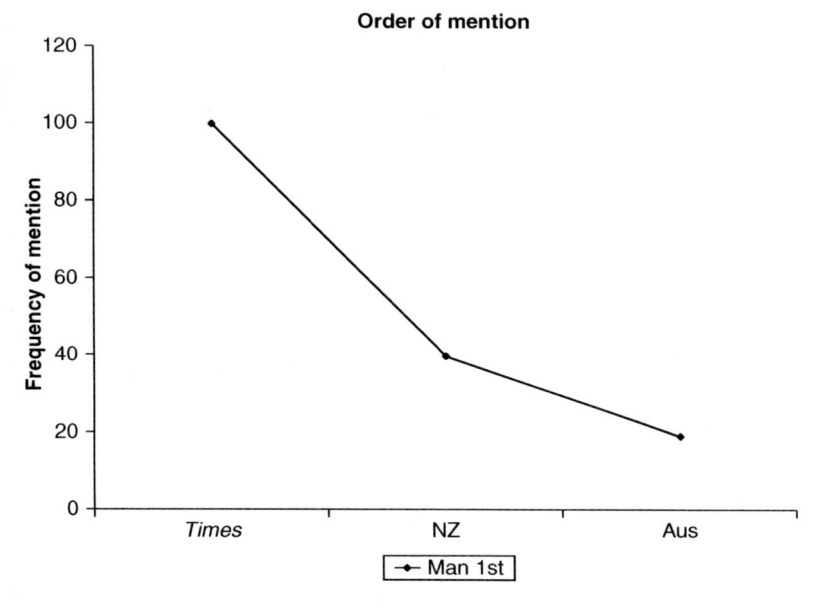

Figure 8.4 Order of mention of couple

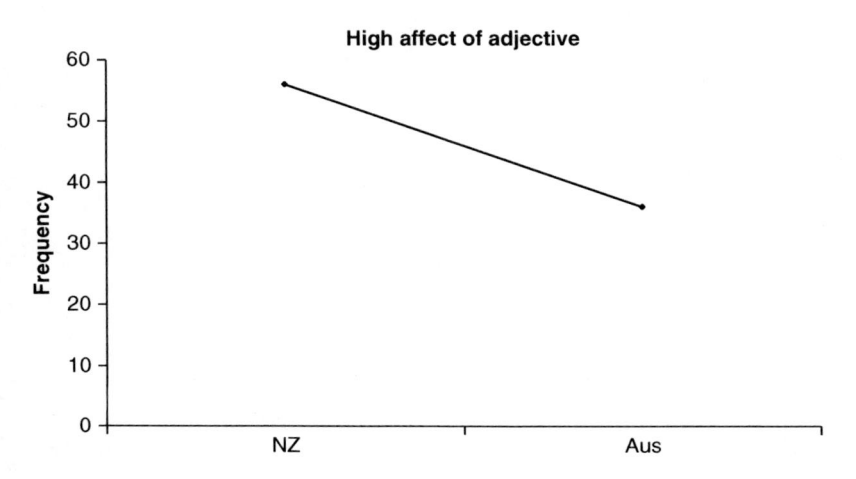

Figure 8.5 Affect of adjective in engagement notices

Parental naming

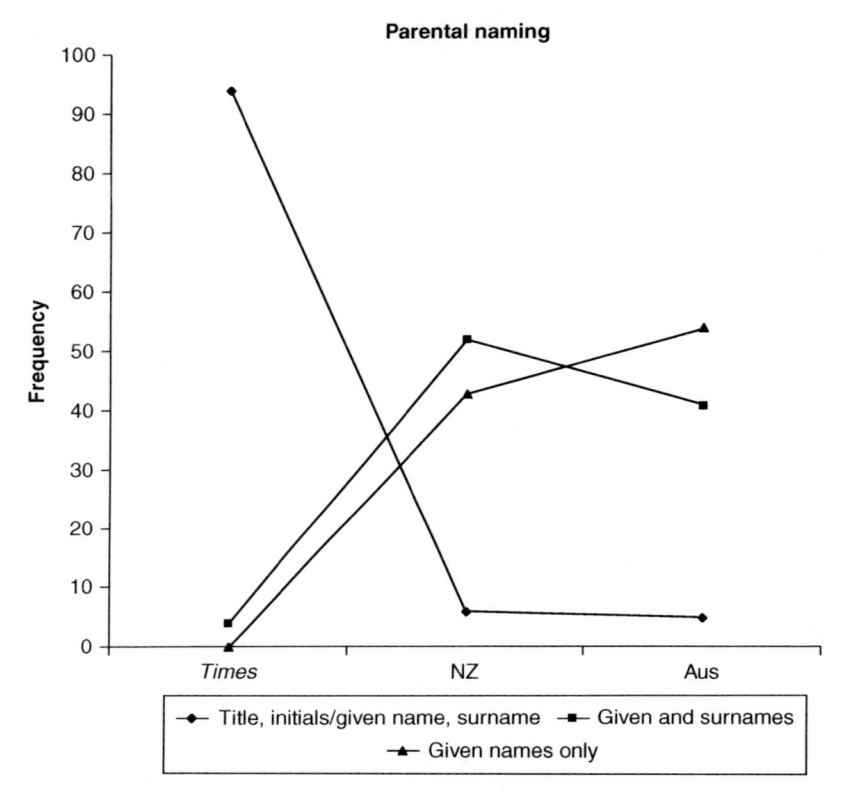

Figure 8.6 Frequency of parental naming

The naming variation described in figure 8.6 shows that Australians have a stronger preference for given names only, again supporting their higher preference for informality. The affective dimension also appears to play a role in whether or not the addition of *to family and friends* is used. In specifying those for whom the notice is intended as 'family and friends', a closer in-group is specified than would be the case if the dative were left out. Figure 8.7 shows the selectional preferences, confirming that New Zealanders are more affectively on record (42:6) in the formal part of the engagement notices than Australians.

However both Australians and New Zealanders, as we saw earlier, may place an addendum after the engagement formula. These addenda often

'to family and friends'

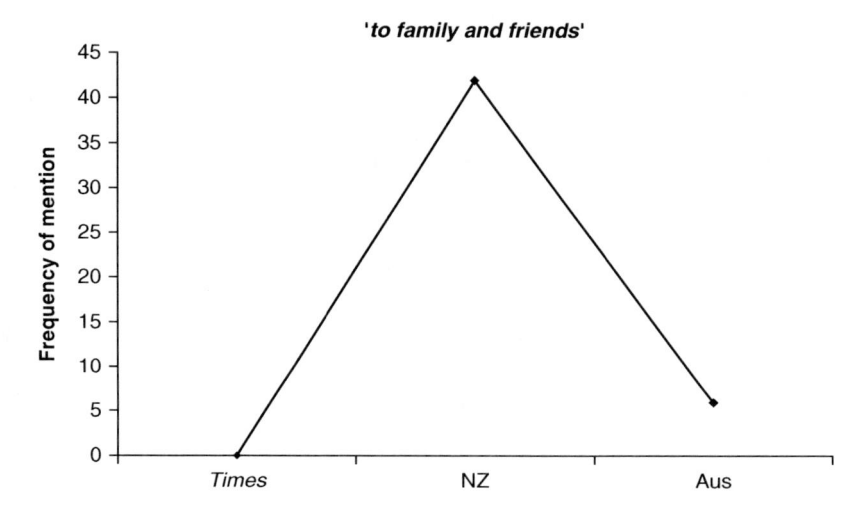

Figure 8.7 'To family and friends'

indicate the affective stance of the people involved. The following are Australian examples:

> *Our wish for them is happiness always and a lifetime of love for each other. Our love to N.J. and Mark, love always, Mum and Dad.*
>
> *Big hugs & kisses from the families. Wishing you good health, happiness, love, peace & prosperity throughout your life together.*

Some of these addenda are very informal, as in:

> *Congratulations. About time!*
> *For once Jill was speechless.*
> *Aya and Sydney think it's a purrfect arrangement.*

(Aya and Sydney appear to be the engaged couple's cats.) This relative informality in addenda is a feature of both the Australian and New Zealand notices. Australians use such addenda twice as often as New Zealanders (42:21), which supports Australian preference for relatively higher levels of informality.

It is manifest from this data that formulaic genres can yield useful data of linguistic variation and that this data can cluster around sociocultural parameters such as formality and affective stance. Generalizing from the data, it seems that *Times* style sets store by control, both formal and affective; New Zealand style is less formal but affectively less restrained, while Australian style is less formal than New Zealand style but affectively more restrained within the engagement formula itself, Australians preferring to place any more heartfelt sentiments in the addendum. This again supports the view that Australian preference is for less formal options.

8.4 Discussion

The text type of engagement notices has a limited set of textual features by which it can be identified. Some of these features are parameters along which the text type may vary. In most cases, the variation is limited. Such formal features are a perceptual template against which actual texts are judged to be members of the text type. These features may be quite abstract. They may, for instance, involve the range within which a textual parameter may vary. In the case of engagement notices there are features which form the set that enables native speakers of the text type to know that a given text is a culturally appropriate engagement notice.

The analysis of variation in text types is not new. Chapter 1 outlined how most theories of genre associate a text type with external sociocultural parameters of situational constraint (Atkinson & Biber, 1994). One of these parameters is geographic dialect. Engagement notices show that such a parameter can be linguistically manifested even in a very restricted text type.

The interpretation of these variables also supports the hypothesis that without examining the text type in detail it may not be possible to understand its parameters of situational constraint (genre properties), supporting the view of Askehave & Swales (2001:204) outlined in chapter 1. We have suggested that Australian placers of engagement notices favour informality more than New Zealander placers do, supporting the contention quoted in chapter 1 that '[t]o avoid reifying "the context" it is necessary to study the textual details that illuminate the manner in which participants are collectively constructing the world around them' (Bauman and Briggs, 1990:69).

Engagement notices are also conventional in many ways, supporting the view of Guenther & Knoblauch (1995). Most of the parameters of formal variation for engagement notices are not necessary ones for the purpose of announcing an engagement. One can think of many ways of announcing engagements that would use none of them. Three of the Australian notices do just that, making up a novel notice instead.

However, once established in a speech community, conventional formal parameters come to be understood as the way to write such an announcement and they come to be understood as having a predictive force on the text type and a perceptual function in guiding how the genre is to be understood socially.

This leads to a further generalization, namely that the relationship between genre features (its dimensions of situational constraint) and a text type are, as again suggested in earlier chapters, not always deterministic, providing counter-evidence for a strongly functionalist approach to the relationship between a genre and an associated text type. One cannot predict in advance precisely what the textual properties of engagement notices might be. However, once the text type exists, one can be much more certain that those who wish to place an engagement notice, in *The Times* for example, will construct a text with particular textual properties.

This raises the nature of the relationship between genre and text type. Biber, as noted in chapter 1, denies that there is a necessary association. The analysis of engagement notices shows that the relationship, while not deterministic in a narrow sense, does show a close association. The variable which may provide a resolution to this apparent contradiction is the level of generality at which both text type and genre are examined. Engagement notices are tightly constrained as both text type and genre. That is because they exist at a low level of generality. If we had looked instead at births, marriages and deaths notices as a single genre, the prediction is that fewer common properties to the text type and genre would have emerged. If all the rest of the public notices in newspapers, such as the shipping news, had been added, the number of common textual features would be decreased still further. If we had supposed the newspapers as a whole were a coherent text type and genre, then we might have been left with very few common features and little if any correlation between text and genre features. Biber (1988:196–7) uses a distinction made in a corpus between broadcasting speech in general and its two sub-genres: sports broadcasting and non-sports broadcasting in particular. But the corpus has no sub-sub-genres as between baseball commentary and, say, football commentary and, within each, of play-by-play versus colour commentary. In other work (Kuiper & Austin, 1990), it has been found that play-by-play has different textual properties from colour commentary. The higher levels of generality will obscure those properties.

This suggests two further generalizations. The first is true definitionally since it is a corollary of the notion 'level of generalization'. Text type commonalities vary in inverse proportion to the degree of generality of the text type; the lower the degree of generality the higher the number of features common to the text type, with the converse also applying. The second generalization is not as obviously the case. It is that correlations between features of text type and genre parameters of situational constraint vary in inverse proportion to the degree of generality of the genre and text type; the more general the genre and text type, the lower will be the correlation between the features of text type and genre. In the case of genres and text types of low generality, such as engagement notices, it can be predicted that there will be a high correlation between genre and text type features and in the case of a text type such as English academic writing and the genre 'English for academic purposes' there will be a relatively low correlation.

By selecting a low level of abstraction in both text type and genre features in the case of engagement notices, it was possible to select a large subset of the total set of formal parameters within which engagement notices may vary. These were mostly specific to the text type. We also selected a single external socio-cultural parameter to correlate with the formal variation which occurs. Australian and New Zealand engagement notices are significantly different along most of the selected parameters. For the New Zealand data, stylistic homogeneity across three different newspapers showed that the variation in the notices is not a function of newspaper house styles.

Furthermore, clusters of variation correlated with the situational parameter of geographical location. These could be interpreted as having to do with the degree of formality favoured by the respective speech communities, New Zealanders favouring a higher degree of formality than Australians, and New Zealanders choosing to indicate their affective stance to the engagement more strongly within the constraints of the formulae they select. This supports further a clear link between the external and internal dimensions of the genre and text type.

It follows, conversely, that a selection of more general parameters, such as those employed by Biber and his associates in the various studies noted in chapters 1 and 6, would not have revealed engagement notices to be a separate text type, because some of the distinctive textual properties of engagement notices appear to play little part in other text types. Thus engagement notices would not emerge as a text type from interrogations of large corpora of newspaper text. This also follows from our correlational hypothesis.

Lastly, the data set was that of a formulaic genre in that engagement notices almost always utilize a formula as the core of the engagement notice. This provided an opportunity to see the variation of the texts as a set of sequential choices where each is potentially affected by the ones preceding it. Almost all the variables selected in section 8.2.2 are contingent in that the earlier choice in the selection of a variable determines what can be done later. This is thus a syntactic fact. It allows for the computation of probabilistic measures for taking any and every path through the formula as a *Times* or Australian or New Zealand placer of engagement notices might. To illustrate: a *Times* writer has a probability of .98 of selecting formula 1. From there (s)he has a zero probability of selecting *It is with great pleasure that* ... or any other affective indicator at the beginning of the formula, a probability of 1 of selecting the preposition *between* rather than *of* in the formula. As far as naming styles of parents go, the probability is that the parents' names will be 'title, given name and surname' in 86 out of 100 cases, i.e. a probability of .86. Since these probabilities are linear, they can be multiplied out to give the likelihood that someone placing an engagement notice in *The Times* will produce a particular sequence. The sequence of probabilities for each string of variables thus becomes an index of the style and the total set of such styles allows for a computational comparison of genrelects.

8.5 Conclusion

Genre theorists differ in the way they explain the relationship between external (genre) and internal form (text type) and the prominence they give to various factors. The tiny genre of engagement notices has yielded data showing it to be a distinctive text type with its own text type parameters of variation. This variation has provided a test to see if engagement notices have different properties in Australia and New Zealand. They have. Furthermore, a number of the parameters of variation cluster and these clusters can be interpreted as having sociocultural significance. A number of generalizations as to the way genres pattern in their external and internal form have also emerged. These are that:

- Text types have identifiable features which form a perceptual template against which actual texts are judged to be members of the text type.
- The relationship between genre features (dimensions of situational constraint) and a text type is not generally deterministic.
- Text type commonalities vary in inverse proportion to the degree of generality of the text type; the lower the degree of generality,

the higher the number of features common to the text type and conversely.
- Correlations between features of text type and genre parameters of situational constraint vary in inverse proportion to the degree of abstraction of the genre and text type; the more abstract the genre and text type, the lower will be the correlation between the features of text type and genre. The final hypothesis is empirically vulnerable in an interesting way and thus worthy of further investigation.

9
Revolutionary Change: Formula Change during the Cultural Revolution, People's Republic of China[1]

> *Anyone should be allowed to speak out, whoever he may be, so long as he is not a hostile element and does not make malicious attacks, and it does not matter if he says something wrong. Leaders at all levels have the duty to listen to others. Two principles must be observed: (1) Say all you know and say it without reserve; (2) don't blame the speaker but take his words as a warning. Unless the principle of 'Don't blame the speaker' is observed genuinely and not falsely, the result will not be 'Say all you know and say it without reserve'.*
> Mao Zedong, *The Tasks for 1945* (December 15, 1944)

9.1 Introduction

The formulaic genres explored in the previous chapters have presupposed a stable social order. But if formulaic genres manifest and code culture, then we would predict that social perturbations should manifest themselves in changes to the formulaic genres of a speech community. This chapter tests this prediction by examining the way in which formulaic genres changed after the Communist government came to power in China in 1949 and specifically during the Cultural Revolution in the 1960s.[2] This is done by looking at the way in which vulnerable day-to-day formulae changed during the Cultural Revolution. It appears that the formulaic inventory underwent interesting changes, in that there were stable elements in Chinese culture existing alongside the revolutionary ones. The stable elements allowed for old formulae to remain in use, although often with changed conditions of use. The Cultural Revolution also highjacked certain older formulae to give them revolutionary significance in the cult of personality surrounding Mao Zedong.

The chapter then analyses the formulaic nature of the Public Criticism Meeting, which was a new formulaic genre of the Cultural Revolution.

9.2 Socio-political background

After a long period of war, including both the Sino-Japanese war and the civil war in which Communist forces fought with those of the Kuomintang, the Communist government took power in China in 1949. The period of war had been a massive upheaval. But the period after 1949 was a period of intensive social engineering, in itself an equal, or perhaps even larger, upheaval. Its aims were to create a new society in which everyone supported the revolution affectively as well as in practice. To create the changes that the Chinese Communist party required, it was necessary to institute practices that were, in part, at odds with traditional values and practices.

New social orders often create new rituals in order to provide a focus for their aims. There were many such rituals in post-revolutionary China. For the most part, these took the form of meetings. As Mu Fu-Sheng (1963:153) puts it, 'everything the Government accomplishes is done by calling meetings'. Those attending them 'would agree that these activities were quite unlike anything they had experienced in the old society' (Whyte, 1974:23). Most of the meetings were of small groups (*hsaie-tsu*) and for the purpose of 'study', and 'mutual criticism' (Whyte, 1974:2). Their purpose, briefly stated, was to change hearts and minds:

> At these meetings everyone is normally given pamphlets to read, an elected leader 'reports' on the contents of the pamphlet under study and all join in the subsequent discussion: why socialism possesses 'incomparable superiority' to capitalism, why 'leaning to one side' (the Russian side) is the only possible solution to China's problem, what 'ideological reform' is and why it is necessary, and so on (Mu Fu-Sheng, 1963:155).

Part of the meeting agenda was to generate a dialectic, and so conflicts had to be created. This was done by having the members of the group candidly express their views. Such views were then criticized. Frequently, the person expressing the views was also criticized. Such mutual criticism was supposed to conclude in a meeting of minds. 'Criticism and self criticism were to go hand in hand with the discussion and were viewed as indispensable from it' (Whyte, 1974:47). However, where serious error or long-term recalcitrance was suspected, special 'investigation' meetings were held. At these, one who was accused of deviating from acceptable norms was faced with members of his or her group. Members of the group were expected to raise with the person all their faults and the person was then supposed to confess. The confession in turn was subjected to close scrutiny for its ideological content.

Whyte (1974:22) suggests that such activities were in conflict with previous social norms:

> The Confucian emphasis on maintaining harmony and avoiding conflict in interpersonal relationships had to be broached in order to get mutual criticism aired. Also the universalistic spirit of Chinese Communist mutual criticism conflicts with the traditional emphasis on favoritism towards primary group members. Now individuals may have to publicly denounce friends and relatives and accept criticism from those to whom they feel no special ties.

So here there was a break of the kind that should result in changes to formulaic inventory.

9.3 Changes in routine interactional genres in postrevolutionary China

Chapters 4, 5 and 6 all made reference to interactional rituals. In this section such rituals and their associated genres again come under scrutiny. The routine politeness formulae discussed earlier, being central to social life, provide one way of testing to see if social change creates linguistic change. To assess whether this is so, routine politeness formulae of the postrevolutionary period can be divided into two sets:[3]

(i) those that were used before the revolution and continued to be used after it;
and
(ii) those that were created and used only after the revolution.

The formulae of the first group are usually those that are used in informal social situations and involve personal communications, such as:

Greetings:
(1)   chi   fan   le   ma?
   LT: eat   meal Aspect Question
   IS: Have you had your meal?

(2)   *ni dao   nar   qu?*
    LT: you to   where   go
    IS: Where are you going?

Leave-taking:
(3)   *hao   zou!*
    LT: well   walk
    IS: Good-bye! or Take care!

(4)   *man   zou!*
    LT: slow   walk
    IS: Good-bye! or Take care!

Name-asking:
(5)   *gui   xing?*
    LT: noble (family)   name
    IS: May I ask your name?

As the revolution wore on, and particularly during the Cultural Revolution, people tended to avoid personal contact and communication unless they were very sure of their ground. This was because various waves of reform tended to pit one group against the other and create increasing uncertainty about who one's friends were. For example, those who had spoken out, as people were encouraged to do, against aspects of Party leadership during the 'Hundred Flowers' movement in 1956–57 often found themselves 'criticized' a year later in the 'anti-rightist' movement that followed it. One learned during the Cultural Revolution that even one's blood relatives might become one's accusers. Thus, routine formulae for casual friendly contact came to be less frequently used. The formulae of the second group, by contrast, are those that are commonly used in formal social situations such as public speeches, official documents, and formal letters. As these were created and used in the postrevolutionary period, they are discussed in more detail.

The new revolutionary formulae had to be pragmatically appropriate to revolutionary norms. Old formulae that lacked revolutionary appropriateness were therefore not used. Take, for example, the following formulae, which appear to function as apologies:

Apologies:
(6)   *qing yu haihan*
    IS: Please be magnanimous enough to forgive.

(7)   *qing duo baohan*
    IS: Please be magnanimous enough to tolerate.

Such formulae were usually used in prerevolutionary China at the end of a formal speech or a formal letter. Though semantically they imply that their user has made errors or had shortcomings, and asks to be excused, they are not necessarily apologetic expressions in a pragmatic sense. They are simply to show the user's modesty and are thus a form of deference behaviour. However, the criticism of the revolutionary meeting set a norm, which was that 'things which are wrong or erroneous must be criticized and corrected'. Accordingly, errors and shortcomings were no longer to be forgiven or tolerated. Thus, the formulae given earlier were replaced by new ones, such as:

(8)   qing   piping   bangzhu
    LT: please criticize help
    IS: Please criticize and help.

(9)   qing   piping   zhizheng
    LT: please criticize correct
    IS: Please criticize and correct.

(10)   huanying   piping
    LT: welcome   criticism
    IS: I welcome criticism.

Compared with the old formulae, these new formulae do not sound like apologetic expressions any more. However, they have the same function and occur in the same context as those of their predecessors. They are, like the old formulae, used at the end of a formal speech or letter as expressions to show the user's modesty. They also imply the user may have made some errors or has shortcomings (again, not necessarily) in speech or in behaviour. But the user of the new formulae takes a different attitude towards the implicit errors or shortcomings. Instead of asking to be excused, the user asks for criticism.

The new formulae are also different from the old formulae in several other respects. First, they have a different degree of formality: the old formulae tend to be used in formal situations, whereas the new ones could be used in formal or informal situations. Second, they have a different degree of idiomaticity: the old formulae are idiomatic, whereas the new ones are not. Third, there is a different restriction on participants: users of the old formulae are likely to be those with higher education, whereas the new ones can be used by people with different degrees of education, ranging from high to low.

It is clear that the new apology or deference formulae are adjusted to meet the revolutionary requirement for subjecting oneself to public and private criticism. They are also adjusted to the proletarian nature of the revolution by being used across the whole social spectrum rather than just being the prerogative of the educated. At the same time, the contexts for the use of these formulae remained much as they had been. This suggests that the proletariat were in fact taking over the social functions performed by the old formulaic apologies and expressions of deference, and using them for their own revolutionary ends. Some old formulae were not completely eliminated but were used instead as a basis from which new formulae were derived. Such formulae had to be syntactically decomposable to allow for the insertion of new constituents. Take, for example, a prerevolutionary greeting formula and its derivatives:

(11)   ci   zhi   jingli!
   LT: here extend   salute
   IS: with high respect

This formula was used at the end of a document or a letter in prerevolutionary times. It was used to pay respect to the addressee if that addressee was old or of higher social status than the sender. Semantically, it is not inappropriate according to the norms of the revolution. But, as its application is restricted to participants with respect to age and social status, and the social attitude towards age and social status changed greatly, particularly in the Cultural Revolution, the formula was an inappropriate one in the revolutionary context. The revolution was a period in which the social hierarchy was ostensibly turned upside down. First, the imperial hierarchy was overthrown. Landlords lost their land and local officials lost their positions while the Communist party elevated the peasantry. In the Cultural Revolution, highranking cadres who had been the new revolutionary elite became the targets and victims of Red Guards and proletariat criticism in turn. The Red Guards and the proletariat rejected the old formula and replaced it with new formulae such as:

(12)   ci   zhi   geming   jingli!
   LT: here extend   revolutionary salute
   IS: With revolutionary greetings!

(13)   ci   zhi   wuchanjieji   jingli!
   LT: here extend   proletarian   salute
   IS: With proletarian greetings!

(14)   ci   zhi   wuchanjieji   geming   jingli!
    LT: here   extend proletarian   revolutionary   salute
    IS: With proletarian revolutionary greetings!'

It is easy to see that such formulae are all derived from the old formula *ci zhi jingli* by the insertion of constituents like *geming* and *wuchanjieji*. This insertion is important as it results in a change of participants in the old formula with respect to age and social status. One's age and social status are not relevant to the application of the new formulae. Instead, one's political identity, or class status, becomes relevant, namely, the participants are restricted to the proletariat or revolutionaries. The change of participants causes a different reading of the word *jingli*. In the old formula, *jingli* means 'respect'; in the new formulae, it means 'greeting'.

Functionally, the new formulae more explicitly support the group identity of their participants via inserted words like *geming* and *wuchanjieji*. By their use of these formulae, users not only identify themselves and the addressee as members of the proletariat or as revolutionaries, but they also rule out the use of these formulae by other groups. Being unable to use both the old formulae and the new formulae, groups other than those of the proletariat and revolutionaries are dishonoured. They receive neither respect nor greetings.

Thus, by insertion of new constituents, new formulae are derived from old. Again, it will be clear that the old social order stands behind the new as the old formulae are part of the new. But since the uses of the new formulae are different, the use of the formulae themselves creates revolutionary change.

The formulae discussed in the previous sections are related to their corresponding old formulae in several ways, either functionally or semantically or contextually. There is, however, an interesting formula which is only contextually related to the formulae it replaces. This is a particular class-greeting formula. To begin with, we will look at the old formulae. In schools, the class greeting was highly ritualized. At the beginning of each class, prerevolutionary students and their teacher exchanged greetings with the following formulaic expressions:

(15)   *tongxuemen   hao!*
    LT: (students)   well
    IS: How do you do, everybody?

(16)   *laoshi   hao!*
LT: teacher   well
IS: How do you do, teacher?
(tongxuemen is a form of address used by a teacher in speaking to students and by students speaking to each other. There is no English equivalent for it.)

The order of the two formulae is fixed. It is the teacher who first greets the student. The greeting must be preceded by nonverbal activity – the students have to stand up – and be accompanied by a nonverbal gesture – the students and the teacher have to remain standing until the greeting is finished.

Functionally, this greeting can be viewed as a means of defining the social relations and social status of the student and the teacher, as the forms of address indicate. As standing up is a cultural way to pay respect to people of higher social status, the teacher's higher social status is explicitly indicated by the obligatory nature of the preceding nonverbal activity. The application of the formula does not necessarily imply familiarity in the relationship between the students and the teacher since they can depend on time (at the beginning of a class) and place (within a classroom) to recognize each other.

However, during the Cultural Revolution, because teachers were regarded as members of the petty bourgeoisie, they lost their high status.[4] Students, on the other hand, became Red Guards who no longer respected their teachers and who, in many cases, wrote wall posters denouncing them or who stood up to criticize them.

> Gang Di denounced the music teacher for her high heels and coquettish voice. Little Monkey said teacher Chen used a Capitalist teaching method by always telling us stories for ten minutes before class to calm us down. The son of a press photographer wrote about how the math teacher wore perfume in the summertime (Liang Heng & Shapiro, 1983:47).

With pupils involved in such activities, the traditional class greeting was inappropriate. The class-greeting formulae were therefore eliminated. A rather different formula, which was used in other situations, not restricted to class greeting in school, came to be used by the students and the teacher.

(17)   *rang women jing   zhu Mao zhuxi   wanshouwuqiang!*
LT: let   us   respectfully wish Mao Chairman   (a long life)
IS: Let's respectfully wish Chairman Mao a long life!

The formula had to be uttered in a particular way such that the first part, *rang women jing zhu Mao zuxi*, was uttered only by the student monitor, and the second part, *wanshouwuqiang*, by all the students and the teacher. The second part of the formula is in fact a dated idiomatic formula, and its application in prerevolutionary China was restricted to the Emperor. The second part was usually uttered three times as a means to express and reinforce the speakers' loyalty to Mao.

This formula replaced the old class-greeting formulae. It was applied in the same way as the old formulae with respect to time (at the beginning of class) and place (within a classroom). Like the old formulae, it was preceded by nonverbal activity (the students had to stand up) and accompanied by a nonverbal gesture (both the students and the teacher are standing). However, in spite of such superficial similarities, the new formula and the old formulae were actually irrelevant to each other. The new formula and the old formulae were different, not only in meaning and syntactic structure, but also in pragmatics. The formula was not restricted to the students and the teacher at the beginning of a class. It was, for example, also used at the beginning of a meeting, with its first part uttered by the chair of the meeting and its second by all the people present at the meeting. Whereas the old formulae defined the social relation and social status of the students and the teacher, the new formula defined the social relation and social status of Mao and all users of the formula (including students and teachers). The new formula was also different from the old formulae in regard to idiomaticity. The new formula was more idiomatic than the old formulae in that it contained another formula that is idiomatic.

To summarize:

- The formulae used in formal situations in prerevolutionary China were more likely to change than those used in informal situations.
- The formulae used in informal situations were less frequently and widely used in people's routine life. Although in general they were not replaced by new formulae, they can still be said to have undergone a pragmatic change in their conditions of use.
- The occurrence of new formulae was usually at the expense of old formulae. The old formulae were eliminated because they were either not semantically appropriate to the revolution, or the social changes of the revolution interfered with their conditions of use.

- New formulae were sometimes semantically or syntactically related to old formulae and occasionally completely novel.
- New formulae often did not keep to the four-character frame that the old formulae had and which is characteristic of high-style literate Chinese.

9.4 The Public Criticism Meeting of the Cultural Revolution

Whereas changes in daily life created by the revolution made an impact on mundane formulae, revolutionary imperatives reveal themselves graphically in one of the central rituals of the revolution, the Public Criticism Meeting of the Cultural Revolution.

We showed earlier how the study and criticism meetings provided a context within which changes in the formulaic inventory of mundane politeness formulae could be understood. There were other meetings that provided a similar context for understanding the formulaic nature of the Public Criticism Meeting, a central ritual of the Cultural Revolution. An early precursor to the Public Criticism Meeting was the 'speak bitterness' meeting where:

> the organising 'political worker' or propagandist calls, for instance, on women to speak of their grievances in the past, apprentices to speak of what they suffered from their capitalists, or prostitutes, or farmers, or 'oppressed people' to speak of their wrongs, till the movement 'reaches its high tide of indignation' and then a women's association or farmers' association is formed and capitalists, landlords and bawds condemned in public trials and punished. Such meetings were held frequently at the beginning of Communist control (Mu Fu-Sheng, 1963:153).

The clearest predecessor to the Public Criticism Meeting was the 'struggle' meeting. Struggle meetings were used early in the revolution to deal with more serious offences than just being mildly out of line. They were, by contrast with the study and mutual criticism meetings, much larger.

> The criminals, such as landlords, Kuomintang agents and counter-revolutionaries (in the narrow sense), that is, people who actually organize resistance to the Party, are shackled, or have their hands tied behind their back. Loudspeakers transmit what is spoken on

the platform to the audience who often sit on the ground in open air, and magnify the shouts for the radio stations which broadcast the proceedings. Speeches are made, the criminals are brought to the platform, accusations are read, slogans are shouted, the reading of the accusations is continued, more slogans are shouted, exhibits are shown, moans are heard, accusations are added to by speakers from the audience, slogans are shouted, an accomplice is led onto the platform, exposure of fresh evidence is made by the accomplice, shrieks are uttered, shaking fists are waved, the accomplice is released to join the audience, hands are clapped and then 'the Leadership' asks through the microphone, 'Comrades, what shall we do with him?' 'Kill him, shoot him!' 'Comrades, should we tolerate such criminals among us?' 'No. Kill him. Shoot him.' And one case is ended. After four, six or even ten hours the meeting is adjourned; sometimes only after executions have taken place 'to the great satisfaction of the people' (Mu Fu-Sheng, 1963:160).

During the Cultural Revolution, the investigation meeting and struggle meeting seem to have merged into a central ritual, which we call the Public Criticism Meeting. It was held regularly in organizations at the basic level, usually once a week, and occasionally on a large scale with hundreds or thousands attending. The victims were accused of wishing to create a new class system or of desiring privilege and generally setting themselves apart from the masses in a counter-revolutionary manner.

The Public Criticism Meeting was a formulaic ritual and, as might be expected, the formulaic character of the Public Criticism Meeting is a joint product of discourse structure, verbal formulae, and the fixed forms of concomitant activity. These three elements are are all determined by the specific characteristics of the Public Criticism Meeting and by the nature of the Cultural Revolution itself.

9.4.1 Discourse structure of Public Criticism Meetings

Public Criticism Meetings shared a common characteristic discourse structure. The sequence was basically as follows. It began with all those who attended standing up and singing the revolutionary song *The East is red*:

The East is red.
The Sun is rising
China has produced a Mao Zedong.

He works for the well-being of the people.
The great emancipator is Mao Zedong.

After the audience was reseated, the criticized, who were known as 'monsters and demons' (class enemies of all descriptions), were brought onto the stage while the audience shouted slogans. Then criticizing began, with spokespeople loudly reading the indictments. As soon as the criticism was over, the accused were taken off the stage. The audience then stood up again, shouting slogans. There followed another revolutionary song, *Sailing depends on the helmsman*:

Sailing depends on the helmsman.
Plants on the sun.
Crops on rain and dew.
And revolution on Mao Zedong thought.

The meeting was then closed.

This discourse pattern (singsong-accused on-shout slogans-criticizing-accused off-shout slogan-singsong) was so common that absence of any one of the elements would be a sign that something had gone wrong. For example, Public Criticism Meetings always began with singing a revolutionary song, which was a symbol of Chairman Mao worship. In fact, during the Cultural Revolution nearly all collective activity, be it a class in high school or a celebratory party or even a wedding ceremony, started with *The East is red*.

Not only was each element of the discourse necessary, the order of the elements of the Public Criticism Meeting was essential and of great significance. For example, the criticized must not be on the stage while the audience sang the revolutionary song. That would be considered profane. However, the criticized must be present when the audience shouted slogans for the first time, because the purpose of shouting slogans was to threaten the accused. However, the criticized were often led away again before the last section of the criticism, which we have termed 'homage to Mao', because, here again, their presence might profane the proceedings. 'According to custom, the worst of the counterrevolutionaries had no right to listen to the sayings of Chairman Mao' (Liang Heng & Shapiro, 1983:121).

Here are a group of slogans typically shouted during Public Criticism Meetings:

(18) *Da duo NP.*⁵
IS: Down with NP.

(19) *NP bi xu tan bai jiao dai.*
IS: NP must confess his (her) crime.

(20) *NP bi xu xiang ge ming qun zhong di tou ren zui.*
IS: NP must hang his (her) head and admit his (her) guilt to the revolutionary masses

(21) *Tan bai cong kuan. Kang ju cong yan.*
IS: Leniency to those who confess their crimes. Severity to those who refuse to.

(22) *Fan dang fan ren min jue mei you hao xia chang.*
IS: Those who oppose the people and the Communist party will come to no good end.

(23) *Jue bu yun xu jie ji di ren fan gong dao suan.*
IS: Never allow the class enemy to retaliate.

(24) *Shi si han wei dang zhong yang. Shi si han wei Mao Zhuxi de ge ming lu xian.*
IS: Pledge to fight to the death in defending the Party central committee. Pledge to fight to the death in defending Chairman Mao's revolutionary line.

(25) *Shi jiang wu chan jie ji wen hua da ge ming jin xing dao di.*
IS: Carry the Great Proletarian Cultural Revolution through to the end.

These slogans form three sets that were sequentially ordered. The first three show the hatred of the audience toward the criticized, which implied that the Public Criticism Meeting was a stage of class struggle where the line between the criticized and the revolutionary masses had to be drawn clearly. The second group of three slogans threatened the criticized so that they should confess their crimes. And finally came the general and abstract slogans expressing the audience's loyalty to Mao and determination to carry the Cultural Revolution right to the end. At this point, those attending might read from the *Little Red Book*, which contained quotations from the writings of Mao. Although all slogans used in different meetings were not necessarily the same in every detail as the samples given here, their equivalents had to be in the order described. It will be clear that the discourse structure of the

Public Criticism Meeting ritual is hierarchical. It can be written as a set of context-free rewrite rules as follows:

R.1 Public Criticism Meeting → song 1 + slogan shouting[1] + criticism + slogan shouting[2] + song 2
R.2 song 1→ *The East is red*
R3. slogan shouting[1]→ hatred + threats to accused
R4. slogan shouting[2]→ homage to Mao
R5. song 2 → *Sailing depends on the helmsman*

For those familiar with revivalist religious meetings, this discourse will look familiar.

9.4.2 Discourse structure and the use of formulae in Public Criticism Meeting speech

The criticism made by spokespeople at Public Criticism Meetings was usually based on a written text that had been carefully prepared before the Public Criticism Meeting.[6] The contents of the written text might vary from Public Criticism Meeting to Public Criticism Meeting according to different accused being presented, but the structure of the text was essentially the same. It usually began with a description of the current political situation, which indicated that, on the whole, everything was fine but nevertheless there were still potential dangers coming from the class enemies such as those on the stage. To support what was stated, a spokesperson would first quote Mao's words and then denounce the accused's 'crimes'. In most of the cases, spokespersons would end their criticism by shouting slogans.[7]

This discourse pattern in the critical speech usually consisted in whole or in part of formulae. The reason for the occurrence of formulae in the written text was that, during the Cultural Revolution, criticism meetings had become one of the most important routine activities, and the speeches made at such meetings were highly ritualized. The use of formulae simplified the whole procedure so that those who attended found it easy to follow. Besides, the petrified forms of speech served as a model. Such forms of speech were politically safer to follow because any personal elaborations in such a speech might turn out to be a political mistake. People had to know not only what to say to whom, but also how to say it and in which part of the discourse. For example, one had to quote Mao's quotations, usually 'fight selfishness, repudiate revisionism', when one greeted one's comrades, members of one's own faction; but one would not greet 'monsters and demons' even if they were relatives or had formerly been friends. This was true in the case of Public Criticism Meetings, at which the obligatory use of formulae served as appropriate tools for saying the right thing at the right time and in the right place. In other words, the explanation for the occurrence of formulae in Public Criticism Meetings lies in the general functions of formulae that are categorized by Coulmas (1979:254) as 'orderliness of communication and group identification'.

Many of the formulae of the Cultural Revolution must have been orally transmitted, since the Cultural Revolution was carried on by workers, peasants and children who would frequently have been at best only partly literate. However, where Red Guards, for example, were literate, they could make use of the Big Character Posters, which were also a feature of the Cultural Revolution and whose slogans were, in many cases, identical to those used in Public Criticism Meetings. Such transmission can be seen in the following account of a group of young Red Guards preparing to do their first criticism of their teachers, on this occasion, by a Big Character Poster:

> faced with the vast open spaces before us, we suddenly discovered that we didn't know what Capitalism or Revisionism really were. Little Li was the only one able to come up with anything, and he painted with a flourish ANGRILY OPEN FIRE ON THE *HUNAN DAILY'S* ATTACHED PRIMARY SCHOOL'S CAPITALIST REVISIONIST LINE!!! We all thought this was just fine, but it was obviously not enough, and we sat in worried silence until my friend Gang Di's older brother, Gang Xian, made a good suggestion. 'Why don't we go down the street and see what other people have written?' (Liang Heng & Shapiro, 1983:46).

9.4.3 Syntactic and semantic aspects of formulae of Public Criticism Meeting speech

One significant feature of Public Criticism Meeting speech was the use of what might be termed empty phraseology. The vocabulary items chosen by spokespersons were often words whose meanings were vague, general, and abstract. For example:

> Nouns: *spirit, soul, revolution, class struggle, revisionism, enemy, destruction, construction*
> Adjectives: *bourgeois, capitalist, indignant, militant, great, profound, revolutionary, etc.*

Meteorological and military terms were also employed for the purpose of building up a momentum and creating a feverish atmosphere symbolizing the mighty power of the Cultural Revolution and of the revolutionary masses. For example, words like *wind, storm, hurricane, tide, sun,* and *cannon, weapon, front, battlefield, battledrum, comrade-in-arms* and so forth were most commonly used in Public Criticism Meeting speech, particularly in the beginning of the speech, which was highly formulaic.

Here are some typical Public Criticism Meeting opening formulae:

(26) *Dong feng jin chui, jie bao pin chuan.*
IS: The east wind blows with mighty power, news of victory keeps pouring in.

(27) *Dang qian quan guo ge tiao zhan xian xing shi yi pian da hao.*
IS: Now a good situation prevails on all fronts in our country.

(28) *Guo nei wai xing shi yi pai da hao.*
IS: The overall situation is glowing and excellent both at home and abroad.

(29) *Shi jie zai dong dang zhong qian jin...*
IS: The world advances amidst turbulence...

(30) *Bu puo bu li.*
IS: Without destruction there can be no construction.

(31) *Di shi di you shi you, wo men bi xu hua qing jie ji jie xian.*
IS: A friend is a friend, a foe is a foe, we must clearly distinguish one from the other.

(32) *Na qi bi zuo duo qiang...*
IS: Taking up the pen as a weapon I now expose...

Apart from the reasons already given, the use of this abstract and specialized vocabulary had the effect of showing a spokesperson's enthusiasm and political attitude. These words had gained new connotations because they represented the revolutionary fashion, the following of which was an indication of one's departure from the old world and enthusiastic entry into the new.

The formulae of Public Criticism Meeting speech also had distinct syntactic properties, among which were the use of short, simple sentences, imperative sentences, antithesis, and four-character idioms. For example, in denouncing the accused's crimes, short sentences were commonly used so that spokespeople could get a quick response from the accused and hold the attention of the audience (e.g., the accused would say 'Yes, yes, that is true, I admit,' and so on), because what the audience wanted to know were the accused's crimes. However, towards the end of the criticism the spokesperson would begin to use threatening formulae and to shout slogan formulae, which were basically imperative sentences. For example:

(33) *Fang lao shi dian!*
   IS: You behave yourself!
(34) *NP bi xu che di tan bai jiao dai!*
   IS: NP must make a clean breast of his (her) crimes!
(35) *Di tou ren zui!*
   IS: Hang your head down!
(36) *Dui fan ge ming fen zi jue bu shi ren sheng!*
   IS: Never mercy to counterrevolutionaries!
(37) *Da dao NP!*
   IS: Down with NP!

9.4.4 The pragmatics of Public Criticism Meeting formulae

Coulmas (1979:242) argues that 'only knowledge of the relevant dimensions of social situations guarantees an understanding of the meaning of formulae which are tied to them'. For example, as we saw in chapter 7.4 directives need not be threatening. Being asked to lower one's head as a warning of an approaching low doorway is not threatening. But the directives directed at the accused in a Public Criticism Meeting were threatening formulae, reflecting the socially asymmetrical relationship between the participants. In this context, being ordered to hang one's head had the conventional interpretation of guilt and submission. Besides, the setting of the Public Criticism Meeting reinforced this effect: (a) at a Public Criticism Meeting the accused was representative of the class enemy of the spokesperson and the audience, and was target of the criticism; (b) the spokesperson and the audience were the overwhelming majority in number; (c) the spokesperson had the power of resorting to force if the accused dared to react against the spokesperson's words. Under these circumstances, the accused could not and would not do anything but 'hang down his (her) head' as low as possible, for hanging down one's head in Chinese tradition is a sign of admitting one's mistakes and of being willing to receive criticism and punishment, as well as being a sign of submission and obedience. Here, we find a case of a social custom that was taken over for revolutionary purposes. In prerevolutionary times, it was the young and the workers and peasants who had to hang their heads. During the Cultural Revolution, the participants took on reversed roles.

The threatening formulae did not occur only in Public Criticism Meeting speech, but they might occur in other situations as well. For example, they occurred whenever there was an encounter between the Red Guards and 'monsters and demons', for then there existed the socially asymmetrical relationship that was the fundamental contextual restriction for the occurrence of the threatening formulae.

In addition, there were always some concomitant activities that accompanied the occurrence of threatening formulae. For example, the spokesperson would point at the criticized with his or her fingers while the accused would go down on his or her knees and nod, which implied the accused was sincerely convinced. The audience might also point at the accused while following the spokesperson shouting slogans, for at this stage of criticism the audience usually got very excited. Carried along by the feverish atmosphere, the spokesperson would raise his or her voice and employ other gestures (e.g., clenching a fist). There were concomitant activities throughout Public Criticism Meetings. For example, before and after speaking the spokesperson always bowed deeply, first to the portrait of Mao hanging on the back wall of the stage and then to the audience. Towards the end of the meeting, all those attending, except the accused, would stand up, shouting slogans while holding the *Little Red Book* in their right hand. All these concomitant activities had the same common function, that is, to build up the fanatical atmosphere for a Public Criticism Meeting.

9.4.5 The Public Criticism Meeting as an oral formulaic genre

It seems that Public Criticism Meeting speech was an orally transmitted formulaic genre in that the formulae of Public Criticism Meeting speech were transmitted from Public Criticism Meeting to Public Criticism Meeting by the Red Guards. Why should a revolutionary movement initiate an oral tradition to convey its central message? If oral traditions are as simple as this one was, then they provide an easy means of cultural transmission. The Cultural Revolution was to be carried chiefly by workers, peasants, and children, many of whom were illiterate or only partly literate. Oral traditions are a perfect vehicle for such revolutionary leaders. Second, oral traditions have an inherent stability, which allows for the tradition to be unchanged in its essentials while being transmitted over long distances and time periods.[8] For example, Haggo and Kuiper (1985) and Kuiper and Tillis (1985) show how the oral tradition of auctioning was transmitted from the United Kingdom to the United States, Canada, and New Zealand, giving rise to various new traditions, each with its own properties.

The amount of variation in Public Criticism Meetings around China is likely, therefore, to have been small, given the rapid transmission of the ceremony, its short historical duration, and the revolutionary imperatives for uniform adherence to revolutionary norms. It is interesting to note that although revolutionary ideologies insist on change, they also insist that it be uniform.

9.4.6 Conclusion

The Public Criticism Meeting, it seems clear, was a ritual which grew out of the need for a new way to provide a focus for the Cultural Revolution. The use of a formulaic genre can be seen as assisting the spread of the ritual since oral formulaic genres are spread by oral transmission. It is also clear how orally transmitted formulae assisted in the ritual itself by ensuring that the ritual was easy to conduct, as all was predictable, and also safe, since the major actors in it did not need to deviate from politically and socially acceptable forms.

9.5 General conclusion

The purpose of launching a revolution is to break down the entire 'old world' together with its social relations, institutions, culture and traditional norms, as well as the established ideology, in order to create a new order. There is ostensibly only one boundary line and that is whether one is a revolutionary or a counter-revolutionary. In the case of the Chinese Communist Revolution, one's revolutionary status depended largely on one's family background and profession; the power and authority lay only in the hands of revolutionaries. Therefore, the formulaic character of Public Criticism Meetings as well as the routine formulaic genres of daily life cannot be seen as isolated linguistic phenomena, because behind them was the revolutionary assumption that the whole linguistic order had to be altered to meet new political imperatives. However, the new world of revolution is linguistically, it seems, not built *ex nihilo*, but of recycled components.

9.6 Methodological epilogue: recalling formulaic data

The study reported in this chapter makes use of memories as data. The two former Red Guards who were the providers of the data were its original co-authors. Memory is often held to be unreliable and in many circumstances it is. However, where formulaic text, over-learned early in life is concerned, memory is often remarkably reliable. We all remember the nursery rhymes we have been read repeatedly. We remember skipping rhymes (if we skipped) and what our teachers said to quieten us down at the beginning of the day. The reasons why formulaic material like this is recalled generally accurately and after long periods is explained by Rubin (1995). It has a great deal to do not just with the fact that formulaic material is repeated, but also that it is often loaded with affect and linguistic mnemonic potential. Pop songs have the same potential. If one thinks of pre-literate speakers, then it is clear why formulaic material should have mnemonic potential. Formulaic traditions must be passed down the generations and the more memorable they are, the better that process is likely to be. In literate societies, some text can be passed on in written form but greetings, leave takings, and apologies are not learned from written text. They are remembered and remembered accurately from generation to generation often with little change. Those memories may be normative in that the outliers are not as likely to be accurately remembered as the central cases. However, for an understanding of normative cases, this is not a problem.

So one need not be as suspicious of informants' memories in the case of their recall of formulaic genres as one should be of their ability to accurately identify people in a police lineup.

10
Historical Variation: The Historical Reconstruction of Proto-English Auction Speech

> *Now folks, today we are going to auction off Miss Pimber's things. I think you all knew Miss Pimber and you know she had some pretty nice things. This is going to be a real fine auction sale and we have a real fine day for it. It may get hot, though, later on, so we want to keep things moving right along. And now I'm going to begin the sale with the things back here by the barn. You've all had a chance to look at everything so let's bid right out for these fine things and keep things moving right along. The sale is cash as usual and Missus Grady is inside to take care of that. The ladies of the Methodist church are kindly providing the lunch. You can see the tables across there in Missus Root's lot and I know you will want to help all these ladies just as they are helping you. It'll be good I know. All right, I'm going to begin the sale back here so if you folks will follow me we'll get started.*
>
> William Gass, 1967 (*Omensetter's Luck*, p.1)

10.1 Introduction

Since formulaic genres are social artefacts, they may evolve over time. Where they are written, as in the case of dating advertisements, such changes can be documented (Vlčková, 2001). Where they are orally transmitted, the task is more difficult. In the case of the formulaic genres of pre-literate cultures such as oral heroic poetry, it is sometimes possible to reconstruct what the genre may have been like from written sources where poems were transcribed when a pre-literate culture became literate. It is, for example, possible to ask how Caedmon's Hymn may have been composed by Caedmon using formulae which were part of the oral traditions of the Old English period (Fry, 1975). Such reconstructions are not unlike those in historical linguistics where one supposes that features of a proto-language are constructed on the basis of common features of that language's likely descendants.

One way to reconstruct earlier versions of spoken genres is to find recordings of them. Clearly that limits the time horizon substantially, given that recording equipment only became available in the twentieth century. But the value of such recordings is great, as Lord shows in his recordings of South Slavic epic (Lord, 1960). In Kuiper (1991), I looked at the history of race calling by way of segments of its history in old recordings. Since this genre was created as a result of the advent of broadcasting, these recordings represented moments in its evolution. This opportunity rarely arises. Usually formulaic genres exist before they are recorded. The second means of coming to conclusions about the evolution of a formulaic genre is to reconstruct proto forms of it through looking at derived forms of a putative common ancestor. That can be done in the case of the auctioning systems which came from England.

10.2 The evolution of the English auctioning tradition[1]

10.2.1 Introduction

Auction traditions are worldwide and of considerable antiquity. Herodotus is the first writer to describe an auction, one in Mesopotamia for brides, where the most attractive attracted high bids and the least attractive were provided with dowries financed from the proceeds of the auction of the more attractive young women. Later the praetorian guard in one of its more disgruntled moods put the Roman Empire up for a Roman auction. Today there are auctioning systems of diverse character in different parts of the world. In parts of Asia, bids are placed by signing into the auctioneer's hand which is hidden under a cloth. At the flower auctions at Aalsmeer in the Netherlands, a clock begins to wind down in descending order; the first bidder to stop the clock by pressing a button is the buyer (Cassady, 1967). The auctioning tradition which is most familiar in the English-speaking world had its origins in England and was exported to the English colonies.

The evidence which will be presented in this chapter for this hypothesis is based on historical reconstruction. By comparing different contemporary auctioning traditions in the English-speaking world some of the central features of the tradition can be inferred and thus a theory about what Proto English Auction Speech (PEAS) was like will be proposed. The range of current traditions which provide the basis for the reconstruction includes livestock auctions from Whateley, Massachusetts, Toronto, Canada, Banbury, England and Christchurch, New Zealand; antique auctions at Sotheby's in London, Douglas Galleries in Deerfield, Massachusetts, and R.G. Bell's auction rooms in Kaiapoi, New Zealand; tobacco auctions in Fuquay-Varina, North Carolina and Danville, Virginia; wool auctions, real estate auctions, and produce auctions all in Christchurch New Zealand. These traditions are not only geographically diverse but also diverse by commodity.

Although the focus of this study is the linguistic character of auctions in the English tradition, such auctions also have a social character since they are formulaic genres. I have given an account of these contexts in Kuiper (1996).

In all auctions in the English tradition, what the auctioneer says and how the buyers respond is predictable in a number of ways. The text type, as will be clear by now, can be defined by the use of discourse structure rules and formulae. As a result, the particular nature of the oral tradition of English auction speech can be traced through the discourse structure rules and oral formulae used by auctioneers in the English tradition. There is a third property of oral formulaic speech which is also significant and that is the prosodic form of auction speech, its intonation, rhythm, and vocal quality. Here too there are particular traditions in the speech of auctioneers who perform in the English tradition.

10.2.2 The discourse structure of the English tradition

All auction systems in the English tradition share at least one, and possibly three, discourse structure rules. The first of these rules to be discussed gives the high-level structure of the individual auction sale. This rule seems self-evident in that those familiar with the English tradition cannot imagine an auction system which does not operate this way. But there are many other auction traditions which are quite different. One example is the candle auction (Cassady, 1967:31–2) where bidding continues until a candle gutters, and one can certainly conceive of auction traditions being other than this.

The rule for the English tradition is:

R3. auction → description + opening bid search + bid calling + sale
     + (epilogue)

It defines the fact that an individual auction always consists of a description of the lot, followed by a search for an opening bid, followed by bid calling, followed by a sale and a possible epilogue. This rule is instantiated in all the diverse English auction traditions.

There are also common features to some of the constituent parts of the auction. The bid calling in the English tradition is characteristically by rising bids with or without fixed increments, but there is evidence that elements of Dutch tradition by descending bids may also have existed in England (Cassady, 1967:32). The contemporary evidence for this comes from one of the derived traditions, the tobacco auctions where the auctioneer uses a descending scale in the Dutch fashion as a way of finding an opening bid and then moves back up the scale in the English fashion to find the highest bid.

There are also two distinct ways of calling bids. In one tradition only the current highest bid is called while in the other both the current highest bid and the bid currently being sought are called. The latter bid calling system is used in most North American auction traditions and in at least one real estate auction in England I have seen. The highest-bid-only tradition is used in many antique auctions in England and New Zealand, and in livestock auctions in the UK and New Zealand. It is therefore probable that both traditions of bid calling existed in PEAS but that younger traditions have chosen to use one or the other.

Let us, for the mean time, say that Rule 3 is a discourse structure rule for PEAS.

There is another rule which appears often enough also to be an interesting candidate for the original tradition. This is an even simpler rule which provides for an introduction to an auction sale in which more than one item is being sold and then for the series of individual auctions to follow it:

> R1. auction sale → (introduction) + auction^n (where n ≥ 1)

The introduction itself appears to have a number of significant constituents which appear in a variety of traditions. Possibly they too belonged to PEAS:

> R2. introduction → [(welcome to buyers) + (description of sale) + (conditions of sale) + (order of sale) + (peripheral practicalities)...] (where square brackets denote relatively free order choices)

For example, some of the peripheral practicalities which appear in various derived auction traditions include informing those who are attending the auction where they may get food and drink and where the washrooms are. The author in the epigraphic quotation for this chapter seems to have a clear recall of what such an introduction sounds like. We can take it then, that the auction which Samuel Pepys mentioned attending in 1662 began with a form of rule 1 in which the auctioneer or an assistant discussed the order of sale and the conditions of sale and possibly also other matters pertaining to the physical circumstances of the sale, after which items were auctioned one after the other, each lot being first described, then an opening bid being sought, bids then being called and a sale being made at the end.

10.2.3 The formulaic inventory

Since auctions are an oral-formulaic genre, auctioneers must have learned an inventory of formulae. These formulae are passed from one performer to the next down the generations. Formulae, as discussed in chapter 1, are set phrases with some degree of flexibility which allow the auctioneers to speak rapidly while attending to many matters other than speaking. The traditions on which this study is based are geographically and occupationally distinct, so if a particular formula occurs in a number of such distinct traditions then it can be attributed to the parent tradition. It is possible that such formulae are borrowed across traditions. However, this seems a less likely explanation given the degree of product specialization in auction traditions and their geographic isolation from each other. New Zealand livestock auctioneers do not go to Canada to sell. Neither do antique auctioneers turn to auctioning cattle very often.

Formulae in auctions have a number of significant properties. The most critical is that each one is appropriate to one and only one part of the discourse structure. Some formulae are used for lot description, others for opening bid search, others for interpolations in bid calling and so on. Since this is the case in all the auction systems in the English tradition, it may be presumed to have been a property of formulae in PEAS. There are a number of instances of formulae which support this hypothesis and which we can therefore assign to PEAS. Examples taken from tobacco auction speech (Kuiper & Tillis, 1985:143) which also occur elsewhere are:

the bid calling formulae: *X I'm bid, X I got* and *I got X*
the bid calling interpolation formula: *Come on, come on*
the bid location formula: *Agin you*

Formulae taken from livestock auction speech in Canada and New Zealand (Haggo & Kuiper, 1985:194) are:

the opening-bid-search formula: *X and go*
the bid-calling formula: *X fer 'em*
the refer-to-vendor formula: *Do I sell 'em?*

Formulae common to both antique auctions and livestock auctions are:

the final-call formula: *Are you all done?*

All these formulae can be assigned to the inventory of formulae in PEAS. There is support for doing so in the case of the last formula from one historical record since this formula was used in the slave markets of the American South (Bancroft, 1959:109–10).

A second property of formulae which occurs in all the derived traditions is that many of them have a structure which can be given in finite state form. For example, the *'em* at the end of the formula *Do I sell 'em* is often omitted. The formula *Agin you* can be augmented by the addition of the word, *Sir* or a locator such as *at the back*. It can be assumed therefore that formulae in PEAS could be structurally modelled by finite state grammars. One of the consequences of modelling them in this way will be explored later.

What, if anything else do the formulae common to PEAS have in common? Not surprisingly they are both discourse-function specific and tradition-neutral. A formula like *Any more bids?* is clearly a bid-calling interpolation used when the bidding stalls. *Are you all done?* is used when the same thing happens but very close to the end of the bid-calling phase to signal to buyers that a sale is about to be made. It is also impossible to tell from the particular formula whether it belongs to the tradition of auctioning tobacco or livestock or antiques, i.e. each formula assigned to PEAS is tradition-neutral.

10.2.4 Prosodic modes

Auction speech in the English tradition has two unusual prosodic features: a shout tune and a drone. These are not found in all of the derived traditions but in enough of them to suggest that they may both have been part of PEAS. The shout tune is used characteristically during the bid-calling phase of an auction when a syllable of a tone unit is very heavily accented, often to the point where there is severe phonetic degradation of the syllable (Kuiper & Haggo, 1984:214–16). For example, in livestock auctions in both New Zealand and Canada a bid-calling formula such as *At X dollars* will have the first word articulated with a significantly higher volume and pitch than the rest of the formula and with a sharp staccato delivery. In saleyards where this happens the air seems punctuated with these shouts.

The second mode is a droned intonation where the auctioneer has a tonal centre to his (or in rare cases her) delivery with some ornamentation. In some traditions this drone is still speech-like, for example in livestock auctions. In others such as the tobacco auctions it is chanted, i.e. has a musical character. This development will be explored later in this chapter. Similar chanting exists in a very large number of oral formulaic traditions. Identical variation in drone traditions exists in horse racing commentaries in New Zealand (Kuiper & Austin, 1990). Some commentators drone while others chant and the two traditions exist alongside each other as stylistic variants. Both these prosodic modes can be attributed to PEAS.

10.2.5 The development of independent traditions

As in the case of linguistic differentiation, there is no reason to suppose that the various geographically dispersed and product-orientated traditions in the English tradition all arose from a totally homogeneous PEAS. It is quite likely the PEAS had already developed diverging traditions in England, depending on what was being sold at auction and where it was being sold. But geographic dispersal and increasing product specialization have certainly given rise to distinctively different oral traditions. This can be illustrated by comparing a tobacco auction from the American South with a fine art auction from Sotheby's in London, and for those not familiar with a range of auction traditions, these two auctioning varieties would appear to have little in common. Indeed it is likely that a novice attender at a tobacco auction would have little understanding of the business in hand, let alone what the auctioneer was saying.

How do such traditions diverge? There is clearly a potential for traditions to diverge in each one of the three areas: discourse structure, formulaic inventory or prosodic modes. But this would be of little real interest if change were unconstrained. It seems that changes in each area are, in fact, limited to a subset of the conceivable.

10.2.5.1 Changes in discourse structure

The implementation of rule 3 can undergo change in a number of ways. The description of the lot can be taken over by non-verbal or pragmatic means. For example, in the tobacco auctions the buyers are able to pick up the leaves of tobacco off the pile which is being auctioned and buyers therefore provide their own assessment of the lot, as can be seen by the fact that the buyer calls the grade of the tobacco after the sale has been made so that the ticket puller is able to note the grade along with the buyer and sale price on the ticket sitting on top of the pile of tobacco. In wool auctions, tests on the wool are included in the catalogue from which the wool is sold, so again description takes place, but not on the basis of a description by the auctioneer.

The first bid search must always be conducted overtly but a variety of implementations of it exist. In tobacco auctioning, the warehouseman who operates the warehouse in which the tobacco is stored and sold calls a trial first bid whereupon, if there is no bid at that level, the auctioneer runs down the scale of values Dutch-fashion until an opening bid is achieved. In livestock auctions in New Zealand, the auctioneer calls, as a trial opening bid, the value he thinks the lot will fetch and follows straight after with a trial opening bid which is lower by the anticipated bidding range, e.g. *Will anyone give me X $ straight out for em? Well, at (X-Y) $ then.* Here X is the anticipated highest bid and Y is lower by the anticipated bidding range. Bid calling is an obligatory function everywhere. It also varies. In the tobacco auctions it involves the auctioneer chanting numbers. In the wool auctions in New Zealand it involves the buyers bidding verbally both concurrently and, later in the auction, antiphonally. Fine art auctions in the great auction houses such as Sotheby's have bid calling conducted genteelly with various kinds of prosodic ornamentation. For example, some auctioneers bid in doublets with the first bid having a rising intonation and the next a falling one.

Sales are made in a variety of ways, by banging the gavel, by striking the order book in the hand, by banging the herding stick on the rail of a pen of cattle, by intonational means. In some auction traditions, e.g. wool sales, both buyer and sale price are called. In others, e.g. tobacco auctions, only the buyer is called.

It appears, from the above account, that rule 3 is inviolable. All the derived traditions have all its constituents in one form or another. The differences are in the implementations of various constituents. The most ornate changes come about when one constituent is itself implemented by a new rule specific to that tradition. This can be illustrated by the case of the livestock auctions of North Canterbury, New Zealand, where the description of the lot has a discourse structure rule of its own, as has the bid calling:

R4. description → [provenance + number] +[(history) + (preparation) + (potential) + ...]

R5. bid calling → bid call + (bid call + (interpolation))^n + (presale) + (bid call + (interpolation) + (presale))^m + (bid by half + (interpolation) + (presale))^o

The presale constituent is either a formula or prosodic tune used to indicate that the auction may finish at any time after it has been used. Bidding by halves involves changing the nominated increments in which the auction is being conducted to a half of the previous value.

So auctioning traditions are bound to maintain rule 3 but may vary its implementation. They may also augment the discourse grammar by creating new sub-rules which implement subroutines to rule 3.

10.2.5.2 Changes in the formulaic inventory

When sub-rules are created, the formulaic inventory undergoes a consequent differentiation. Recall that all formulae in PEAS were discourse-function specific. They stay that way where the discourse structure rules are augmented. In livestock auctions there are specific formulae to indicate the number of beasts in a pen, e.g. *22 in the line* and other formulae to indicate their provenance, *the property of Mr X from Y*. Specific formulae used as interpolations in the bid calling which re-describe the lot do not recapitulate the formulae used in the lot description phase of the auction. Other formulae are used instead.

A second way formulaic inventories can be altered is by the addition of new formulae and, possibly, the loss of old ones. Recording the loss of old formulae is possible only with long-term recording. However, new formulae appear to be added when one notices a particular formula which is the property of only one auctioneer being taken up by younger auctioneers. The late Alistair Hopkinson, formerly head auctioneer for Pyne Gould Guinness in Canterbury, New Zealand had a number of such formulae and one notices some of them creeping into the auctioning speech of his younger colleagues, e.g. the formula *You can all be in the party*.

A further possible way in which formulae can change is by new tracks appearing in the finite state grammar of a formula. Take, for example, the formula given in figure 10.1. A new track through the formula could be created as in figure 10.2. New tracks can also be created by augmenting the formula through accretion. It seems that some formulae of a tradition are rich in paths and accretions while others have only a single path. It also seems that oral traditions within a spoken formulaic genre

186 *Formulaic Genres*

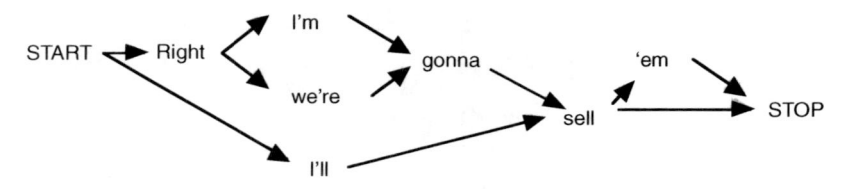

Figure 10.1 Sample formula

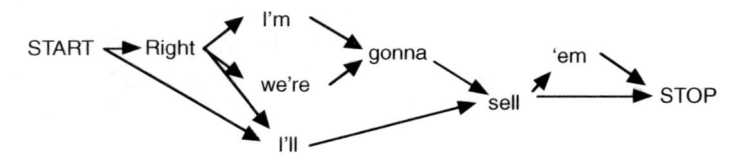

Figure 10.2 A new track through the formula

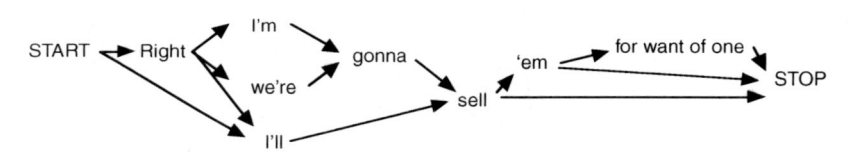

Figure 10.3 Lexical addition to the formula

develop formulae in this way from simple finite state diagrams created by individuals which are then developed in the tradition over the years. The limits on length and path structure will depend on memorability, (i.e. a formula must not become too complex to remember), and functional constraints, (i.e. a formula must not become too big to serve its discourse function economically). Figure 10.3 illustrates the process of lexical addition to formula 1.

10.2.5.3 Changes to prosodic modes[2]

There are many ways in which, if a formulaic genre has specialized intonational patterns, these may change and differentiate over time. For example, a sub-genre may develop specific tunes such as the detour tune used in livestock auctions to signal that bid calling is to be interrupted for an interpolation of some kind, and the end tune which signals that the bidding is about to close (Kuiper & Haggo, 1984:216–19). These are akin to the development of sub-routines in the discourse of the formulaic genre.

Here we will illustrate one interesting development of a highly specialized way of chanting auctions explored by Kuiper & Tillis (1985), namely that of the tobacco auctioneers as recorded in the early 1980s. Tobacco auctions were then conducted in tobacco warehouses all over the tobacco country of the American South. Tobacco was brought in to a warehouse by the grower and packed in a cloth which was placed on the floor of the warehouse and a ticket naming the vendor placed on top. The piles of tobacco were arranged in long rows down the length of the warehouse with enough room between the rows for the auctioneer and his party to walk down one side of the row and the buyers who buy for tobacco companies to walk down the other side of the row.

As a formulaic genre, tobacco auctioning is no different from a number of the formulaic genres discussed in earlier chapters. The auctions have a fixed discourse structure and apart from the chanting of numbers for each bid, the auctioneer speaks in formulae, such as the opening formula *Dance with me, darlins*. Unlike the greeting genres we looked at earlier, however, tobacco auctions are chanted musically and it is this musical tradition which shows an idiosyncratic development. Tobacco auctioneers are not the only performers of formulaic genres who chant, as suggested above. Livestock auctioneers do, and so do singers of oral epics. Tobacco auctioneers have their own chant which is heavily influenced by Afro-American musical traditions. Within this general tradition each auctioneer has his individual family of chants.

Musically the chants have a strong tonal centre, a note to which the auctioneer returns and which is ornamented by various departures. The musical scale used for the chant is essentially pentatonic. The rhythm is often syncopated with speech patterns being used to provide the syncopation. The melodic range normally encompasses a major sixth while major and minor thirds and seconds are also prevalent. All of these musical characteristics of the tobacco auctioneer's chanting are shared with the chants of Afro-American church ministers and leaders of congregational singing and camp meetings. Yet all the auctioneers I recorded in the early 1980s were white. Typical chants of three tobacco auctioneers are given in figure 10.4.

The answer to the question of how tobacco auctions came to sound the way they did has to be sought in the way in which the tobacco auctioning genre evolved. Since many auctions are chanted, particularly rapid ones, one can presume that when the auctioning genre was transported to the USA, some such auctions may also have been chanted.

Figure 10.4 The chants of three tobacco auctioneers

Tobacco auctioning began in the mid nineteenth century, well after auctioning traditions had been established in the USA. Tobacco auctioning is also rapid, with a lot being sold on average every three seconds, and auctioneers selling for around six hours a day. Tobacco warehouses in which the tobacco was sold in the mid nineteenth century had a labour force consisting almost entirely of Afro-American workers and 'visitors entering one of the huge dusty tobacco factories of the slave country noticed first of all the chant of the Negro spirituals which filled the dusty air' (Robert, 1967:86). Since the 'home' chant of the tobacco warehouses was Afro-American, the chant of the tobacco auctioneers became Afro-American, creating a creolized chant. The strong tonal centre which is characteristic of all auction chanting is present also in Afro-American musical traditions. Only the syncopated rhythms and ornamentation have to be added to provide the contemporary chant of the tobacco auctioneer.

10.3 Conclusion

Because auctioning is an oral formulaic genre, it is not only possible to reconstruct central aspects of the English auction tradition, but also to show how the changes in the tradition are constrained by it. The changes in the discourse structure are constrained by the necessity to maintain the central rule of the English tradition and by the fact that the rule is the kind of rewrite rule which allows for sub-rules to implement particular discourse constituents. Because formulae are long-lived and because they are discourse function-specific, some of them appear to have come down through the centuries relatively unchanged. The changes that do take place are constrained by the fact that formulae are finite state units which allow for lexical accretion and path augmentation. Even the historical changes in prosodic modes appear to be constrained by the tradition in allowing only implementations of the drone and shout modes to change but not the basic character of the modes themselves.

10.4 Methodological epilogue: collecting historically relevant data

The historical analysis of formulaic genres, as in all other study of formulaic genres, requires data collection. That data collection has to be informed by at least some prior knowledge of the history of the genre. I knew that certain auctioning traditions could be traced back to England. Colonial exportation of these traditions was likely to have taken place since the English colonial expansion brought so many traditions with it. Recording auctions in the various places that Doug Haggo and I did then confirmed that there were strong family resemblances in the various commodity auctions in the US, Canada, England and New Zealand. We supposed that these resemblances were the result of the common origins of the traditions and that the differences were the result of the idiosyncratic developments of those traditions in various places and in various commodity markets. On the strength of this rather obvious hypothesis, we would suppose that you could go elsewhere in the English-speaking world and look at other commodity markets and corroborate these hypotheses, documenting in increasing detail, if that is what you wanted to do, what is traditional and what is unique about each tradition. With the introduction of on-line auctions, for example, it is interesting to see how the common features of the English tradition have found their way into the on-line forms of auctioning (Boyd, 2001).

So how many places do you have to visit and how much recording must you do to corroborate a hypothesis? Sample size is again determined by purpose. Suppose you were studying a particular commodity market, such as real estate, in one country. You could travel around recording house auctions in major centres. You would likely find that the practices differed slightly from city to city. The transmission of oral traditions is a function of an apprenticeship system and, so long as auctioneers do not move from place to place in the country you are studying, you would be able to do a sociolinguistic regional geography of the genrelect of real estate auctions. Ten or twenty auctions by a single auctioneer is often sufficient to provide quite a good sketch of their individual style. But individual auctioneers have idiolects in their genre, so you would need to record a number of auctioneers from the same place. Auctioneers can also have house styles related to the company for which they are selling, so some control for that would have to be considered. The reason I mention these complications is that every formulaic genre has its own traditions and, consequently, its own complications. You need to get familiar with a formulaic genre tradition before you collect historical or comparative data.

Collecting old recordings is a matter of luck. There are archives of old recordings of various kinds. Folklorists sometimes have such collections, as do broadcasting outlets, particularly state-run ones. The old recordings I used to trace the history of race calling came from the latter source by way of Reon Murtha who thought I might be interested in them. As far as the size of the data set of old recordings goes, you are limited by whatever people chose to record and to archive. Sometimes this can be scanty but scanty evidence is better than no evidence at all. That being so, it is better first to see what you can find before you decide which formulaic genre you want to study the history of.

11
Volitional Variation: Humour and Formulae[1]

> Conventional, formulaic, and memorized expressions of all kinds play a large role in language play and linguistic creativity. The innumerable phrases known to fellow speakers are alluded to, toyed with, and varied just a little for emphasis and effect. Such phrases arise within families, organizations and groups of all kinds. Humorists and cartoonists draw on them constantly and journalists rely on them as 'eye catchers' in their story titles.
>
> (Van Lancker, 1987:103)

11.1 Introduction

Chapter 1 suggested that in contrast to single word lexical items which have word structure, phrasal lexical items have phrase structure. For example, *dog-eared* is a compound adjective and therefore a word while *a dog's breakfast* is a lexicalized phrase. Phrasal lexical items, as we saw in chapter 1, not only appear in formulaic genres but make an appearance in almost all text, written or oral. Like all lexical items, phrasal lexical items are coined at a particular point in time and may come to be lexicalized when some use is found for them. It might be that they express a complex predicate such as, for example, *make allowances for*, or that they perform a useful social role, such as, for example, *Make sure you....* Unlike single word coinages, however, potential phrasal coinages occur almost every time someone constructs a new phrase or clause since any phrase which is uttered is potentially a new phrasal lexical item.[2] Creativity in terms of the coinage of new phrasal lexical items is, therefore, hard to study. As Noam Chomsky has tirelessly pointed out, speakers are being creative every time they put a new phrase or sentence together. However, that creativity is not in itself intentional.

If we make a distinction between intentional and unintentional creativity then there are certainly coinages which are intended to be creative. In domains such as new product onomastics, slogan and pop song lyric writing, it may be possible to discern an intent to be creative. Frequently, this is manifest in the coined word or phrase(s) being repeated so many times by its creator(s) that it becomes lexicalized, sometimes reposing in our mental lexica like a skipping CD. John Lennon's *Give peace a chance* and MacDonalds' *You deserve a break today* or *I'm lovin' it* come, regrettably, to mind.

In this chapter another form of lexical creativity will be explored, namely the creativity which takes an existing lexical item and performs an operation on it which is not conventionally permitted. Lexical items, since they are stored and retrieved from the mental lexicon, generate stable expectations on the part of their users as to what may conventionally be done with and to them. *Finnegan's Wake* shows that these stable expectations may be tampered with in a variety of ways. Such word play involves a form of intentional lexical creativity.

This chapter is an exploration of the genre of cartoons in which phrasal lexical items (PLIs) and formulae play a central role in being artistically deformed.

11.2 Potential for word play in PLIs

Chapter 1 provided an account of the properties of PLIs which may be idiosyncratic. These are rigidities of various kinds and thus can be potentially a source of 'artistic deformation' (Mel'čuk, 1995).[3] Such deformation is local in space and time. Therefore the deformation of PLIs has a unique creative aspect, as being local, it is normally context-dependent. For example, subeditors who create headlines based on PLIs normally use the particular changes once only.

The approach taken in this chapter builds on the description of PLIs in chapter 1 and then explores which of them are further available for humorous manipulation. Then we will see how one cartoonist actually does manipulate them. Cartoons are a complex genre involving both images and words. Where they involve formulae, they are a formulaic genre of a kind. This approach is thus theory-driven as compared with studies which provide taxonomies of humour based on the study of examples (Alexander, 1997; Chiaro, 1992).

In order to drive the study from its origins in the linguistic resources of the phrasal lexicon, it is necessary first to understand what the relevant properties of PLIs are. In the following discussion it will be supposed that each PLI is a lexical item with its own entry in the mental lexicon of a speaker who knows it. Such knowledge is potentially complex. Furthermore, not all native speakers of a language who know a particular phrasal lexical item will necessarily know it in exactly the same way, i.e. some will know it as having properties which other speakers will not (Fraser, 1970; Mel'čuk, 1995); but for every speaker there must be the mental equivalent of what Naciscone (2001) terms the item's *base form*. Without such a base form a number of the kinds of creative lexical play could not be recognized. That they are, corroborates the claim that PLIs have base forms.

This leads to two more observations. The first is that a speaker must know the PLI in order to be able to perceive 'artistic deformation' of it. That seems obvious but it needs saying. All intentional deformation has as its intent that a perceiver perceive the difference(s) between the base form and its variant. That can only happen if the perceiver knows the item and its base form. For this reason many second language learners cannot perceive such lexical play since they do not know the items on which it is based. I shall term this *the accessibility condition*.

The second observation is that, if the base form of a PLI is to be recognizable perceptually, then, after artistic deformation there must remain sufficient perceptual cues to allow the item to be recognized. I shall term this *the recoverability condition*.

11.2.1   Creative artistic deformation of PLIs

So which of the properties of phrasal lexical items which were enumerated in chapter 1 is available for artistic deformation?[4] Since these items have syntactic structure, that may be deformed by, for instance, adding a modifier where conventionally the PLI is not permitted to take such modifiers. For example, the phrase *as scarce as hen's teeth* cannot have the modifier *red* added before *hen* or the word *white* before *teeth* however appropriate these adjectives might otherwise be. The semantic properties of a PLI may be independently deformed. For example, a lexicalized constituent of a PLI may be semantically ambiguous in the general case but have only one reading in the PLI. The PLI may be re-contextualized in such a way that the other reading becomes accessible. In many instances, however, both kinds of deformation may occur together. A pun created by the substitution of a homophone for a lexicalized constituent of a PLI has both structural and semantic affects. As Chiaro (1992) suggests, many of these kinds of deformation are closely paralleled by kinds of slips of the tongue.[5] The leading hypothesis of what follows is that, in general, artistic deformation will be of this kind.

11.2.1.1 Phonological deformation

It is possible to create phonological deformation through substitution and exchanges in the same way as these are found in slips of the tongue. Spoonerisms are a classic example in which the onsets of stressed syllables are exchanged.

11.2.1.2 Structural deformation

(a) Lexicalized constituent substitution. Lexicalized constituents might be substituted for. For example, the clause *It takes a thief to catch a thief* might have the word *cop* substituted for *thief*. Recall that a crucial aspect of such deformation, as with all the other processes to be outlined below, is that the original PLI must still be identifiable or else the deformation is not identifiable as such. For example, if one substituted the word *bus* for the word *cake* in the PLI *to take the cake* then the original PLI would not be accessed by any hearer, whereas if the word *biscuit* were substituted and the PLI was used in a context where the speaker's intent that the phrase should be taken as an expression of astonishment was clear, the substitution could then be seen as a kind of lexical play. That rests on the fact that *biscuit* and *cake* are co-hyponyms whereas *bus* has no relationship with the PLI's lexicalized constituent *cake* for which it has been substituted. In this regard, puns can be seen as being of two kinds; either a lexical substitution of a homonym (homophone or homograph) has taken place, or a non-conventional sense of a polysemous lexicalized constituent within a PLI has been accessed. I will suppose that, in every case, some preferred sense or lexical item has been substituted for the one in the PLI. There are clearly complexities here that have to do with the accessing of lexical items and word senses in the mental lexicon. Since this chapter deals with the way in which the properties of PLIs are utilized, such complexities will be ignored.

Substituting for a bound word would normally yield a freely formed phrase since the rest of the phrase would give no clue that the word substituted for was a bound word. For example, if one substituted the word *offence* for *umbrage*, *take umbrage at* would not be recoverable. Hence such a form of lexical substitution is unlikely in the kind of lexical creativity under discussion here.

The same holds for addition to a lexical selection set. Such a creative addition can essentially be seen as a lexical substitution for all the members of the set. Here again the recoverability of the PLI may be impaired. For example, if one substituted *equilibrium* for *cool/rag/temper* in *to lose one's cool/rag/temper* the PLI would not be recoverable. But of one substituted *cloth*, there is potential recoverability on the basis of the fact that *rag* is unilaterally idiomatic in this PLI and in its literal sense it is semantically closely related to *cloth*. That allows for recoverability of *rag* in the appropriate context.

Optional lexicalized constituents provide little opportunity for artistic deformation since any lexical substitution in an optional constituent would likely lead to it being read as a normal adjunct.

Lexical substitution may be further examined in terms of the characteristics of the lexicalized constituent and what is substituted for it. A number of characteristics of the word might be similar or related. For example, they might rhyme or be synonyms. Since restricted collocation is a kind of minimal idiosyncrasy for a PLI, substituting for either of the words which are involved in such a collocation is likely to be perceived as non native-like selection (Pawley & Syder, 1983). For example, the substitution of *accept* for *take* in the PLI *take offence* would probably not be taken as a form of artistic deformation. A native speaker would generally know that the conventionally prescribed verb is *take* and so recoverability can be maintained.

(b) Lexical exchanges. Some PLIs allow for words of the same syntactic category to be exchanged. For example the proverb *A bird in the hand is worth two in the bush* might have its nouns exchanged to read *A bird in the bush is worth two in the hand*.

(c) Violating slot restrictions. While filling in, say, a noun phrase in an open slot in a PLI would not yield anything remarkable, breaching arbitrary slot restrictions in a PLI would. Consider, for example, the PLI *take NP to task*. The noun phrase slot has the conventional restriction that it can only be a human NP. If one inserted an inanimate NP, say, *the rock*, this would be akin to the violation of a selectional restriction. In other cases, slots are restricted in terms of co-reference. Many possessive PLIs have arbitrary restrictions on their antecedent co-referent. For example, in *get NP's goat* the goat which is being got must not be co-referential with the subject of the verb *get*. So the sentence *Andrea got her goat* cannot be read as involving the subject of the PLI in question.

(d) Modifying unmodifiable PLIs. If a PLI is conventionally unmodifiable then modifying it can be done as a form of artistic deformation. For example indicating that someone is *a moderately bad egg* could be seen as a form of artistic deformation.

(e) Transforming inflexible PLIs. One could also transform an inflexible PLI provided the recoverability condition was met. For example, in a context where it was clear that the death of a person was involved, one could indicate that *the bucket was kicked by old uncle Maurice* which involves passivizing *kick the bucket*, a PLI that is conventionally unable to be passivized. But if one clefts *take for granted* as in *Granted for he certainly was not taken* then the resulting construction is barely recognizable as a form of *take for granted* and thus on the border of irrecoverability.

(f) **Blending two PLIs.** Sometimes two PLIs are semantically related and this allows for them to be blended. For example, *cross that bridge when NP come(s) to it* and *burn NP's bridges* can be blended *to burn that bridge when NP comes to it*.

(g) **Foregrounding structural ambiguity.** PLIs can be syntactically ambiguous (Alexander, 1997). However, conventionally, only one of the possible readings is normally available. In such a case the ambiguity may be foregrounded by artistic deformation. For example, the PLI *hail-fellow-well-met* is conventionally used as a pre-nominal modifier. But if it were written *Hail, fellow. Well met*, then an alternative parsing of the phrase would have been foregrounded without the form of words being altered.

Not all of these options are mutually exclusive. It is possible to perform both a lexical substitution and transform an inflexible PLI at the same time. Some of the humour illustrated below shows multiple structural deformations.

11.2.1.3 *Semantic deformation*

(a) **Literalizing of idiomatic readings.** PLIs may be idiomatic in whole or in part. Various means are available to bring to mind the literal sense of either one of the lexicalized constituents which is conventionally metaphorical or of the whole PLI (Alexander, 1997). For example, the PLI *raining cats and dogs* can have attention drawn to its literal meaning by lexical substitution as in *raining moggies and hounds*. Speaking of his intimations of the whereabouts of Brünhilde, Siegried could say, *A little bird told me* which, in Wagner's opera, is literally the case, a little bird did tell Siegfried where Brünhilde was. Being a rather simple soul, Siegfried did not mean that he wished not to disclose the source of his knowledge, which is what the figurative meaning of the idiom imports. Such literalizing is a function of substitution under the analysis conducted here. Usually, if a lexicalized constituent is a metaphor and is literalized the whole PLI is then also re-parsed in a literal sense.

(b) **Pun on a constituent lexeme.** PLIs often contain lexemes which are polysemous but which in the PLI have only one reading. By providing a targeted context the unconventional sense can be foregrounded.

Conventionally *being left speechless* involves being bereft of speech but a speaker who has left his or her notes behind is also left speechless since the word *speech* is ambiguous as between the power to speak and a public address.

Puns, as suggested above, can be forced through the use of homonyms in lexical substitutions. For instance, by substituting the word *soul* for the word *sole* one can indicate that an elderly jazz singer is the soul survivor of a group. Such puns are common in newspaper word play (Alexander, 1997; Cowie, 1991, 1998).

The relationships between structural and semantic deformation are not mutually exclusive. While a structural deformation may not have a semantic effect, it often will, particularly in cases where the intent is to create humour.

11.3 Tonsorial onomastics

The volitional variation of formulae can be illustrated initially from an unlikely source. Hairdressers in New Zealand have a tendency to name their salons in punning ways. For example, one salon is named *Streaks Ahead*. The idiom on which this name is based is, of course, *streets ahead*, meaning 'in advance of', 'better than'. Some hairdressers will put colour streaks in hair and *ahead* has been punned on by the re-analysis giving *a head*. The original meaning of the idiom is also drawn on to suggest that the salon is better than its competitors.

Another salon is called *Hair Today*. The pun here relies on the fact that, in New Zealand English, the diphthongs in *here* and *hair* are merging making *here* and *hair* homophones. So *hair today* sounds just like *here today*. But if one performs a cloze test on *here today* then the rest of the formula is *and gone tomorrow* which is what happens to your hair when you go to the hairdresser. *In Hair, Hair 'n' Beyond* and *Here for Hair* make use of the same diphthongal merger to create a pun while *Ahead of Hair* makes use of the re-analysis option.

Then there is *Hair Port* where the pun relies on the fact that, in some dialects of English the initial *h* is dropped, giving *airport*. *Making Waves* probably does perms. Here the figure of speech is the literal use of a figurative expression, a literalization, as is *Cut Loose*. *Shylock's Hairdressers* is again based on a re-analysis pun.

There are other communities of practice which also indulge in this kind of word play. Newspaper subeditors commonly do so (Cowie, 1998). It is evident that the hairdressers of New Zealand have particular preferences for the way they pun for effect. They like the merger of the diphthongs in *here* and *hair* and they like the re-analysis option. How should we deal with this kind of volitional variation? One way is to look at the work of one artistic deformer in detail.

11.4 Word play in a corpus of cartoons by Cathy Wilcox

While all of the options in section 11.2 appear to be available, it is not necessarily the case that all are equally likely to lead to humour or that, even when they are, a humorist will be equally drawn to all. Particular humorists may prefer some kinds of deformation to others. What follows aims at two goals. The first is to illustrate how an artist might use artistic deformation of PLIs for humorous effect. In place of an inductive approach this will be done deductively by allowing the analysis to proceed in a resource-based way from the above possibilities for artistic deformation. The second is to provide a model of the way in which a particular humorist exploits the resources of the phrasal lexicon. The leading hypothesis is that such exploitation differs from one humorist to another and from one medium to another. We would suppose that Cathy Wilcox's cartoon art differs in this respect from that of Giles or Gary Larson and that the humour of Wallace and Gromit differs from that of the Muppet Show.

Cathy Wilcox is an award-winning Australian cartoonist whose work is to be found in the *Sydney Morning Herald* and *The Age*. The data for this study is the complete set of cartoons from her first collection (Wilcox, 1991). Only those cartoons were selected where there was clear reference to one or more PLIs and then those where such reference was evident were coded for the various artistic deformations that they had undergone. Cartooning is a medium which has its own potential for PLI humour in that the PLI must normally be in a caption, in the balloon text of the characters, or both, while the drawing can shed a contextual light on the text(s). There is a substantial tradition of word play in cartoons. *Punch* and the *New Yorker* both publish cartoons of this kind. In one *New Yorker* cartoon two men are sitting behind identical desks facing one another on opposite sides of an otherwise featureless office. One says to the other, *One day you will be sitting where I am now sitting*. Conventionally this PLI is used by a senior member of an institutional hierarchy to a junior member of the same hierarchy as a way of indicating that the junior is on his way up the institutional ladder. However the featureless office invites the statement to be taken literally and, since one cannot see any difference between the situation of the two men, to examine the nature of promotion. On the front cover of *Punch* a doctor is writing a script for a Japanese patient who is dressing behind a screen. The doctor says, *It's all right, Mr Hayakawa. I'll just give you something to open your bowels.* Mr Hayakawa has just produced a samurai sword and appears to be going to commit harakiri. In both cases a PLI is being literalized.

The Wilcox corpus consists of 240 PLIs of which 90 contain reference to one or more PLIs. The rest also involve humour based on varieties of word play but these lie outside the scope of this chapter; see table 11.1.

11.4.1 Phonological deformation

There are four cases of phonological deformation in the data in table 11.1. Three involve exchanges. In one a dog is leaning on a crutch and the caption reads *The leaning piece of towser* where the exchange source is *the leaning Tower of Pisa*. In the other, one cow is saying to the other, *I am just a tense simmental fool* where the exchange source is *I'm just a sentimental fool*. In a third an approaching ocean liner named HMS Pinafore is hailed from a small boat with the words, *Your ship is slowing*. This last exchange is a Spoonerism. Phonological addition occurs in a cartoon showing a cow on a hillside with a caption reading *A ruminant with a view*. This latter case can also be seen as a lexical substitution, in which case it is a malapropism. The next set involves structural deformation (and possible attendant semantic effects).

11.4.2 Lexical substitutions

Of the 90 cartoons containing a PLI, 53 contained one or more substitutions for a total of 72 substitutions; see table 11.2. One of the more ingenious cases of substitution is a cartoon showing a mother, father and small child around the dinner table. The caption is *Nuclear family*. The child asks, *What's for DNA?* Here the substitution is the acronym *DNA* for the word *dinner*. In Australian English these are close to homophonous. The mother replies, *You're just like your father*, picking up the DNA substitution and producing an ambiguity as to whether the

Table 11.1 Number of PLIs per cartoon

Number of PLIs	Instances
1 per cartoon	73
2 per cartoon	14
3 per cartoon	3
Total number of PLIs	110

Table 11.2 Substitutions within a PLI

Number of substitutions/cartoon	Instances	% of substitutions
single substitution	39	73.6
double substitution	10	18.9
triple substitution	3	5.7
quadruple substitution	1	1.9
Total number of substitutions	72	
Total number of cartoons containing substitutions	53	

child has the same DNA as his father or whether that is what the father always asks at dinner time. I take it that the word *nuclear* in the PLI *nuclear family* has the conventional sense 'parents plus children' but has been substituted for by the word *nuclear* with the sense 'pertaining to the cell nucleus'.[6]

Lexical substitutions also allow for an examination of the relationship between the original word and its substitute. Here the relationship was usually homonymous. Where the substitute was also a homophone, there is a clear case of punning. Where the phonological relationship is close, i.e. the words are paronyms (Attardo, 1994), the closeness allows for the recoverability condition to be met thus producing a near pun; see table 11.3.

A typical example of lexical substitution involving a phonological relationship is a cartoon in which the male protagonist says, *What say we burn some hedges?* The substitution here is *hedges* for *bridges*. Both words are disyllabic and they share the coda of their first syllable and all of their second syllable. The female protagonist then says, *Sterling idea,*

Table 11.3 Relationship between the lexical items

Type of relationship	Instances	% of insertions
homonymy	39	54.2
homophony	39	54.2
homography & homophony	26	36.1
homography only	0	0
paronymy	21	29.2
co-hyponymy	2	2.8
antonymy	1	1.4
same semantic/pragmatic field	1	1.4
syntactic	2	2.8
none	6	8.3

alerting us to the ambiguity of *hedge* as between a physical entity and a financial institution.

Homophony without homography is found in cases such as a cartoon where two men are on board a speeding boat. One says, *I'm afraid I've thrown away the bits that slow us down.* The other replies, *Them's the brakes.* Semantic relationships are created when a substitute is, for example, a converse, as in a cartoon showing the start of a race at a dog track where one hound says to the other, *This is where the buck starts.*

Syntactic relationships occur in these cartoons when one pronoun is substituted for another, as in a case where *your* is substituted for by *my* in the Muir and Nordenesque Mae West misquotation, *Is that a gun in my socket or are you just pleased to seize me?* which shows a soldier placing the muzzle of a rifle in the speaker's eye.

In some cases, for example where there are PLI blends, the substitutions have no individual relationship. Here the relationship often arises from the context. For example a dog is scratching itself and the caption reads *Scratch and smell.* Here the PLI target is the game of chance *Scratch and win.*

11.4.3 Lexical exchanges

Five of the 90 cartoons contain exchanges. Two of these are lexical. In one, one sheep says to the other, *Do you know 'Click go the shears'?* The other replies, *No, but if you baa a few hums...* where the exchange source is *hum a few bars*. In another, two dogs are bemoaning the state of urban living. One says to the other, *This dog's going to the country*. Here the exchange source is *This country is going to the dogs*; see table 11.4.

11.4.4 Violating slot restrictions

There are three cases which can be interpreted this way. The phrasal verb *let NP out*, when its complement is a domestic pet means, that the pet is to be allowed/made to leave the house; when its slot is a garment it means that the garment is to be made larger. In the cartoon the husband,

Table 11.4 Exchanges

Type	Instances
Spoonerism	1
syllabic exchanges	2
lexical exchanges	2
Total exchanges	5

in bed with his wife with a large cat sitting on the bed, asks, *Didn't you let that cat out?* The wife replies, *No dear, I just bought a bigger one.* The phrasal verb *NP go off* has two sets of slot restrictions; if the NP is food then it means the food has become unfit to eat and smells; if it is an explosive then it means that the explosive has exploded. The cartoon shows a woman bending over a fish. She sniffs and says, *I think this fish has gone off.* In the next frame the fish has exploded and her face and hands are covered with black soot.

11.4.5 Adding a modifier where none is conventionally permitted

No cases were found.

11.4.6 Transforming a frozen PLI

One case only occurs where the one hound says to the other, *This is where the buck starts.* The canonical form of the source PLI is *The buck stops here.*

11.4.7 PLI blends

There were four PLI blends. In one *The Lone Ranger* was blended with *loan shark* to make *The lone shark.* In another *The Bermuda triangle* was blended with *Bermuda shorts* to give *The Bermuda shorts.*

Figure 11.1 Cartoon by Cathy Wilcox

11.4.8 Structural re-analysis

There are nine cases where a non-conventional structural representation of a PLI is foregrounded. *The Queen's English* comes up for re-analysis in a cartoon in which the lady says, *I was taught the Queen's English.* Her disreputable-looking male interlocutor replies, *I already knew she was.* The following cases involve semantic deformation (much arising from structural deformation).

11.4.9 Literalizing the sense of a metaphor within a PLI

There are seven cases of punning using this device. At a bar the gentleman asks the lady, *What do you do for a crust?* The lady replies, *Eat out the soft bit.* Note that literalizing one word in a PLI usually involves reparsing the meaning of the whole PLI.

11.4.10 Literalizing the sense of a figurative PLI

There are eighteen such cases. In many cases where an individual substitution has taken place the reading of the whole PLI has become literal. A brain surgeon holding up the whole of a brain says to an assistant, *This is the stuff that dreams are made of.* A man delivering a box of underpants to a prison says to the guard at the gate, *200 pairs of Y fronts for maximum security, Sir.*

11.4.11 Calques and other paraphrases

There is one ingenious case of a loan translated PLI. The lady asks an academic-looking gentleman, *Do you speak Latin?* The gentleman replies, *Pontifex catholicus est?* the latter being a loan translation of *Is the pope a Catholic?* In another cartoon, the PLI *rose-tinted glasses/spectacles* is paraphrased as *pink contact lenses.*

11.4.12 Pragmatic incongruity

Many PLIs have conventional conditions of use, i.e. these are formulae, and these conditions can be foregrounded by placing the PLI in an unconventional context. For example, under the caption *Humane lobster cooking* a chef is looking into a boiling pan saying, *I hear what you're saying.* Many other cartoons also show unconventional contexts alongside other verbal deformation. In one cartoon a hunter in a pith helmet and holding a gun asks a lion, *Why won't you talk to me?* The lion replies, *You've hurt my pride.* The pun on *pride* exists alongside the pragmatic incongruity of a hunter asking a lion why the lion won't talk to him. The pragmatic incongruity is partly occasioned by the pun to come.

11.4.13 Inferred PLIs

In some measure any PLI which has been artistically deformed must be inferred and accessed from the mental lexicon on the basis of what is left of it after the deformation. However, in the majority of cartoons a PLI is directly quoted in whole or in part. Occasionally, however, the PLI must be largely inferred in that it is not stated, just hinted at. There are four such cases among the PLIs found in the cartoons. In one ingenious case one snake says to the other, which has a large bulge in its middle and a dummy in its mouth, *Spit it out, Bill, that's only the garnish*. The only word of the PLI *spit the dummy* which is overt is *spit*. The dummy is in the picture and the baby, which once sucked the dummy, must be inferred to be the bulge in Bill's middle and which is therefore the main course that has the garnish. In the Bermuda shorts cartoon above, the word *triangle* in the PLI *the Bermuda triangle* must be inferred from the fact that the wife has lost her husband in his Bermuda shorts. The contextual real word 'knowledge' that things disappear without trace in the Bermuda triangle has to be brought to bear to make this inference.[7]

11.5 Conclusion

It is clear that Cathy Wilcox has a preference for puns and near puns over other forms of artistic deformation. Since puns are a function of substitutions, this is borne out by the fact that the total number of substitutions (given that there can be more than one per cartoon) is almost as large as the total number of cartoons under analysis and that more than half of the cartoons contain substitutions. That is not to say that Wilcox is unaware of the other avenues for deformation. This is evidenced by the fact that the only deformation device unrepresented in the data is where a modifier is added where none is conventionally permitted. Given the long list of potential sources of deformation, it is noteworthy that so many of them can be used humorously.

Looking at table 11.5, the selective preferences Wilcox demonstrates in this dataset of 90 cartoons are evident. This provides a comparison against which other cartoonists who work with PLIs might be compared. Note that, since a given PLI can undergo more than one of these processes, the index is calculated in terms of the number of cases that appear per PLI in the data. Lexical creativity can therefore be seen to manifest itself not only on each occasion that a cartoonist produces a new cartoon involving lexical play but also by the personal set of preferences for certain kinds of creativity.

Table 11.5 The PLI deformation signature of Cathy Wilcox

Type of deformation	Instances	Type/PLI
substitutions	72	.655
literalization of a PLI	18	.163
structural ambiguity	9	.081
literalization of a lexical sense	7	.063
phonological	4	.036
PLI blends	4	.036
slot restriction violations	3	.027
lexical exchanges	2	.018
calques and paraphrases	2	.018
frozenness violation	1	.009

11.6 Artistry and artistic deformation

The conclusions above are fine as far as they go, but that is not far enough. Artistic deformation, i.e. intentional changes to the stable expectations arising from the idiosyncratic properties of PLIs in the mental lexicon, do not quite give us enough sense of the artistry which a fine cartoonist like Cathy Wilcox displays. Here we are drawing on the kind of distinction between *performance* used in the Chomskian sense and *performance* in the sense of Bauman (1975). A sense of artistry is essentially qualitative and not all artistic deformation is qualitatively alike. Such quality is not easy to analyse in linguistic terms and, furthermore, to do so is quite often to do violence to the intuitive sense one has with many of Wilcox's cartoons that the cartoonist is doing something which is really clever. Analysis can also be seen as 'brushing the bloom off the butterfly'.

Another instance, shown in figure 11.2, will perhaps suffice to show what is meant here. In a hold-up with a hostage the PLI *hand over the...or the...gets it* is conventionally understood to mean that the addressee should hand over the money, diamonds etc to the speaker, the man with the gun, or else the hostage will be shot. In the cartoon, a mother is the addressee and her small son is the hostage. By uttering a second PLI to her son the mother uncovers a multiple ambiguity in the PLI which it does not conventionally have. Conventionally *hand something over* in this case is taken to mean hand it over to the robber. That is what the phrase appears to mean here. But there are three participants: robber, hostage and person being held up. The phrase could therefore be taken as an instruction to hand the cash over to the hostage.

206 Formulaic Genres

Figure 11.2 Cartoon by Cathy Wilcox

Conventionally the phrase *so and so gets it* means that the hostage will be shot or killed. But if the cash is to be handed over, then structurally *the kid gets it* could be an alternative to handing it over to the robber since the two clauses are connected by *or*. Since the mother would, naturally, prefer her small son to get her money rather than the robber, she exhorts her lad not to spend all her money at once. Here the second PLI, *Don't spend it all at once*, is used to expose the structural ambiguity of the first PLI. This is, clearly, a clever and creative use of the two PLIs, but it is also totally unexpected. One expects a mother to want to protect her son who has a pistol aimed at his head. One does not expect him to be exhorted to fiscal responsibility at such a time. It is this element of surprise and delight which comes from 'making it new', in the sense of seeing a hackneyed scenario and its attendant language anew through its creative deformation, that gives one a sense of real artistry.

Notes

1 What are Formulaic Genres?

1. This example is taken from Kuiper & Tan (1989).
2. Parents are not invariably mentioned.
3. Note too that, while this is the house style of *The Times*, *The Daily Telegraph* follows the same house style.
4. This section is based on the work of Kuiper & Haggo (1985).
5. The data and observations below are based on commentaries of televised National Hockey League games. The NHL is the premier ice hockey competition in North America, with teams from both Canada and the USA competing. The NHL season finishes with the playoffs, the winning team receiving the Stanley Cup.
6. This section is taken from Kuiper (2007).
7. In German these are termed *unikale Komponenten* (Soehn, 2003).
8. Bakhtin (1986:68).
9. *Christchurch Press*, Friday, 25 June 2002.

2 A Day at the Races

1. I take the definition of ritual to be a 'formal procedure of a communicative but arbitrary kind, having the effect of regularizing a social situation' (Firth, 1972:3). There are anthropologists who view all rituals as being religious (Rappaport, 1999). In societies where religion plays a significant role that may be so. However in essentially secular societies there are still rituals of the Firthian variety. These may also be significant in the way suggested by Wilson when she says that, '[r]ituals reveal values at their deepest level...men express in ritual what moves them most, and since the form of expression is conventionalized and obligatory, it is the values of the group that are revealed. (Wilson, 1954:241). It may also, conversely, be that '[t]he only cultural values that rituals transmit are rituals' (Staal, 1990:123). I take it that this is a matter of looking at particular rituals and their place in a society. In this study I look at a vernacular ritual in a society of which I am a native.
2. Harness racing involves a horse pulling a sulkie on which the driver sits. There are two kinds of harness race, trotting and pacing, depending on the gait of the horse.
3. We will see later that this name may be apposite.
4. Strappers are employees of the training stable where a racehorse spends its non-racing days. Strappers exercise the horse, feed it and groom it. In English racing parlance they are called 'lads' (regardless of their gender).
5. Fortune's wheel as a topos goes back at least to Herodotus (Robinson, 1946). It is alluded to in Chaucer and Shakespeare and finds contemporary form in the proverb *What goes round comes round*.

6. 'Tis a manly thing to bear bad fortune lightly' (Accius, 140 BC).
7. Formulae will be given without opening and closing punctuation. X is a variable representing the name of a horse.
8. It also needs to be noted that, for much of the race, the distance from the rail is more difficult to assess since the field is more or less perpendicular to the caller.
9. Horses 'break up' in harness races when they lose their trotting or pacing step. This can be dangerous because their loss of rhythm then often interferes with the running of other horses, who may trip and fall.
10. Cat fancy involves 'showing' pedigree cats at cat shows.
11. See, for example, Kuiper (1996).
12. In the case of *The Times* engagement notices analysed in chapter 1, 100 seemed a nice round number to deal both with constant features and variation such as it was.

3 Forecasting the Weather

1. This chapter is based on Hickey (1991) and Hickey & Kuiper (2000).
2. For accounts of other forecasting traditions see Crystal (1995:385) and Wray (2002:79–83).
3. Although there are female forecasters at the Met. Office, only male forecasters appeared on the National Programme at the time of this study.
4. The following notation applies to the rules used in this chapter:

    \\: Items enclosed in reverse slashes may be repeated up to three times. In most cases different phrases must be used on each repeat.

    [ ]: Items enclosed in square brackets may be in any order.

    Numerals: When identical items occur more than once in a rule and are accompanied by numerals, only one of the items may be chosen.

    *: Phrases which are not in the MOG are indicated by a preceding asterisk.

    +: Items which are adaptations of phrases from MOG are preceded by a plus sign.

5. Only one of these finite state diagrams is given here by way of illustration although many of the weather forecasting formulae can be similarly represented.
6. This information about the training of forecasters was provided by Peter Lechner of the New Zealand Meteorological Service.

4 Polite Genres in a Multilingual Community: Greeting and Eating in Singapore

1. An earlier version of this chapter appeared in Kuiper & Tan (1989).
2. Strategy 15 is to be incomplete or use ellipsis, i.e. not being direct by not saying fully what you intend.
3. Negative politeness involves ways of making it up to the hearer that you are wanting them to do something which constrains their own preferred activities.

5 Playing a False Part: Projecting and Perceiving Fraudulent Identities on the Internet

1. The research reported in this chapter was conducted with Georgie Columbus. An earlier version of part of this chapter has appeared in Kuiper & Newsome (2006).
2. The term 'error' is being used here as a shorthand for 'non-native linguistic usage' (Richards, 1974). Individual cases of 'errors' may also be usages in native but non Anglo-American varieties of English. The crucial matter is to see these usages as contrasting with those of the recipients of the e-mail in the 'west' and thus as projections of 'foreignness'.
3. A quick web search for this exact phrase on Google revealed that the *only* use of this phrase on the internet was either this letter (by varying authors) or referencing this letter (invariably as a warning against being taken in by this con artist). 1 August 2005. Plagiarism and editing of fraud letters is common, as a Google search for Mrs Mariam Sese Seko will show. The nature of the editorial processes which change one letter into another is a different but interesting topic.

6 Idiolectal Variation: Ritual Talk at the Supermarket Checkout

1. This chapter has been previously published as Kuiper & Flindall (2000).
2. Before initially publishing this study in 2000, some intervening years passed so that, given the turnover of checkout operator staff at supermarkets in New Zealand, few of the operators if any would be identifiable from any transcript.
3. This is not true in all countries. In the Netherlands the whole transaction may be accomplished without any talk.
4. Occasionally items lose their barcode labels.
5. The checkout operator was fitted with a lapel microphone and the customers were recorded using a semi-directional microphone, the two channels being fed into a stereophonic cassette recorder. The hedge of *about* is necessary because some of the interactions were chats with supervisors and other operators which fell outside the normal transactional data we were using as the basis of this study. These interactions were not used for this study.
6. A number of operators were only 'on' for short periods filling in for others who were on a break.
7. We have given only an orthographic transcription of the speech we recorded since our interest was and is primarily in the formulae used by speakers.
8. The use of a finite state approach to the structural properties of formulae is explained in Kuiper (1996:45-6). Many formulae have variant forms and a speaker who knows a set of structurally related formulae knows the finite state diagram which generates them and can thus select any of the available tracks through the diagram from left to right following the arrows. It may be that not all of the possibilities in such a diagram will appear in a sample of speech recorded from a particular speaker. But the diagrams can be set up on the basis of a particular speaker's performance, as we will see later.

Finite state approaches to structural representation in syntax were first used by Chomsky (1957). The eagle-eyed will notice that some of the finite state diagrams in the chapter slightly overgenerate beyond the data actually collected and shown in the tables. The diagrams are therefore to be read as claims about what the operators could say as well as what they do say from within their personal formulaic competence. Our claim is that the finite state diagrams are a representation of the formulaic tradition which is available within the community of speakers. We will see later that different speakers have a preference for their own tracks through the diagram, each having a characteristic set of these.
9. We follow the rules of openings and closings devised by Smith (1991) because they are based in part on New Zealand conversational data and that seems the appropriate basis for seeing how conversations at New Zealand supermarkets are organized.
10. Context-free re-write rules generate, i.e. explicitly characterize, an allowable set of tree diagrams, e.g. in syntactic analysis. For our purposes we can regard these rules as those which the speakers have internalized and which they use to structure their discourse. We have shown the utility of such rules elsewhere (Kuiper & Haggo, 1984; Kuiper, 1996).
11. Justine Coupland (personal communication) suggests that these utterances 'seem to indicate prior acquaintance' otherwise they look 'unusually intrusive and beyond the bounds of "safe" talk...displayed here.' We feel that a New Zealander can safely assume that the customer is older, having had a hip replacement operation. She would probably be a 'regular' at this supermarket. The acquaintanceship would only need to be of this order to make such utterances perfectly safe. The customer would be known from her previous visits to this supermarket. Beyond that no further acquaintanceship would be necessary. Again this may suggest a different metric for what constitutes verbal safety in New Zealand service encounters from that which prevails in the UK.
12. It would have been interesting to note at the time whether the interlocutor was male although this is not a concern of this study.
13. We have noted other examples of this kind of accretion to existing formulae in Kuiper (1992).
14. Each cell contains the raw number of these greetings used in the sample followed by its percentage of the total number of greetings used by this operator.

7 Genrelects, Gender and Politeness: Form and Function in Controlling the Body

1. This section is based on Kuiper & Lodge (2004).
2. Both may have the same effect on the fitness of the body.
3. At an extreme level, the desire for control of the body can be found in body builders (Guthrie & Castelnuovo, 1992).
4. Delin (1998) provides a sensitive account of this situation. Here no loss of body control is involved. Rituals, voluntarily undergone, which involve a humiliating loss of body control also exist (Hodges, 1985). Torture, by way

of contrast, often involves rituals not voluntarily undergone which involve a humiliating loss of body control. This suggests that there is a rich area of ethnography involving body control, its aims and consequences, its social mores and practices (Douglas, 1982).
5. In contrast to the step aerobics instructors studied by Delin (2001).
6. Les Mills is a consortium of gymnasia in New Zealand now also responsible for a set of fitness programmes marketed worldwide. This set includes a pump aerobics workout.
7. Delin (2001) used transcripts from three hours of step aerobics with two live freelance instructors and one videotaped session produced by Reebok.
8. The speech of four different instructors, all freelance, has been used for this study. All of them produce almost entirely formulaic speech of this kind to cue their routines. There is some personal variability. Not all the instructors use the same set of formulae. But all of them do use formulae for each discourse node of the routine. As is usual in formulaic genres, each formula is restricted to particular discourse nodes and cannot be used in others.

8 Regional Genrelects in Engagement Notices

1. For a comparative account of wedding invitations in two different Muslim societies see Clynes & Henry (2004) and Nahar Al-Ali (2006). Obituaries are also a formulaic genre in some societies (Nwoye, 1992).
2. Sample size in the case of formulaic varieties can be determined by 'rate of return'. The more rigid the variety is, the less likely it is that more data will present novelty. We believe that the sample of one hundred texts is fairly representative of the large majority of variation which may take place within the confines of the formulaic elements of the notices. That is not to say that a study of the non-formulaic addenda which are present in many Australian and New Zealand notices would not repay larger sample sizes. But that is not the primary area of focus.
3. 2% of cases.
4. Note that this creation, which is an actual example, is constructed of three formulae: *Be very happy with, welcome to our NP* and *with love.*
5. Sometimes only one parent appears, for various inferable reasons not given in the notice.
6. Negative affect is not permitted to be expressed in engagement notices however strongly it may be felt by a parent.

9 Revolutionary Change: Formula Change during the Cultural Revolution, People's Republic of China

1. An earlier version of this chapter was originally published as Ji, Kuiper & Shu, (1990). A more extended study of linguistic engineering is to be found in Ji (2004).
2. Data for this study were obtained from the memories of the two Chinese authors and from their discussions with fellow Chinese students at the University of Canterbury during 1987. Many of these students were at school

during the Cultural Revolution and were thus able to act as informants and provide a control on the memories of the Chinese authors. Some of the cited slogans for Public Criticism Meetings are also to be found in Liang Heng & Shapiro (1983). There is a partial account of two Public Criticism Meetings in their publication (1983:78–9, 120–1).
3. We shall have nothing to say about those formulae that were used before the revolution and thereafter abandoned, as they are not formulae of the revolutionary period.
4. There is debate about the exact period covered by the Cultural Revolution. Whyte (1974:4) gives dates from 1966 to 1969. Liang Heng & Shapiro (1983), however, suggest from their personal chronicle of Liang Heng's youth that the period of turmoil associated with the Cultural Revolution had a long aftermath.
5. NP stands for a noun phrase slot that would usually be filled by an accused person's name.
6. For an account of other oral formulaic performances where writing plays a significant role in providing a means for verbatim production, see Finnegan (1981).
7. Many of the slogans used at the meeting were also used in other situations, as, for example, by Red Guard children talking to their parents:

> Father emerged when he heard voices and was glad to see Liang Fang.
> 'How have things been going?' he asked. 'We haven't seen you in a long time.'
> 'The situation is excellent,' she answered in the language of the Revolution. 'We're washing away all the dirty water. But I never sleep. Every night we're out making search raids.' (Liang Heng & Shapiro, 1983:69).

8. We do not wish to imply that such traditions are more stable than written texts; just that oral formulaic traditions can be very stable (Rubin, 1995).

10 Historical Variation: The Historical Reconstruction of Proto-English Auction Speech

1. An earlier version of some of this chapter was published in Kuiper (1992).
2. This section is based on Kuiper & Tillis (1985).

11 Volitional Variation: Humour and Formulae

1. An earlier version of this chapter was originally published as Kuiper (2007).
2. I ignore for the purposes of this chapter the possibility that PLIs are subject to constraints on their structural representations (Kuiper & Everaert, 2000).
3. See Naciscone (2001:7–8) for a discussion of various approaches to such manipulation.
4. We will only survey deformation of those PLI properties which PLIs have as a result of being PLIs.

5. See Kuiper (2004) for some examples of PLI slips which parallel cases of the artistic deformation of PLIs. Note that not all slip types are plausible conscious artistic deformations and so not all slip types will be used in this study. For example, anticipation and perseveration slips arise as the result of activation patterns which are unlikely to be replicated as a conscious process while metathesis and exchanges such a Spoonerisms can be.
6. Whether these are two senses of one word or two different words, i.e. homonyms, is not material to the argument.
7. There is more research to be done on the nature of such inference and the way in which perceivers access the phrasal lexical item's lexical entry on the basis of less than a full input of it.

References

Accius. (140BC). *Meleanger*.
Aijmer, G. (1997). *Ritual Dramas in the Duke of York Islands: An Exploration of Cultural Imagery*. Göteborg: Institute for Advanced Studies in Social Anthropology.
Aijmer, K. (1996). *Conversational Routines in English*. London: Longman.
Alexander, R. J. (1997). *Aspects of Verbal Humour in English*. Tübingen: Gunther Narr.
Aronoff, M. (1976). *Word Formation in Generative Grammar*. Cambridge, MA: MIT Press.
Askehave, I. & Swales, J. M. (2001). 'Genre identification and communicative purpose: a problem and a possible solution'. *Applied Linguistics, 22* (2): 195–212.
Atkinson, D. & Biber, D. (1994). 'Register: a review of empirical research'. In D. Biber & E. Finegan (eds.), *Sociolinguistic Perspectives on Register* (pp. 351–85). New York: Oxford University Press.
Attardo, S. (1994). *Linguistic Theories of Humor*. Berlin: Mouton de Gruyter.
Austin, J. L. (1976). *How to Do Things with Words*. London: Oxford University Press.
Bakhtin, M. M. (1973). *Problems of Dostoevsky's Poetics*. Ann Arbor, MI: Ardis.
Bakhtin, M. M. (1986). 'The problem of speech genres' (V. W. McGee, trans.). In C. Emerson & M. Holmquist (eds.), *Speech Genres and other Late Essays* (pp. 60–102). Austin, Texas: University of Texas Press.
Bancroft, F. (1959). *Slave Trading in the Old South*. New York: Ungar.
Bao, Z. (2003). 'Social stigma and grammatical autonomy in non-native varieties of English'. *Language in Society, 32* (1): 23–46.
Bates, E. & Deverscovi, A. (1989). 'Crosslinguistic studies of sentence comprehension'. In B. MacWhinney & E. Bates (eds.), *The Cross-linguistic Study of Sentence Processing* (pp. 225–53). Cambridge: Cambridge University Press.
Bauman, R. (1975). 'Verbal art as performance'. *American Anthropologist, 77*: 290–311.
Bauman, R. & Briggs, C. L. (1990). 'Poetics and performance as critical perspectives on language and social life'. *Annual Review of Anthropology, 19*: 59–88.
Bayard, D. & Green, A. J. (2005). 'Evaluating English accents worldwide'. *Te Reo, 48*: 21–8.
Becker, J. (1975). *The Phrasal Lexicon*. Report No. 3081. Boston: Bolt Beranek and Newman, Inc.
Bell, A. (1991). *The Language of News Media*. Oxford: Blackwell.
Bell, A. & Kuiper, K. (eds.) (2000). *New Zealand English*. Wellington/Amsterdam: Victoria University Press/John Benjamins.
Bergmann, J. R. & Luckmann, T. (1995). 'Drama and narration'. In U. Quasthoff (ed.), *Aspects of Oral Communication* (pp. 289–304). Berlin: De Gruyter.
Bhatia, V. K. (2001). 'The power and politics of genre'. In A. Burns & C. Coffin (eds.), *Analysing English in a Global Context* (pp. 65–77). London: Routledge.

Biber, D. (1988). *Variation Across Speech and Writing*. Cambridge: Cambridge University Press.
Biber, D. (1989). 'A typology of English texts'. *Linguistics, 27*: 3–43.
Biber, D. (1994). 'An analytic framework for register studies'. In D. Biber and E. Finegan (eds.), *Sociolinguistic Perspectives on Register* (pp. 31–56). New York: Oxford University Press.
Biber, D. (1995). *Dimensions of Register Variation: A Cross-Linguistic Comparison*. Cambridge: Cambridge University Press.
Biber, D., Conrad, S. & Reppen, R. (1998). *Corpus Linguistics: Investigating Language Structure and Use*. Cambridge: Cambridge University Press.
Blair, D. & Collins, P. (eds.) (2001). *English in Australia*. Amsterdam: John Benjamins.
Blum-Kulka, S. (1997). *Dinner Talk: Cultural Patterns of Sociability and Socialization in Family Discourse*. Mahwah, NJ: Lawrence Erlbaum Associates.
Blum-Kulka, S., House, J. & Kasper, G. (eds.) (1989). *Cross-Cultural Pragmatics: Requests and Apologies*. Norwood, NJ: Ablex.
Boyd, J. (2001). 'Virtual orality: how ebay controls auctions without an auctioneer's voice'. *American Speech, 76* (3): 286–300.
Brown, P. & Levinson, S. (1978). 'Universals in language usage: politeness phenomena'. In E. N. Goody (ed.), *Questions and Politeness: Strategies in Social Interaction*. Cambridge: Cambridge University Press.
Brown, P. & Levinson, S. (1987). *Politeness: Some Universals of Language Usage*. Cambridge: Cambridge University Press.
Cassady, R. (1967). *Auctions and Auctioneering*. Berkeley: University of California Press.
Cassidy, R. (2002). *The Sport of Kings*. Cambridge: Cambridge University Press.
Chagnon, N. (1977). *Yanomamö: The Fierce People* (2nd edn). London: Thomson.
Chase, P. et al. (1998). *Effective Business Communication in New Zealand* (2nd edn). Auckland: Longman.
Chiaro, D. (1992). *The Language of Jokes: Analyzing Verbal Play*. London: Routledge.
Chomsky, N. (1957). *Syntactic Structures*. The Hague: Mouton.
Chomsky, N. (1965). *Aspects of the Theory of Syntax*. Cambridge, MA: MIT Press.
Chomsky, N. (1981). *Lectures on Government and Binding*. Dordrecht: Foris.
Chomsky, N. (1986). *Knowledge of Language: Its Nature, Origin and Use*. New York: Praeger.
Chomsky, N. (1996). *Minimalism*. Cambridge, MA: MIT Press.
Clynes, A. & Henry, A. (2004). 'Introducing genre analysis using Brunei Malay wedding invitations'. *Language Awareness, 13* (4): 225–42.
Coulmas, F. (1979). 'On the sociolinguistic relevance of routine formulae'. *Journal of Pragmatics* 3: 239–66.
Coulmas, F. (ed.) (1981). *Conversational Routine: Explorations in Standardized Communication Situations and Prepatterned Speech*. The Hague: Mouton.
Coulthard, M. & Ashby, M. (1975). 'Talking with the doctor, 1'. *Journal of Communication, 25* (2): 140–147.
Coupland, J., Coupland, N. & Robinson, J. D. (1992). '"How are you?": negotiating phatic communion'. *Language in Society, 21*: 207–30.
Cowie, A. P. (1991). 'Multiword units in newspaper language'. *Cahiers de l'Institut de Linguistique de Louvain, 17* (1–3): 101–16.

References

Cowie, A. P. (1998). 'Creativity and formulaic language'. *Linguistica e Philologia,* 8: 159–70.
Crystal, D. (1995). *The Cambridge Encyclopedia of the English Language.* Cambridge: Cambridge University Press.
Crystal, D. & Davy D (1969). *Investigating English Style.* London: Longman.
Delin, J. (1998). 'Facework and instructor goals in the step aerobics workout'. In S. Hunston (ed.), *Language at Work* (pp. 52–71). Clevedon: British Association for Applied Linguistics, in association with Multilingual Matters.
Delin, J. (2001). 'Keeping in step: task structure, discourse structure and utterance interpretation in the step aerobics workout'. *Discourse Processes,* 31 (1): 61–89.
Douglas, M. (1982). *Natural Symbols.* New York: Pantheon.
Drew, P. & Heritage, J. (1992). 'Analysing talk at work: an introduction'. In P. Drew & J. Heritage (eds.), *Talk at Work: Interaction in Institutional Settings.* Cambridge: Cambridge University Press.
Dutton, K. R. (1995). *The Perfectible Body: The Western Ideal of Physical Development.* St Leonard, Australia: Allen and Unwin.
Dwyer, J. (2000). *The Business Communication Handbook* (5th edn). Frenchs Forest, NSW: Prentice Hall.
Edwards, V. & Sienkewicz, T. J. (1990). *Oral Cultures Past and Present: Rappin and Homer.* Oxford: Basil Blackwell.
Ferguson, C. (1976). 'The structure and use of politeness formulas'. *Language in Society,* 5: 137–51.
Ferguson, C. (1983). 'Sports announcer talk: syntactic aspects of register variation'. *Language in Society,* 12: 153–72.
Fiedler, S. (2007). *English Phraseology: A Coursebook.* Tübingen: Gunther Narr.
Fillmore, C. J., Kay, P. & O'Connor, M. C. (1988). 'Regularity and idiomaticity in grammatical constructions'. *Language,* 64: 501–38.
Finnegan, R. (1981). 'Literacy and literature'. In B. Lloyd & J. Gay (eds.), *Universals of Human Thought* (pp. 234–55). Cambridge: Cambridge University Press.
Firth, R. (1972). 'Verbal and bodily rituals of greeting and parting'. In J. S. La Fontaine (ed.), *The Interpretation of Ritual: Essays in Honour of A.I. Richards.* (pp.1–38). London: Tavistock.
Flyvbjerg, B. (2001). *Making Social Science Matter: Why Social Enquiry Fails and How it can Succeed Again.* Cambridge: Cambridge University Press.
Fox, K. (1999). *The Racing Tribe: Watching the Horse Watchers.* London: Metro Publishing.
Frankenberg-Garcia, A. (2000). 'Using a translation corpus to teach English to native speakers of Portuguese'. *A Journal of Anglo-American Studies,* 3: 65–78.
Fraser, B. (1970). 'Idioms within a transformational grammar'. *Foundations of Language,* 6: 22–42.
Fraser Gupta, A. (1998). 'Singapore colloquial English or deviant standard English?' In J. Tent & F. Mugler (eds.), *SICOL: Proceedings of the Second International Conference on Oceanic Linguistics: Volume 1, Language Contact (Vol. C-141)* (pp. 43–57). Canberra: Pacific Linguistics.
Fry, D. K. (1975). 'Caedmon as a formulaic poet'. In J. J. Duggan (ed.), *Oral Literature* (pp. 41–61). Edinburgh and London: Scottish Academic Press.
Gennep, A. van (1960). *The Rites of Passage.* Chicago: University of Chicago Press.
Gläser, R. (1986). *Phaseologie der englischen Sprache.* Tübingen: Max Niemeyer Verlag.

Gläser, R. (1995). 'The stylistic potential of phraseological units in the light of genre analysis'. In A. P. Cowie (ed.), *Phraseology: Theory, Analysis, and Applications* (pp. 125–143). Oxford: Clarendon Press.

Goffman, E. (1967). *Interaction Ritual*. New York: Anchor Books.

Goffman, E. (1969). *The Presentation of Self in Everyday Life*. Harmondsworth: Penguin.

Goldberg, E., Driedger, N. & Kittredge, R. I. (1995). 'Using natural-language processing to produce weather forecasts'. *Expert, IEEE*, 9 (2): 45–53.

Gruber, M. C. (2007). 'A linguistic and ethnographic analysis of apology narratives performed in the context of federal sentencing hearings'. Unpublished PhD thesis, University of Chicago, Chicago.

Guenther, S. & Knoblauch, H. (1995). 'Culturally patterned speaking practices'. *Pragmatics*, 5 (1): 95–127.

Gullen, Z. (ed.) (2002). *Debrett's Correct Form* (2nd edn). London: Headline.

Guthrie, S. & Castelnuovo, S. (1992). 'Elite women bodybuilders: models of resistance and compliance'. *Play and Culture*, 5: 401–8.

Haggo, D. & Kuiper, K. (1983). Review of F. Coulmas (ed.), *Conversational Routine*. *Linguistics*, 21: 531–51.

Haggo, D. C. & Kuiper, K. (1985). 'Stock auction speech in Canada and New Zealand'. In R. Berry & J. Acheson (eds.), *Regionalism and National Identity: Multidisciplinary Essays on Canada, Australia and New Zealand* (pp. 189–197). Christchurch: Association for Canadian Studies in Australia and New Zealand.

Hanks, W. F. (1987). 'Discourse genres in a theory of practice'. *American Ethnologist*, 14 (4): 668–92.

Harrah, J. (1992). 'The landscape of possibility: an ethnography of the Kentucky Derby'. Unpublished PhD thesis, Indiana University.

Herdt, G. H. (1980). *The Guardians of the Flutes*. New York: Macmillan.

Hickey, F. (1991). 'What Penelope said: styling the weather forecast'. Unpublished MA dissertation, University of Canterbury, NZ.

Hickey, F. & Kuiper, K. (2000). '"A deep depression covers the South Tasman Sea": New Zealand Meteorological Office weather forecasts'. In A. Bell & K. Kuiper (eds.), *New Zealand English*. Wellington/Amsterdam: Victoria University Press/John Benjamins.

Hodges, I. (1985). 'Drinking rituals and the negotiation of intimacy'. *Sites*, 11: 13–19.

Holmes, J. (1994). *Women, Men and Politeness*. London: Longman.

Howarth, P. A. (1996). *Phraseology in English Academic Writing: Some Implications for Language Learning and Dictionary Making*. Tübingen: Max Niemeyer Verlag.

Hymes, D. (1968). 'The ethnography of speaking'. In J. Fishman (ed.), *The Sociology of Language* (pp. 99–138). The Hague: Mouton.

Ji, F. (2004). *Linguistic Engineering, Language and Politics in Mao's China*. Honolulu: University of Hawai'i Press.

Ji, F., Kuiper, K. & Shu, S (1990). 'Language and revolution, formulae of the Chinese Cultural Revolution'. *Language in Society* 19: 61–79.

Johns, A. M. (1997). *Text, Role and Context: Developing Academic Literacies*. Cambridge: Cambridge University Press.

Kane, P. (1987). 'Is the weather report an oral formulaic variety?', Unpublished ms. University of Canterbury, Christchurch.

References

Klemperer, V., Nowojski, W. & Klemperer, H. (1995). *Ich will Zeugnis ablegen bis zum Letzten* (1. Aufl. ed.). Berlin: Aufbau-Verlag.
Koopman, H. & Sportiche, D. (1991). 'The position of subjects'. *Lingua*, 85: 211–58.
Kuiper, K. (1990). 'New Zealand sporting formulae: two models of male socialisation'. In J. Cheshire (ed.), *English Around the World: Sociolinguistic Perspectives* (pp. 200–9). Cambridge: Cambridge University Press.
Kuiper, K. (1991). 'The evolution of an oral tradition: racecalling in Canterbury, New Zealand'. *Oral Tradition*, 6: 19–34.
Kuiper, K. (1992). 'The English oral tradition in auction speech'. *American Speech*, 67: 279–289.
Kuiper, K. (1996). *Smooth Talkers: The Linguistic Performance of Auctioneers and Sportscasters*. Mahwah, NJ: Lawrence Erlbaum Associates.
Kuiper, K. (1998). 'Star Wars: an imperial myth'. *Journal for Popular Culture*, 21 (4): 77–86.
Kuiper, K. (2004). 'From intent to malutterance'. *Landfall*, 207: 90–6.
Kuiper, K. (2007). 'Cathy Wilcox meets the phrasal lexicon'. In J. Munat (ed.), *Lexical Creativity, Texts and Contexts* (pp. 93–112). Amsterdam: John Benjamins.
Kuiper, K. & Austin, J. P. M. (1990). 'They're off and racing now: the speech of the New Zealand race caller'. In A. Bell & J. Holmes (eds.), *New Zealand Ways of Speaking English* (pp. 195–220). Bristol: Multilingual Matters.
Kuiper, K. & Everaert, M. (2000). 'Constraints on the phrase structural properties of English phrasal lexical items'. *PASE Papers in Language Studies: Proceedings of the 8th Annual Conference of the Polish Association for the Study of English* (pp.151–70). Aksel: Wroclaw.
Kuiper, K. & Flindall, M. (2000). 'Social rituals, formulaic speech and small talk at the supermarket checkout'. In J. Coupland (ed.), *Small Talk*. (pp. 183–207). Harlow: Longman.
Kuiper, K. & Haggo, D. (1984). 'Livestock auctions, oral poetry, and ordinary language'. *Language in Society*, 13: 205–34.
Kuiper, K., & Haggo, D. (1985). 'The nature of ice hockey commentaries'. In R. Berry & J. Acheson (eds.), *Regionalism and National Identity: Multidisciplinary Essays on Canada, Australia, and New Zealand* (pp.167–175). Christchurch: Association for Canadian Studies in Australia and New Zealand.
Kuiper, K. & Lodge, M. (2004). 'Formulae of command: form and function in controlling the body'. In C. Földes (ed.), *Res humanae: Proverbiorum et sententiarum: Ad honorem Wolfgangi Mieder* (pp. 141–54). Tübingen: Gunther Narr.
Kuiper, K. & Newsome, G. (2006). 'Subverting the self: standard and non-standard phraseology in "African" fraud letters'. In L. Jinhua, K. Henshall & X. Hong (eds.), *Ethnic Identities and Linguistic Expressions: Languages, Literatures and Cultural Interaction in an Age of Globalization* (pp. 524–41). Beijing: Renmin Wenxue (People's Literary) Press.
Kuiper, K. & Small, V. (1986). 'Constraints on fictions'. *Poetics Today*, 7 (3): 495–526.
Kuiper, K. & Tan, D. (1989). 'Cultural congruence and conflict: acquiring formulae in second language learning'. In O. Garcia & R. Otheguy (eds.), *English Across Cultures: Cultures Across English* (pp. 281–304). Berlin: Mouton de Gruyter.

Kuiper, K. & Tillis, F. (1985). 'The chant of the tobacco auctioneer'. *American Speech*, 60: 141–9.

Labov, W. (1972). *Sociolinguistic Patterns*. Oxford: Basil Blackwell.

Laver, J. D. M. H. (1981). 'Linguistic routines and politeness in greeting and parting'. In F. Coulmas (ed.), *Conversational Routine: Explorations in Standardized Communication Situations and Prepatterned Speech* (pp. 289–304). The Hague: Mouton.

Levelt, W. J. M. (1989). *Speaking: From Intention to Articulation*. Cambridge, MA: MIT Press.

Liang Heng & Shapiro, J. (1983). *Son of the Revolution*. New York: Knopf.

Lord, A. B. (1960). *The Singer of Tales*. Cambridge, MA: Harvard University Press.

MacDonald, B. A. (1981). 'A robot learns by being led through movements'. *Man Machine Studies* (No. 19). Christchurch, NZ: University of Canterbury.

Mackin, R. (1978). 'On collocations: "words shall be known by the company they keep"'. In P. Strevens (ed.), *In Honour of A.S. Hornby* (pp. 149–65). Oxford: Oxford University Press.

Malinowski, B. (1922). *Argonauts of the Western Pacific*. London: Routledge and Kegan Paul.

Mel'čuk, I. (1995). 'Phrasemes in language and phraseology in linguistics'. In M. Everaert, E.-J. van der Linden, A. Schenk & R. Schroeder (eds.), *Idioms: Structural and Psychological Perspectives* (pp. 167–232). Hillsdale, NJ: Lawrence Erlbaum Associates.

Mel'čuk, I. (1998). 'Collocations and lexical functions'. In A. P. Cowie (ed.), *Phraseology: Theory, Analysis, and Applications* (pp. 23–53). Oxford: Clarendon Press.

Merritt, M. (1976). 'On questions following questions in service encounters'. *Language in Society*, 5: 315–57.

Merritt, M. (1977). 'The playback: an instance of variation in discourse'. In R. W. Fasold & R. W. Shuy (eds.), *Studies in Language Variation: Semantics, Syntax, Phonology, Pragmatics, Social Situations, Ethnographic Approaches*. (pp.198–208). Washington, DC: Georgetown University Press.

Miller, C. R. (1994). 'Genre as social action'. In A. Freedman & P. Medway (eds.), *Genre and the New Rhetoric* (pp. 23–42). London: Taylor & Francis.

Mitkov, R. (1991). 'Generating public weather reports'. Paper presented at the International Conference on Current Issues in Computational Linguistics, Penang, Malasia.

Moon, R. (1998). *Fixed Expressions and Idioms in English: A Corpus Based Approach*. Oxford: Clarendon Press.

Mu Fu-Sheng (1963). *The Wilting of the Hundred Flower: The Chinese Intelligensia under Mao*. New York: Praeger.

Naciscone, A. (2001). *Phraseological Units in Discourse: Towards Applied Stylistics*. Riga: Latvian Academy of Culture.

Nahar Al-Ali, M. (2006). 'Religious affiliations and masculine power in Jordanian wedding invitation genre'. *Discourse and Society*, 17 (6): 691–714.

Nesbitt, C. & Plum, G. (1988). 'Probabilities in a systemic-functional grammar: the clause complex in English'. In R. P. Fawcett & D. J. Young (eds.), *New Developments in Systemic Linguistics* (Vol. 2, pp. 6–38). London: Pinter.

Newsome, G. (2006). 'Estimating the size of the phrasal E lexicon of aircraft engineers'. Unpublished MA dissertation, University of Canterbury, Christchurch.

Nicolas, T. (1995). 'Semantics of idiom modification'. In M. Everaert, E.-J. van der Linden, A. Schenk & R. Schroeder (eds.), *Idioms: Structural and Psychological Perspectives* (pp. 233–252). Hillsdale, NJ: Lawrence Erlbaum Associates.

Nunberg, G., Sag, I. & Wasow, T. (1994). Idioms. *Language*, 70 (3): 491–538.

Nwoye, O. G. (1992). 'Obituary announcements as communicative events in Nigerian English'. *World Englishes*, 11 (1): 15–27.

Orwell, G. (1953). *Politics and the English Language*. London: Secker & Warburg.

Paltridge, B. (1997). *Genre, Frames and Writing in Research Settings*. Amsterdam: Benjamins.

Paolillo, J. C. (1998). 'Gary Larson's Far Side: Nonsense? Nonsense!' *Humor*, 11 (3): 261–90.

Pawley, A. & Syder, F. (1983). 'Two puzzles for linguistic theory: nativelike selection and nativelike fluency'. In J. Richards & R. Schmidt (eds.), *Language and Communication* (pp. 191–226). London: Longman.

Platt, J. (1975). 'The Singapore English speech continuum and its basilect "Singlish" as a "creoloid"'. *Anthropological Linguistics*, 17: 363–74.

Platt, J. (1984). 'The Chinese background to Singapore English'. In B. Hong (ed.), *New Papers on Chinese Language Use* (pp. 105–117). Canberra: Australian National University.

Platt, J., Weber, H. & Ho, M. L. (1983). *Singapore and Malaysia*. Amsterdam: John Benjamins.

Python, M. (2000). *The Brand New Monty Python Papperbok*. London: Methuen.

Rappaport, R. A. (1999). *Ritual and Religion in the Making of Humanity*. Cambridge: Cambridge University Press.

Richards, J. C. (1974). *Error Analysis: Perspectives on Second Language Acquisition*. London: Longman.

Robert, J. C. (1967). *The Story of Tobacco in America*. Chapel Hill: University of North Carolina Press.

Robinson, D. M. (1946). 'The wheel of fortune'. *Classical Philology*, 41: 207–16.

Rubin, D. C. (1995). *Memory in Oral Traditions: The Cognitive Psychology of Epic, Ballads, and Counting-out Rhymes*. New York: Oxford University Press.

Salmond, A. (1976). 'Rituals of encounter among the Maori: sociolinguistic study of a scene'. In B. Stolz & R. Shannon (eds.), *Oral Literature and Formulae* (pp.192–12). Ann Arbor, MI: Center for the Coordination of Ancient and Modern Studies, The University of Michigan.

Sapir, E. (1924). 'The grammarian and his language'. *American Mercury*, i: 149–155.

Schegloff, E. A. (1972). 'Sequencing in conversational openings'. In J. J. Gumperz & D. Hymes (eds.), *Directions in Sociolinguistics: The Ethnography of Communication* (pp. 346–80). New York: Holt, Rinehart & Winston.

Schegloff, E. A. & Sacks, H. (1973). 'Opening up closings'. *Semiotica*, 7: 289–327.

Scherzer, J. (1974). 'Semantic systems, discourse structures, and the ecology of language'. In R. W. Fasold & R. W. Shuy (eds.), *Studies in Language Variation: Semantics, Syntax, Phonology, Pragmatics, Social Situations, Ethnographic Approaches* (pp.283–93). Washington, DC: Georgetown University Press.

Schiffrin, D. (1987). *Discourse Markers*. New York: Cambridge University Press.

Schipper, K. (1994). *The Taoist Body* (K. C. Duval, Trans.). Berkeley, CA: University of California Press.

Shilling, C. (1993). *The Body and Social Theory*. London: Sage.

Smith, C. W. (1989). *Auctions: The Social Construction of Value.* London: Harvester Wheatsheaf.

Smith, J. (1991). 'Salutations, felicitations, and terminations: a study in communicative performance'. Unpublished MA dissertation, University of Canterbury: Christchurch

Soehn, J.-P. (2003). 'Von Geisterhand zu Potte gekommen: Eine HPSG-Analyse von PPs mit unikaler Komponente'. Unpublished MA dissertation, Universität Tübingen, Tübingen.

Staal, F. (1990). *Rules Without Meaning: Ritual, Mantras, and the Human Sciences.* New York: Peter Lang.

Stubbe, M., & Holmes, J. (1995). 'You know, eh and other "exasperating expressions": an analysis of social and stylistic variation in the use of pragmatic devices in a sample of New Zealand English'. *Language and Communication,* 15: 63–88.

Subbiah, I. (1989). 'Occasional showers and fine periods: an analysis of weather bulletins'. Unpublished MS, Auckland University.

Swan, M. & Smith, B. (2001). *Learning English, a Teacher's Guide to Interference and other Problems* (2nd edn). Cambridge: Cambridge University Press.

Thorne, A. & Coupland, J. (1998) 'Articulations of same-sex desire: lesbian and gay male dating advertisements'. *Journal of Sociolinguistics,* 2: 233–57.

Van Lancker, D. (1987). 'Non propositional speech: neurolinguistic studies'. In A. W. Ellis (ed.), *Progress in the Psychology of Language* (Vol. 3, pp. 49–118). Hillsdale, NJ: Lawrence Erlbaum Associates.

Veblen, T. (1994). *The Theory of the Leisure Class.* Mineola, NY: Dover.

Verstraten, L. (1992). 'Fixed phrases in learners' dictionaries'. In P. J. L. Arnaud & H. Béjoint (eds.), *Vocabulary in Applied Linguistics* (pp. 28–40). Basingstoke: Macmillan.

Vine, B. (2001). 'Workplace language and power: directives, requests and advice'. Unpublished PhD thesis, Victoria University of Wellington, Wellington.

Vlčková, J. (2001). 'The language of personal advertisements in Australian newspapers'. Unpublished PhD thesis, Masaryk University, Brno.

Weinreich, U. (1969). 'Problems in the analysis of idioms'. In J. Puhvel (ed.), *Substance and the Structure of Language* (pp. 23–81). Berkeley: University of California Press.

Whorf, B. L. (1956). 'The relation of habitual thought and behavior to language'. In J. B. Carrol (ed.), *Language, Thought, and Reality: Selected Writings of Benjamin Lee Whorf* (pp.134–59). Cambridge, MA: MIT Press.

Whyte, M. K. (1974). *Small Groups and Political Rituals in China.* Berkeley: University of California Press.

Wilcox, C. (1991). *Throw Away Lines: Cartoons by Cathy Wilcox.* North Ryde: Collins/Angus and Robertson.

Williams, E. (1994). 'Remarks on lexical knowledge'. *Lingua,* 92 (1): 7–34.

Wilson, M. (1954). 'Nyakysa ritual and symbolism'. *American Anthropologist,* 56 (2): 228–41.

Wray, A. (2002). *Formulaic Language and the Lexicon.* Cambridge: Cambridge

Yates, J. A., & Orlikowski, W. J. (1992). 'Genres of organisational communication: a structurational approach'. *Academy of Management Review,* 17: 299–326.

Index

accessibility condition 193
apology formulae 160–1
artistic deformation 192–7

Bakhtin 24–5,
base form of PLI 193
body control 116–17, 137
business letters 80–1, 91

carnival 38
checkout operators 23
class 88–9, 173
colour commentary 10–11, 33
commencing a meal 66–71
communicative competence 3, 26
conditions of use 1–2, 21, 203
consultants 73–4, 114–15, 211–12
convention 16
cueing 122–36

data collection 189–90
directives 116
 parade ground 117–20
 pump aerobics 120–30
 dance calling 130–6
discourse structure rules 7, 12, 49, 101, 210
 of auctioneering 179–85
 of aerobics instructors 123–5
 of checkout operators 106–10
 of face-offs 12
 of Public Criticism Meetings 170
 of weather forecasts 44–53

e-mail 76, 80–5, 91
engagement notices 7–10, 138–52
English as a foreign language 81, 86–7
ethnography 27, 41
exercise 120–1

fieldwork 73
face 59–60, 71, 121–2

finite state systems 101–8, 110, 142, 182, 185–6, 209–10
formality 82–4, 140, 147–55, 161
formulae 6–7
 discourse indexing 13
 of aerobics instructors 125–9
 of auctioneering 181–6
 of business 82–5
 of checkout operators 101–10
 of classroom greeting 163–5
 of the Cultural Revolution 159–73
 of dance callers and cuers 131–3
 of engagement notices 140–2
 of ice hockey commentary 13–14
formulaic genres 3, 17
fortune's wheel 32–8, 207
fraud 76–7
frequency 40
 of checkout formulae 111
 of engagement formulae 141–4, 147–52

gambling 30
generalization in social science 137, 153–4
gender 136–7
genre 13–18
 genre variation 95, 153–4
 genrelect ix
Goffman 22–4, 77, 81, 136
greeting 61–6, 95, 100–1, 159–60

historical reconstruction 177–8
house style 144–6, 207
human ethics processes 115, 209

ice hockey commentary 10–15
idiolect 109–13, 127–8, 134–5, 204
idiom 21, 119, 161
imperative 119

language acquisition   3–4, 55–6,
   72, 123
leave taking   99, 107–9, 160
lectal continuum   58, 61
literalization   196
loan translation   61, 72

meal beginnings   66–71

native speaker   3, 21, 24, 26,
   72, 73–4

oral tradition   56, 109, 123,
   174, 183

participant observation   39
perception of a persona   88–91
performance   205
phrasal lexical items   5–6, 18
   properties of   19–21
play-by-play commentary   10–11, 33
politeness   121, 136–7
politeness genres   59–72
prosody   119, 182–3, 187–8
Public Criticism Meeting   166–75

'rate of return'   211
recording speech   39–40, 99,
   124, 178
recoverability condition   193
restricted collocation   20, 84–5
rite of passage   138–9
ritual   27, 99–100, 130, 158, 166,
   175, 207
routines   22–4, 97–9, 119

sample size   40–1, 190, 208
scripts   24, 42
service encounter   96
sincerity   71, 102
slips of the tongue   193–4
small talk   96–7, 103–5
social change   157–8
style   83–4, 89–90, 144–7, 155

text type   9, 138, 152–4

variability   17–18, 152–3
variables   140–2
verbatim recall   123
vocabulary   3–5
   structurally complex   5